Praise for *Change-Focused Leadership*

"*Change Focused Leadership* rates 10 out of 10 for strategies to lead in times of uncertainty. Dr. Hanes goes beyond the mere invitation to step up and embrace change, he provides readers with a comprehensive and practical tool kit to decisively lead in new and better ways. Whether you see yourself as a leader and agent of visionary change or as a team player and willing participant in the pursuit of change for the better, this book is an indispensable 'must read.'"

> — Dr. Michael Burns, President & COO,
> Ferndale Pharma Group

"*Change Focused Leadership* provides managers and leaders essential information for success that is relevant to a broad spectrum of organizations. I intend to make this an integral part of our management development program at CNA."

> — Christine Fox, President,
> The Center For Naval Analyses

"*Change Focused Leadership* offers clear, succinct, and hard hitting advice for leaders who are motivated to improve any organization from any managerial level. Dr. Hanes' insights are derived from years of his personal work assisting real organizations and real leaders. As a participant in several of his programs, I can assure you that you will be a more effective leader after reading this book, which could not have been published at a more perfect time."

> — Ed Harper, Chairman Of the Board,
> Avocent Corporation

"All leaders need coaching... Dr. Hanes' experience working with executives really comes through in *Change Focused Leadership*, making it a great tool for leaders at any level to improve their performance. His insights are practical, no-nonsense steps that will improve your ability to become a stronger leader."

— Jake St. Philip, Former CEO
Biolase Technology, Inc.

"The link between leadership and performance is even more important today as we take our teams through difficult economic times while continuing to restore trust. Dr. Hanes clearly outlines the importance of building relationships to enhance collaboration among the ranks. *Change Focused Leadership* helps leaders see their situation from a different perspective and provides the tools to implement strategies they might never have considered. This book is a fantastic resource for executives and educators."

— Jay Hesse, President & CEO
Blue Ox

"A succinct and superb set of leadership strategies essential for success of high performing leaders and their organizations. Exhilarating real life examples make this book a 'high energy read' for top performers in pursuit of excellence."

— Reza Meshgin, President & CEO
M Flex Corporation

CHANGE-FOCUSED LEADERSHIP:

**Ten Proven Strategies For Success
In Uncertain Times**

CHANGE-FOCUSED LEADERSHIP:

Ten Proven Strategies For Success In Uncertain Times

By Dr. John W. Hanes

AUTHORITY
PUBLISHING

Change Focused Leadership:
Ten Proven Strategies for Success in Uncertain Times
By John W. Hanes
1. Business and Economics – Leadership 2. Education – Leadership
3. Business and Economics – Management
ISBN: 978-0-9819510-4-1

Cover design by Cynthia Nicholson

Printed in the United States of America

Authority Publishing
11230 Gold Express Dr. #310-413
Gold River, CA 95670
800-877-1097
www.AuthorityPublishing.com

To my son Chad,

A young leader for change
and the inspiration for
this book. I am very
proud of the fine young
man you have become.

CONTENTS

Introduction
Change Focused Leadership

We find ourselves in a most challenging time. Intense global competition, fear of a deepening and protracted recession, dwindling natural resources and the radically different expectations of Generation X and Millennial workers cry out for leaders to reject business as usual approaches. Even before the current worldwide economic crisis, which rocked the financial markets and brought dozens of once-proud institutions to their knees, the reality was that many organizations were poorly managed and their people led uninspiringly. Figure one illustrates the gap between life in modern day organizations against the veritable barrage of demands placed on them.

FIGURE ONE

Demand - Reality Gap

Current Demands On Organizations	Ineffective Organizational Reality
Speed in Decision-making	Mind-numbing Bureaucracy
Competitive Pressure to Lower Costs	Continually Rising Overhead
Tolerance for Reasonable Risk	Hesitancy & Indecisiveness
Excellence in Serving Customers	Appalling Indifference
Radical Innovation	Marginal Improvements
Near Perfect Quality	Frequent Errors
Transparency of Everything	A Cloak of Secrecy
Sustainability	Wasted Natural Resources
Personal Connection Between Leaders & Associates	Walled-off & Impersonal Between Leaders & Associates

Facing these realities head on before your competitors do will dramatically increase the odds of your organization's continued viability. In the current environment, few executives can count anymore on growth to bail them out of bad decisions or apathy. A major leadership imperative is to make sure that when the dust settles after this lousy stretch passes, that your organization is not part of the carnage, that it will emerge more competitive, not less.

The most innovative and globally successful enterprises have always been led by leaders with the courage to adopt unconventional approaches to leading their organizations. However, these innovators who push the envelope have always been few and far between and were seldom listened to within the entrenched bureaucracies of the day. The Tesla electric vehicle was not invented by Detroit's big three automakers. Federal Express was not the brainchild of the U.S. Postal Service, and Paypal did not evolve from a bank. Think of nearly every major innovation and behind it you will find a courageous break from mainstream ways of thinking.

The root cause of organizational ineffectiveness today is that many people in "leadership" positions actually behave as guardians of the status quo. Through their caution and self-serving behaviors, they delay, dilute or destroy initiative. It is almost as if they feel some divine obligation to defend "the way we do things around here." This institutional inertia is particularly dangerous in times of extreme challenge such as we are facing right now.

I firmly believe that a pioneering, change-focused style of leadership needs to become more widely practiced throughout all levels of organizations, not just by one visionary at the top.

Change-Focused Leadership

Changed-focused leaders attract and jell. They inspire and empower. They are the enemy of the status quo. They become a catalyst that brings unity out of chaos and confusion.

Change-focused leaders are about big ideas, but also about vigorously grabbing the reins and making things happen. Their leadership is exercised more by visible example than by edicts or directives. The leader's mantra becomes, "Stop preaching — start doing."

A foundational quality of change-focused leaders is trust. The assurance that the leader will serve the interests of those who follow, as well as those who pay the bills. The authenticity and integrity to reject political expediency by making difficult decisions that benefit the greater good. How many leaders do you see today that live up to those qualities?

Change-focused leaders succeed through a formula rife with paradox. They yield power to their people to increase their own power overall. They realize that firing the appropriate people can often be the most humane thing they can do for those that remain. By passing around more credit to others, they end up getting more kudos themselves. Where lesser leaders see human resource development as an expense, they view it as an investment. They gain control by minimizing controls. While human nature causes many managers to hide problems, select associates who aren't threats, and to lay low during a crisis, change-focused leaders confront reality, select people more talented than themselves, and become the visible focal point when disaster strikes.

While many managers' temptation is to get caught up in the trappings of success, a change-focused leader retains his humility. If others insist on comparing themselves to the competition, the change-focused leader compares himself to excellence. Where many "Western" executives pride themselves on speed out of the gate with a "planning as we go" mentality, the change-focused leader takes a page out of "Eastern" culture and plans for important contingencies.

While "managers" spend countless hours deciding how to divide up the pie, the unconventional leader endeavors to make the pie larger. When conventional wisdom says to cut back, the change-focused leader believes it might be a great time to expand. If other CEOs can't find the time to interview, coach, and mentor, the change-focused sees these activities as much of the core job as vision and strategy. Sensing that competitors innovate exclusively through the research lab, the change-focused leader unleashes all associates to contribute to the innovation process.

The conventional leader is a proponent of internal competition, where the change-focused leader understands the value of collaboration. If standard practice is to understand an organization's culture and set goals that fit within it comfortably, the unconventional leader does not shy away from changing the culture to fit his aims.

In short, change-focused leaders continually stand convention on its ear and opt to take the path less traveled. They courageously do the heavy lifting needed without regard to pain or gain.

CONVENTIONAL	CHANGE-FOCUSED
Divide the Compensation Pie Fairly	Make the Pie Larger
Hunker Down in Uncertain Times	Invest
Tackle Issues As They Arise	Plan for Contingencies
Compare Against Peers	Compare Against Excellence
Fight for All Deserved Credit	Liberally Credit Others
People Development Is An Expense	People Development is An Investment
Lay Low In a Crisis	Be Visible & Available When Incidents Occur
Hoard Power	Yield Authority to Gain Overall Power
Create Internal Competition	Increase Collaboration
Select Associates Who Are Not Threats	Surround Self With Exceptional Associates
Sweep Problems Under the Rug	Confront Unpleasant Reality
Measure Everything	Generate Data on the Critical
Fiduciary Responsibility Requires Tight Controls	Control Through Values
It's Almost Impossible to Fire People	Coach or Eliminate Substandard Performers
Culture is Tough to Change So Learn to Adapt	Change the Environment to Be Supportive of the Mission

Innovation is the Job of R&D	Enlist All Associates In Innovation
Interviewing, Coaching & Mentoring Are Important But Not Critical	Interviewing, Coaching & Mentoring Are As Important As Vision & Strategy
It Is A Sign of Weakness To Seek Help & Ideas From Others	Assemble A "Cabinet" Of Strategic Advisors

A common reaction to the daunting challenge presented by the global economic crisis was to slash headcount, trim the sales travel budget, stretch out research programs, suspend associate development and kill initiatives with a time horizon longer than six months. To be sure, a swig of this bitter medicine had to be swallowed, but the change-focused leader senses there are plenty of opportunities as well. A recession creates winners and losers just like in more bullish times. If a leader acts prudently, he will find that the strong can actually get stronger while the weak perish.

In surfing, an "impact zone" is the point where the wave begins to crash. This is where there is maximum danger, but also the ultimate opportunity for the surfer to catch the ride of his life. We find ourselves at just such a place today. Perhaps by adopting a slight change in perspective we might see opportunity where all that others seem to sense is danger.

This book presents ten innovative yet proven approaches that will give leaders strategies and tactics to survive and flourish in this era of uncertainty. It details the essential qualities needed to lead for change. The concepts, models, tools and advice you will read about have formed the nucleus of my consulting practice over the past twenty-three years along with nuggets gleaned from the entirety of my thirty-two-year career in business. And, because of the uncharted waters we find ourselves in, applying these insights could not possibly be more critical.

Introduction

Over the span of my life I have had the good fortune to meet, coach, and develop thousands of leaders from hundreds of diverse organizations, many of which are regarded as the nation's finest in their areas of focus.

These encounters were no mere "meet and greet." More than 23,000 managers have attended my seminars over the years. Each submitted to a battery of psychological profiles, and each received extensive confidential feedback on a 360-degree instrument from their boss, direct reports and key peers. They spent three exhausting days engaged in group simulations battling the elements and each other in the Amazon Rainforest, attempting to get elected to the United States Senate and fighting it out in a complex computerized business simulation, all in a quest to better themselves as leaders.

They learned that by adopting pioneering approaches that defied so-called conventional wisdom they could in fact become leaders for change. They saw that leadership could emerge at any level in the toughest of times and in the most dysfunctional or repressive organizational cultures.

This book is specifically targeted to leaders at all organizational levels, not just the fortunate few who ascend to the "C Suite." It is centered on the ten essential things that leaders need to do to win in this extremely challenging competitive climate.

1. Be bold where others fear to tread
2. Jealously guard the crown jewels, then acquire more
3. Gain traction through teamwork
4. Use trust as the glue that cements relationships
5. Change the playing field through culture
6. Grow your seed corn, don't eat it
7. Energize the workforce
8. Plan ahead or plan to fail
9. Generate the power of the pyramid
10. Avoid "one size fits all" performance management

I have also included three "special circumstances" chapters. One deals with taking over a new organization. Another is for leaders who find themselves in a situation that requires an immediate and drastic turnaround. The final one deals with avoiding the "burnout" that can come with being a change agent.

My hope is that this book will give leaders and aspiring leaders in all fields the inspiration, ideas, and courage to break out of the mold of conventionality to chart a path that will make a game-changing difference in themselves and their institutions.

In a speech given at the University of California over forty years ago, Robert F. Kennedy said something amazingly prescient:

You are living in one of the rarest moments in history — a time when all around us the old order of things is crumbling and a new world society is painfully struggling to take shape.

If you shrink from this struggle and its many difficulties, you will betray the trust which your own position forces upon you. You live in the most privileged nation on Earth. You are the most privileged citizens of that privileged nation, for you have been given the opportunity to lead.

You can use your enormous influence and opportunity to seek purely private pleasure and gain. But history will judge you, and as the years pass, you will ultimately judge yourself, in the extent to which you have used your gifts and talents to lighten and enrich the lives of your fellow men.

In your hands lie the future of your world and the fulfillment of the best qualities of your own spirit.

May your journey be a productive and profitable one.

CHAPTER 1

BE BOLD WHERE OTHERS FEAR TO TREAD:
Go On the Offensive

At one time Montgomery Ward and Sears were about of equal size. Aaron Montgomery Ward feared that a recession was coming and stopped building new stores. Sears used the opportunity to acquire the choicest properties and continue its expansion program unabated. Sears prospered for decades while Wards was on perpetual life support and finally succumbed altogether. Then Sears executives made the same mistake and their lack of courage opened the door for Wal-Mart.

In the mid-70s, Schlitz was No. 2 in market share in beer sales in the United States. During a recession, instead of continuing to build their brand, they attempted to maintain profitability by cutting costs. They substituted corn syrup for the more expensive barley malt. The result was beer that had visible flakes of yeast, less of a head, and a taste that consumers deemed inferior. By 1985, Schlitz was down to 1 percent market share. While cost cutting is sometimes necessary, it is almost impossible to simply cut your way to excellence in any business, even in difficult times.[1]

After every recession, a fundamental lesson learned is that the most successful enterprises never cut funding in their most critical areas of competence. In fact, they strategically plan to improve customer service when others are cutting back. They invest more heavily in research and development so they are nicely positioned when the economy rebounds. And, they make acquisitions while others stand pat. For example, Mark Hurd, CEO of Hewlett Packard, recently cut costs in non-core areas so he could fund *more* research and development. He also bought Electronic Data Systems for a bargain price to strategically move the company into tech outsourcing. On February 10, 2009 with the economy still in free fall, Intel's Paul Otellini announced plans for the company to invest $7 billion to retool plants to position itself to capture new markets for chips in telecommunications and HDTV.

In government, President Obama's Chief of Staff, Rahm Emmanuel, lives by the dictum that "one should not let a crisis go to waste." Despite the grim economy, Emmanuel pressed ahead with plans to dramatically increase renewable energy production, overhaul education, and totally revamp the nation's healthcare system all while cutting the federal deficit in half in four years. While this is undoubtedly overly ambitious, and violates my own dictum that "one should only pursue change where one cannot afford to fail," it nonetheless demonstrates aggressive leadership when others are paralyzed. Emmanuel understands that change can be brought about more quickly when everyone feels the pain associated with having their backs up against the wall.

A recession creates the perfect opportunity to challenge your people to think "out of the box." Hard times tend to sharpen the senses, increase focus, and spur creativity if the associate's sense of despair can be channeled properly. For instance, the sales function may choose to give away loads of product free of charge to generate goodwill and perhaps create a sense of psychological obligation for the future. Marketing could look to develop partnerships with companies offering complementary but non-competing products as a way to tap new markets. Research & Development might be tasked with fast-tracking products that can be sold in a down economy. Purchasing can use the desperation of their suppliers to lock in favorable prices. In short, courageous leaders keep everyone productively engaged in activities that have both short and long-term impact.

Not including our current economic implosion, there have been ten official recessions from 1945-2007. The average duration, peak to trough, was only 10 months. Even though our current recession has already lasted longer, the window of opportunity to leapfrog competitors will close quickly.

Charles Lazarus chose to open his first Toys "R" Us superstore during the recession of 1957. In the midst of the 1973 Arab oil embargo downturn, Ron Rivett and Dennis Brown opened Super 8 Motels. In the early '80s recession, Gary Hendrix was able to convince tight-fisted venture capitalists to spring for $3 million to fund a spin-off from Machine Intelligence Corporation, which became known as Symantec. During the Dot Com bust, Fred Chang started Newegg.com, a company that has grown into a $1.5 billion computer components enterprise while Jimmy Wales and Larry Sange started Wikipedia.

Leaders are people who purposely avoid following the crowd. If they have a product, service or idea they believe in, they demonstrate the courage to place a more aggressive bet, not a more timid one. They balance this with the prudence to abandon the highest risk initiatives and cut out marginally productive activities. They frugally pore over every expense to eliminate waste.

Leaders who successfully navigated their organizations through tough stretches in the past give almost without exception, the same advice. They say that managers need to be bold enough to make changes that associates, customers, or suppliers are likely to perceive as being negative quickly. In hindsight, most say their mistakes came from moving too slowly, and not going deep enough to take all their hits in one fell swoop. They advise to avoid doing things in drips and drabs. To cut swiftly to a defensible core of the operation, and begin rebuilding from there.

Leadership Tales from the Workplace

A large public utility would seem to be an unlikely place to find a courageous, resilient, leader at the helm. But that is exactly the type of person that Anaheim, CA, has in Public Utilities General Manager Marcie Edwards.

In January 2001, Marcie became one of the first women in the nation to be chosen to head an electric and water utility. The industry's leaders have historically been Good Ole Boys, predominately white, older, risk averse, technically proficient men chosen from a pool of internal candidates after years of grooming. Marcie was young, female, an outsider and carried herself as if she were a woman on a mission, which sent a message that she was more than willing to challenge the status quo.

One of Marcie's defining characteristics is that unlike her perception of most women, *she has the courage to take on jobs she has never tried.*

During the early part of her career, Marcie would don coveralls out in the field, earning her stripes. She had to endure hazing at first but soon learned that it was a ritual that all members were expected to go through to show the others that they are a stand-up person. As Marcie explains, "When there is a fire in a hole you don't pick up a phone and call 911. You put on an oxygen tank and rush to get the guys out of the hole. They need to know you have their backs."

Along the way, Marcie learned about legislation, lobbying, media relations, transmission, distribution and deregulation, to name but a few of the disciplines she tackled with little in the way of prior knowledge.

Her courage is currently being put to one of its biggest tests. On June 24, 2008, after extensive study and analysis of many options, Marcie recommended to the Anaheim City Council that they enter into a contract worth approximately $103 million with GE to purchase four massive turbines and related equipment/services. The kicker: There is no guarantee that the Canyon Power Project where these engines are slated to be placed, will receive the licenses and permits required to begin operation in the summer of 2010.

Marcie's dilemma was that there are only forty of these giant turbines built each year and other buyers had already secured most that will be produced in the next eighteen months. In order to get a favorable price and ensure delivery in time to make a summer of 2010 fire-up date, the contract had to be signed immediately. Yet, the licensing and permits necessary to make the project a reality would not be completed for at least another year.

Most general managers of utilities facing a similar decision would have done the safe non-controversial thing and waited until the permits were in hand before they signed a contract of that magnitude. As Marcie pointed out, "In our industry the do-nothing option is safe almost all of the time." But, as the philosopher Goethe said, "The dangers in life are infinite, and among them is safety."

If Marcie had waited for the permits, there would have been a guaranteed delay of the project by at least a year with associated costs to her organization of a minimum $25 million for having to obtain power from alternate sources plus a probable increase in the price of the turbines of $15-20 million. Waiting for the permits would have been the "safe play," but it sure would have been an expensive one.

Marcie's advice — good judgment is the byproduct of experience. Experience comes as a result of having the courage to overcome your fear of failure and make decisions. You have got to learn to fail and recover; to develop resilience. As author Edwin Louis Cole said, "You don't drown by falling in the water; you drown by staying there."[2]

Among the many differences between change-focused leaders and conventional managers is their philosophy regarding stability. A manager's prime focus is minimizing variation in process. It is hard to find fault with that goal. Like many seemingly worthwhile endeavors though, it can sometimes extinguish the desire to make vital changes.

Look at McDonald's. For many years, their entire company was set up to follow standardized procedures. Workers who were able to work within the system became promoted to supervisor followed by assistant manager, restaurant manager, district manager, regional manager, etc. They had a "promote from within" philosophy, which was a major factor in lowering turnover and providing a large pool of candidates to choose from at every level. However, there was an unintended consequence. By the time associates made it into the senior management ranks, anyone with maverick tendencies had long since washed out. It is no wonder that McDonald's ended up with a senior team practically devoid of creative thinking or approaches. Same-store sales stagnated and they fell behind their more innovative rivals. It took an infusion of outside talent at the highest levels to get the giant headed in a new and more profitable direction.

Change-focused leaders, by contrast, are all about having the courage to push the organization to take quantum leaps. If you don't need or want change, then a leader, especially a maverick one, is very dangerous indeed. Good managers may be able to implement enough incremental change to keep an institution competitive unless something truly disruptive happens. But change-focused leaders seem to be essential in turbulent times such as we find ourselves in today when revolutionary changes are called for and nothing short of dramatic increases in effectiveness will do.

Tales From the Workplace

Brian Burke, president of The Toronto Maple Leafs and former executive vice president and general manager of the 2007 Stanley Cup Champion Anaheim Ducks, believes that leading for change begins with a leader having the courage to follow his convictions. When Burkie first took over as general manager of the Ducks, he envisioned an explosive, daring team built on speed together with mental and physical toughness. To handle such a team, he determined that his head coach must be a confident, combative *warrior type*. He wanted a leader who was willing to take chances and capable of handling the pressure that would come from the overly aggressive mistakes his players would likely make. Burkie could have chosen any number of coaches who already had some success as an NHL head coach. But, none matched the high-risk, high-reward style profile he had in mind. So, he boldly rolled the dice in tapping Randy Carlyle, who had no previous head coach experience, to be his frontline leader.

Burkie also believes that leading for change involves having the courage to clarify expectations, even those that may be unpopular with associates. He is unapologetic in his demand for excellence in everyone from the Zamboni driver to his senior executives. He believes that there is a *loneliness of command* that leaders who set high expectations must endure.

On the day of my meeting with Burkie, the 2008 rookie crop made their first appearance at the team's facilities. He imparted a stern and unambiguous message. He said, "The Ducks are not run as a democracy. If you want to be on that type of team, we will accommodate you with a trade to an organization run like that, but you will probably be joining a loser. We expect you to be a vital part of our community. We expect you to follow direction, play within our system and to competently handle your role, whether it be four minutes or thirty-six minutes of ice time per game. Becoming a champion is hard, and work is not always going to be fun. The enjoyment comes from winning with others. Nothing less will be tolerated." Now that's what I call drawing a line on the ice!

Burkie used an interesting analogy with the players to make his point. He said, "A hockey team operates a lot like a symphony orchestra. Center stage up front is the first violinist. She is extremely talented and bathed in the spotlight. Having someone like that is critical to the symphony. But also important are the tubas and french horns in the rear. Everyone must accept their defined roles for the whole orchestra to produce a beautiful sound. All the musicians need to follow one person's direction. And, from a conductor's standpoint, he can't lead people who don't want to be part of his team."

Burkie says, "Don't be afraid of the moaning and groaning of your associates when they see you setting high expectations. Their enthusiasm will come when they see their dedication to excellence starting to pay off in their performance."[3]

A change-focused leader has to generate some pain associated with people's continuing with the status quo. If the discomfort of the present is not great enough, inertia will probably win out. Years ago when Mike Walsh was alive and CEO of Union Pacific Railroad, he went to every whistle-stop where the railroad had associates and explained to them that the alternative to cutting pay, benefits, and jobs was the bankruptcy of the company. People got the message. Recently, General Motors did the same thing to get the UAW to take over the company's pension obligations, though in their case GM executives probably waited too long to summon the courage to push for needed change.

Tales From the Workplace

A vivid example of administering a dose of reality occurred with one of my manufacturing clients. For years they were considered to be the undisputed worldwide leader in their industry. Even though their prices were often 50 percent higher than their competition, customers continued to buy, though market share had been slipping for a few years. They thought their quality and features were unsurpassed and, for that reason, their customers would continue to pay these ridiculously high premiums. Traditionally, every year the company would invite its top several hundred managers to travel to headquarters for the unveiling of the year's new products. In effect it was a giant pep-rally designed to whip people into a frenzy with upbeat speeches and a multimedia extravaganza.

As everyone settled into their seats in the darkened auditorium, the video production began. In the foreground were senior executives of very large companies giving testimonials. They waxed eloquently on the quality, features, and service plans of the products silhouetted in the background. As you might imagine, everyone was getting all pumped up. There were periodic shouts of "That's what I'm talking about," and "Cha-ching" echoing through the auditorium. After many minutes of this hoopla, the lights came up on the products that had been in the darkened background. People literally gasped when they realized every piece of equipment that the customers had been raving about in such glowing terms were those of their *competitor*. You could feel the air rush out of the arena and could have heard a pin drop. At that instant there was a collective sense of "Oh my god, the threat is real." These were high-level executives from potential customers talking about competitors in terms heretofore reserved for them — at a price 50 percent lower. Now that is how you get people to face reality!

Essential Knowledge

In their zeal to make an impact quickly, too many leaders use a shotgun approach where they try to change too many things at once. One of the most important lessons I try and impart to my clients is that they should never attempt to institute a major change unless they cannot afford to fail. Time, executive attention, money, people's absorption capacity, equipment and energy-- among other things -- are all limited. It takes great courage to choose not to pursue certain business initiatives even though they may have merit. Major change efforts are often stopped dead in their tracks as an organization's precious resources are spread too thin among lower value added propositions.

Perhaps the most powerful barrier to change of any kind is vested interests. Many leaders seem more interested in fitting in with their peers and direct reports than they do about implementing needed changes that will go against their "friends" interests. They often convince themselves that it is easier to "go along to get along."

People in the United States instinctively realize that the current Social Security system is unsustainable, tort reform is sorely needed, we need to lessen our dependence on foreign oil, and that a healthcare system that leaves tens of millions of people uninsured is a disgrace. Yet, who wants to pay more taxes, see their benefits reduced, have a nuclear power plant built nearby, or open up miles of our coastline to offshore drilling?

Failure to take into account whose vested interests are most likely to be threatened is the biggest mistake most would-be change-agents make. But once known, the leader has got to summon the courage to put a plan together to deal with these entrenched interests.

To most effectively drive home change, lots of communication is needed. People need to know how they will be affected personally and why doing what they are being asked to do is the best available option. Jack

Welch, the legendary former leader of General Electric, said, "You don't get anywhere if you keep changing your ideas. The only way to change people's minds is with consistency. You communicate, you communicate, and then you communicate some more. Consistency, simplicity, and repetition are what it's all about."

Since people tend to hate ambiguity it is imperative that key decisions are communicated to all affected parties. In the months leading up to Desert Storm, the morale of soldiers in the Persian Gulf was low, since they had no idea when they would be asked to fight. The minute the troops learned the date when the ground war would begin, morale skyrocketed even though it was much more likely that they might die. The soldiers could now focus on preparing for battle. It seems that people CAN handle the truth.

The default setting for many executives faced with uncertainty is to delay communication until they have greater visibility of unfolding events. This is the opposite of what is needed. Associates fear that they will be laid off. Investors wring their hands that the stock price will plunge. Suppliers lose sleep over whether their invoices will go unpaid. And community leaders become nervous that the whole operation might be shuttered. In the absence of official communication, anxiety increases. The rumor mill fills the void with inaccurate information that often makes things seem more dire than they really are.

The Importance of Perseverance

Changing an organization is like pulling on a "slinky" toy. If you pull one end, a few rings will immediately get pulled along, a few others will be stretched, but the bulk will stay relatively unchanged. If you let go, all the rings will snap back to their original positions. So, a key is to keep pulling. When you do, a few more rings will come to your side, a few more will stretch, and ultimately there will be so few rings left that they will "whoosh" over to your side all at the same time. As a change-focused leader you need to be persistent, otherwise the critical mass necessary to ingrain institutional changes will never be achieved.

When all is said and done, organizational change really is about getting *individuals* to alter the ways they are doing things. Resistance often starts because all human beings fall into *comfortable, habitual* ways of doing things. This is not only normal, it is essential. Without patterns to our behavior we would be faced with creating conscious responses every time we encountered a situation. A leader cannot change an organization directly. He can only do it by attempting to change the individual behavior of its members, many of whom will resist mightily.

Do a quick experiment. Cross your arms. Once you have done this, uncross them and re-cross them the opposite way. For most of us, the second way is somewhat uncomfortable. If you are like most people, you probably have slipped into a pattern of crossing your arms in the same manner every time you do it even though right over left is no better than left over right. But this habit keeps you from having to consciously think about it each time you do it. And if you were to try and break the habit, it is going to be a bit uncomfortable for a while. As the leader, you need to have the tenacity to keep challenging people to break their ineffective habits. Otherwise, people will naturally fall back into their habitual comfort zone.

💡 Don't Forget This 💡

Past history can determine whether change can be accelerated. Associates working in high tech industries are more accustomed to rapid change than say folks working in the Social Security Administration.

Wall Street looks for 90-day results. Fast-track military officers have a two-year window before their next assignment and high potential corporate leaders spend about two and a half years in each rotation. Most elected officials have about three years before they have to "run on their record" the final year of their term if they are seeking re-election or desire a higher office. Yet, fixes to really big problems often require payment of a short-term price. And, someone else may end up getting the credit for the results down the road. Thus the temptation is great for executives to use delay tactics and hope that things don't totally fall apart until someone else's watch. It takes courage to resist short-term pressures and do the necessary things — not the expedient ones.

Consider the poor state of infrastructure (roads, bridges, sewer systems, power plants, etc.) in many U.S. cities. The funds necessary to keep up with, let alone get ahead of the demands, are usually enormous and will certainly require a reduction in the day-to-day benefits for citizens in other areas. Infrastructure issues are somewhat invisible until they crash completely and any paybacks from a forward thinking city council that does address the issue come in long after the current council members are gone. Being a change-focused leader requires courageous long-term thinking and perseverance in an increasingly short-term world. No wonder Lee Iacocca asks, "Where have all the leaders gone?"

Tales From the Workplace

Former Federal Communications Commission Chairman Kevin Martin will likely go down in history as one of the most courageous FCC chiefs ever to hold the position. Historically the FCC was known for catering to the needs of the industry moguls, not to consumers. By contrast, Martin pushed through a blizzard of initiatives aimed at stimulating competition for the benefit of consumers.

Charles Dolan, founder and chairman of Cablevision, said he admires Martin for his willingness to make tough decisions. "He's not in there to do anybody's bidding. He's in there to do what's right for the agency and the public, and he's very bold about it."

Martin says that while his positions upset some companies or even whole industries, "That's just part of being a leader. When you are deciding controversial issues, nobody remembers when you were with them, they only remember when you were against them. You have got to follow your own convictions."[4]

To act boldly when others are hunkering down requires a healthy dose of self-assurance. It is an unmistakable fact that confidence is contagious. People are drawn to President Obama as much or more because of his self-assurance as they are to his philosophies.

If there is one characteristic that all highly successful change agents possess, it is the ability to project a level of confidence that serves to both comfort and inspire others. Some leaders such as Donald Trump, Carly Fiorina, Dallas Cowboys owner Jerry Jones, Sir Richard Branson, and Dallas Maverick's owner Mark Cuban display a charismatic bravado that at times makes them seem larger than life. Others including Condoleezza Rice, GE's Jeff Immelt, future Hall of Fame NFL Coach Tony Dungy, Michael Dell and Playboy Enterprises CEO Christie Hefner exude confidence in the more humble and self-effacing manner that I highly recommend. Regardless of the style leaders choose to project their confidence, it is impossible to overstate its importance.

In *every* high-level executive assessment I have ever conducted, an important charge I am given by the CEO or board of directors is to find them a courageous leader with gravitas who inspires confidence in others. And why not? Leaders have to deal with diverse constituencies that include Wall Street analysts, elected officials, regulatory watchdogs, environmental and consumer activists, dissident shareholders, powerful board members, union leaders, demanding customers, world-class associates, and relentless members of the media.

Leadership Tales from the Workplace

Christine Fox, president of The Center for Naval Analyses, the U.S. Navy's "think tank," is a leader with conviction.

Christine was appointed by NASA Director Sean O'Keefe to the Stafford-Covey Task Group to perform independent assessments of the implementation of the Columbia Space Shuttle Accident Investigation Board's recommendations. For the first time in many years she was involved in an organization foreign to her, NASA. Also, her job was supposed to be oversight, not problem solving. Despite her given role, Christine said the most valuable thing she learned was that you have got to have the courage to stay true to what you believe. Initially when she would overstep her bounds in providing recommendations, she was put in her place by others who told her that she should stick to her job, which was to stand back and critique — not solve problems.

Eventually her courage won the day. Christine said, "Look, our first goal is to get the shuttle to fly safely. If I have an idea that I think will help accomplish that goal I am duty bound to present it." In the end, Christine proposed several creative changes in procedure that were incorporated into the group's final report.

She told me that, initially a newcomer to a heavyweight group should watch and listen. But, at some point you have to demonstrate your confidence by speaking up regarding things you don't believe are right. "As an 'outsider,' whenever I did, that certainly had everyone's attention — even if for some I may have appeared to come on too strong." People would later corner her and say, "I am so glad you made that point today." As Martin Luther King Jr. once said, "Our days begin to end when we become silent about things that matter."[5]

CHAPTER 2

BE BOLD WHERE OTHERS FEAR TO TREAD:
Project Confidence

The Seven Habits of Confident People

Executives who do not feel self-assured are very unlikely to project the level of confidence that will inspire others to take risks in these uncertain times. The following are seven habits of "perception management" that courageous, change-focused leaders seem to have developed to mask any feelings of insecurity they might be experiencing.

Habit One — Speaking Clearly and Concisely

Leaders who under-communicate seek to shift the spotlight off of themselves as quickly as possible. Their speech seems abrupt and their answers incomplete. They create stress in the people they interact with since the other party has to find ways to carry the entire conversation.

Folks who tend to the opposite extreme and over-communicate are essentially trying to dominate the "airtime." Some love the sound of their self-perceived greatness. Others fear losing control of the argument or conversation. The other party dealing with such a person often becomes bored, frustrated, or completely turned off by the lack of sensitivity.

Fluid brevity should be the style that leaders aspire to project. In the harried environment of business, crisp and clear communication is essential to a leader's success.

Habit Two – Don't Waffle

Donald Trump says, "If you equivocate, it's an indication that you're unsure of yourself and what you're doing. I find it inappropriate, insulting, and condescending."[1]

Trump tells the story of one of his executives who was presenting data on the merits of a proposed development. The presenter had visited the city on several occasions and had done considerable due diligence. He proceeded to outline the pluses, the minuses, the pros and the cons, the good and the bad in mind-numbing detail. At times Mr. Trump thought the guy was advocating that the project be green lighted while at others he sensed the fellow thought the project might be a bad idea. On-and-on this man droned, seemingly straddling the fence. Finally in the throws of frustration Trump asked, "In ten words or less, what do you think of the project?" The man replied, "It stinks."

It is usually a mistake to *prematurely* share your opinion around powerful people. They like to feel as if they are in some semblance of control. However, once asked for your "take" on the situation, there shouldn't be the slightest hesitation or waffle. Clearly and concisely share your views and be prepared to defend them. Successful people love to probe others so they can gauge the depth of one's commitment. Even if they may not share the same point of view, winners tend to be impressed with a person of conviction.

Habit Three
Proper Pronunciation and Crisp Enunciation

Nothing says sloppy, unprepared, and stupid quite like butchering the language and mumbling. In 1972, presidential candidate Senator George McGovern had just taken the stage at the packed field house at the University of Cincinnati. Fourteen thousand students eagerly awaited his message. The first words out of his mouth were, "It's great to be here in Cin-sa-nat-ah." A collective groan echoed throughout the field house. This guy couldn't even properly pronounce the name of the city. He did the same thing in Spokane, Wash., pronouncing it Spo-kane instead of the proper Spo-can.

It is also amazing how many executives mumble when they give speeches. If someone is brilliant, perhaps he can get away with it. But for the rest of us it is a killer.

Depending upon where a leader was raised, he may have to shake some bad habits. I was raised in Pittsburgh, Penn., and we have our own accent and vocabulary called "Pittsburghese." I had to learn not to say "Yun's," "Gumband" and "Warsh," among many other things. In Chicago, it's "Dems" and "Dohs" that need to be avoided. And, in some cultures, the words come out "Bid-ness" or "Ax me." If a leader wants to project professionalism, he should attempt to develop excellent diction and make sure he knows the proper pronunciation of words *before* he finds himself in the middle of a presentation.

Habit Four – Dress for the Situation Appropriately

I always advise clients to dress a half-level above the people they supervise. This means if a leader's direct reports work in jeans and T-shirts, he should dress in slacks and a long sleeve blouse or golf shirt. If the leader's people come to work in pants and polo shirts, he might want to consider a blazer. If the associates are typically dressed in blazers then the leader should go with a suit. The problem arises when "suits" supervise people who work in jeans. There is too much distance projected. The idea is to let your dress communicate comfort with just a hint of authority.

Due to a bureaucratic snafu I found myself having to physically go down to the county courthouse to straighten things out in front of a traffic court judge. There were 80 of us packed into the tiny courtroom. Druggies, gang bangers, alcoholics and other assorted lower echelons of society dressed accordingly were one-by-one called before the judge to plead their case. It was clear the judge was impatient and had little respect for people who clearly projected little respect for themselves based upon how they dressed.

One young man asked the judge if he could do his community service in the adjacent county. The judge replied, "We don't accept their trash and we don't send our trash over there." The few of us who had dressed a bit more respectfully for being in a court of law were treated quite differently. When I was called before the judge he looked me over, glanced at my file and said, "So, Dr. Hanes, what can the court do for you today?" When I was finished he said, "Sorry for the inconvenience in having to spend the morning in court." He even reduced the cost of my traffic citation by two-thirds. The only thing that was different was my appearance. While it was not fair for the judge to act in that manner, he was only being human.

Habit Five – Smile and Project Your Voice Solidly

A smile is irresistible. When someone smiles at us we feel an unconscious urge to smile back. This reduces tension for both parties. Have you noticed that people who are nervous seldom smile? All their energy is focused inwards on their feelings of insecurity.

When we are nervous three things tend to negatively impact our speech. First, the throat tightens up and we feel an urge to swallow hard. Second, mucus builds up causing an unconscious reaction to clear our throats. Third, voice pitch gets higher. You can reduce your own anxiety by being aware of these things and by focusing your attention outside yourself, perhaps by looking to see if the other person is projecting their own signs of nervousness.

People with confidence learn to modulate their voice. At times it helps to be able to "boom" one's voice, while at others, toning down to a near whisper can best serve the purpose. Mostly a strong steady push of the voice from the diaphragm is the way to go. Don't let yourself get lost in the crowd.

Habit Six – Make Eye Contact Appropriately

If a person's eyes were truly the window to one's soul, then making effective eye contact would seem to be an important thing for a leader to focus upon. Of course what constitutes appropriate eye contact may vary from culture-to-culture throughout the world. Perhaps the biggest non-verbal cue to a person's lack of self-confidence in the United States is the aversion of eye contact. A person who can't look someone in the eye is subconsciously afraid that the person they are interacting with can see right through them. It is also a tip off to lack of interest in the person. A surprising number of people at all organizational levels find it difficult to look the person they are speaking to in the eyes.

Have you noticed how some people always seem to be looking past you when in conversation? Their eyes flit around the room as if searching for someone who they feel might better meet their needs. At the opposite extreme are the people whose eyes seem to "radar lock" on yours to the point of creating extreme discomfort. Some people try to use their eyes to bore through you with laser-like intensity. This is usually an intimidation tactic. The worst offenders are the people whose gaze is directed sideways and downward. Few things say "nervous" in a more telling way than that.

In the United States the idea is to generally look the other person squarely in the eye with the periodic breaking of contact so as not to create tension. Leaders should attempt to get frequent insight from others as to the appropriateness of their eye contact. *Used effectively*, eye contact is a major factor in projecting self-assuredness.

Habit Seven – Sustain A Symphonic Flow

Observe effective CEOs over an extended period of time and a calming sensation begins to envelope you. Unlike most mere mortals, they appear to glide effortlessly through their day as if they were floating on air. Most of them have a clean, well-organized desk. They routinely make time for the unexpected drop-in visitor or choose to linger for a few minutes at the end of a meeting before heading on to the next one.

When great CEOs give speeches or make points in a meeting their communication style is seldom haphazard or herky-jerky. It is fluid and symphonic with a steady predictable rhythm. You can sense their comfort and feel their command of the situation.

Especially in times of uncertainty, associates at all levels carefully scrutinize a leader's behavior to help them interpret the severity of a given circumstance. A leader's behaviors should signal that things are under control. If your desire is to ascend to the C-suite, forcing yourself to become the eye of the hurricane when all the crap is flying around you is a trait worth developing.

In the field of psychology, the word "priming" describes framing a situation in such a manner that other people are likely to see what one wants them to see. In Western society we have been "primed" to expect leaders to exhibit certain characteristics. In fact the previous seven attributes are emblematic of what many people's stereotype of an effective leader looks like. It is immediately noticeable when one or more of our "expectations" are violated. Authoritative yet relaxed posture, a firm handshake, steady and projected voice, crisp speech, appropriate eye contact, and professional mode of dress are merely the "table stakes" to allow entry into the game.

Essential Knowledge

Courageous Leaders:

Make decisions and live with them without second-guessing.

Do their homework by painstakingly developing and working through options.

Think about the impact of decisions on the larger organization.

Display a calm demeanor when things don't go according to plan.

Operate from a strong ethical base that causes them to always consider the potential fallout on all parties that might be affected if things were to go wrong.

Keep themselves energized in tough times by having the chutzpah to believe that there is no way they are going to let the enterprise fail on their watch.

Challenge their people to look for creative, "out of the box" solutions to seemingly intractable problems. In essence, channeling associates fear and despair into an opportunity to re-conceptualize all aspects of the organization.

Whether it is a calculated risk in signing a contract before absolute certainty prevails or committing to a potentially brilliant gamble fraught with risk, change-focused leaders have the courage of their convictions and through their boldness serve to inspire actions that often cause those risks to pan out. In tough times, prudent risk taking can set an organization up for accelerated success once the recession passes.

💡 Don't Forget This 💡

Once you lose your courage, your effectiveness as a leader decreases very quickly. There are few things sadder to watch than a person who has the potential for success but lacks the courage to try, or an opportunity squandered due to fear of failure. Leaders who are consumed with fear of being fired will never be bold enough to make a meaningful difference. Thus it behooves you to become financially and intellectually independent of your organization as soon as possible.

CHAPTER 3

JEALOUSLY GUARD THE CROWN JEWELS, THEN ACQUIRE MORE: Retain Your Best Talent

Philip Schoonover, CEO of Circuit City, fired 3,400 of his most experienced employees in 2007, arguing that they made too much money. By the end of 2008, Circuit City was bankrupt.[1] In a downturn, the smart play is to attempt to lure the best talent away from your competitors while doing all that you can to make sure they don't attract yours.

An organization cannot usually become world-class without at least a few star players. Their talents are vital, but their egos often create unique challenges, which must be handled in a very sophisticated way by the leader of the institution. It is ironic that while your stars are the last people you would ever consider laying off, in these tough times when they see thousands of workers getting *pink slips* they often get nervous about their own job security and are tempted to jump ship. It is critical that you, as a leader, do all that you can to prevent this from happening. With all the pressure to downsize, it is easy to lose sight of the critical importance of talent retention.

One thing organizations can do is to make sure that bonus payment formulas are set around results that star associates can control. Things like customer satisfaction survey scores or production quality/efficiency levels can be directly influenced regardless of the state of the overall economy. And, while it is critical that regular communication come from the CEO in a crisis, it is equally important to hear from the direct boss. Often an associate's supervisor is not only better known, but also more highly respected and trusted than the CEO.

If you are fortunate, at some point in your career you will be promoted to a level or join an organization where *everyone* you are asked to lead will be stars in their own right. Some will be brilliant, others supremely talented, and a few may even be famous or extremely wealthy. Many may be considered by others to be terrific leaders themselves.

In certain collectives such as elite universities, prestigious think-tanks, world-class consulting firms, professional sports teams, or the best medical, legal, accounting or investment banking institutions, it is a virtual guarantee that large numbers of people you are responsible for will be more successful than you in some way.

Can these people be led in the same manner as we attempt to lead more "normal" folks? Will they follow even the best of leaders?

During my career I have done consulting work with the Brookings Institution, the American Academy of Physician Executives, the Battelle Memorial Institute, Science Applications International, The Center for Naval Analyses, and other storied organizations. I have conducted seminars with hundreds of "rocket scientists" from ATK Launch Systems, General Dynamics, and Lockheed Martin. An Academy Award winner, numerous company presidents and several NFL All Pro players have called me their personal coach. Attempting to influence the "best of the best" is indeed worlds apart from what would be considered our usual leadership challenges.

Stars Are Different

To successfully lead stars it helps to know how they differ from the norm, and they *are* quite different. Think of Phil Jackson's challenge in trying to coach Michael Jordan, Scottie Pippin, Dennis Rodman, Shaquille O'Neal, and Kobe Bryant. Clearly they are rich, famous, and influential players. Or imagine Strobe Talbot, president of the Brookings Institution, attempting to "manage" Michael O'Hanlon, perhaps the nation's foremost expert on Middle East policy.

First, stars are difficult if not impossible to replace, and as such they have enormous leverage. They cast a halo over the institutions that are lucky enough to land them. They are needed by others far more than they need what their organizations offer in return. Many come to expect special perks and treatment. In the case of sports stars or Hollywood celebrities, they often make as much or more money from commercial endorsements as from their contracts to play or act. Star associates in business often identify more with their profession than their organization. They are usually well known, well connected and have seemingly endless options. Most have pretty healthy egos and don't see themselves as working *for* anyone.

Don't abuse your current market power. Yes, stars are more readily available and less expensive during a recession. But beware of letting your commanding position cause you to do things you may later regret. According to a 2008 study done at Vanderbilt University, associates treated poorly during the hiring process are twice as likely to leave the company as soon as the market changes. Things that especially raise ire are a slow and unresponsive selection process, "shotgun" offers that expire at the end of the day if not accepted and an "attitude" that says, "You need us more than we need you." Like all forms of power, if you abuse the temporary advantage the recession confers upon you, it can come back to haunt you when times get better.

Understand Their Dreams

Despite your stars' power, you should not acquiesce to their every whim and demand. Keep in mind, the reason they chose to associate with your enclave in the first place is that they felt it would give them an image boost or enhance their ability to achieve their personal goals in some, or many ways. So, it is vital that you understand their interests and objectives and take great pains to show them how you and your organization can help them achieve their aims. In the summer of 2008, hockey star Marian Hossa turned down a lucrative multi-year contract with the Pittsburgh Penguins and accepted a one-year deal for less money to join the Detroit Red Wings solely because he felt he had a better chance to win the Stanley Cup there than with the Penguins.

A recent example would be NBA stars Kevin Garnett, Paul Pierce and Ray Allen who were each the main attraction on a pitiful team. They came together to win a championship with the Boston Celtics.

Don't Forget This

Most stars would rather be part of an ensemble cast of other great players that blend their talents to win championships than be the standout performer on a losing team.

Forget Your Title

Position power or formal authority means very little in the business world today and almost nothing to stars. They need to feel they are choosing to be led. Stars will not make such a choice unless they know and trust the person attempting to lead. Therefore it is vital that the leader spend considerable effort over a long period of time trying to develop a one-to-one relationship. This implies that the leader open up about his or her background, family, goals, and desires, while seeking to learn the same from the star. This is not easy for many leaders to do as they have been sold a bill of goods somewhere along the way that says to keep a distance from the people they lead and that openness will create too much vulnerability.

Get Face To Face

Whenever possible, it is important to deal with stars in person versus over the phone, in writing, or by e-mail. The visit itself shows that you consider the person to be important.

When Kobe Bryant was demanding a trade from the Los Angeles Lakers in 2007, team owner Dr. Jerry Buss got on a plane and flew to Europe to meet Bryant in person. According to Bryant, this personal attention was the critical action that caused him to cease to pressure for a trade.

With stars, it often comes down to feeling respected.

Co-Op Their Expertise

Another leadership technique that works well with stars is to frequently ask them their opinions on issues, or their advice on decisions. This will show that you confer a special status on them. It will also make your job of implementing whatever decisions are made so much easier. The goal is to tap into their unique insight and expertise to stretch your own thinking.

When future Hall of Fame Coach Phil Jackson was thinking of offering a contract to Dennis Rodman to join the NBA Chicago Bulls, he approached the team's stars Michael Jordan and Scottie Pippin for advice. He told them that he thought having a great rebounder like Dennis, who had just led the league in rebounding for the third consecutive year, might just be the piece needed to bring a championship to Chicago. But, he warned, Dennis will create a media circus, probably skip practice on occasion and get thrown out of key games at critical times. If we make this move, you will have to support my treating Dennis a bit different from the rest of the team. Are you willing to do this?[2]

Phil Jackson was smart. He shared the decision with his key players, an almost unheard of act in sports at the time. The stars were now aligned in support of the organization's decision because it was also their decision. The move paid off handsomely, bringing the Bulls six NBA Championships with Rodman as a key component.

Forge A Bond

Leaders of exceptionally talented people should create vehicles where these stars can share their backgrounds and interests with each other as a means of solidifying their connection to the organization. One of my favorite team-building activities is to gather people together and ask them to stand and speak to the group for five minutes. They are to talk about their lives and interests outside of work (or including work if it makes sense). Usually there are at least a couple things that each person in the group will have in common with other members. I have found that the thickest of bonds can develop between persons that have even just one simple passionate interest in common. And, if you pay close attention, this exercise will give you invaluable insight into their background and goals in life. They literally lay out for you the keys to their motivational engine.

Leverage History

Another thing leaders of stars should do is to make visible the history of the organization. Perhaps creating a museum of memorabilia like Mary Kay Cosmetics does, inviting past stars to address current day associates like the Los Angeles Lakers do, or publishing a history of the enterprise as Science Applications International does would make sense. Obviously organizations with a rich past like the Pittsburgh Steelers, Boston Celtics, IBM, Harvard University, the Boston Philharmonic or the Cleveland Clinic would be in a better position to leverage this asset, but all organizations should make the attempt. If the institution is going through a down cycle, you should look for the stars who may be drawn to the challenge inherent in trying to turn around an organization with a recent history of losing.

One last thing that usually works well is to create exceptional internal and external communication systems. Blue Ox companies' terrific quarterly magazine, the Brookings Institution's coveted roundtable lunches, LanDesk Software's weekly e-mail blasts and the like will keep everyone focused on the goings-on inside the organization and remind people of the benefits of the collective.

Hall of Fame Coach Pat Riley "guaranteed" to the media a "three-peat" when he was coach of the NBA's Los Angeles Lakers as a way to challenge his stars. Lance Armstrong wanted to win more Tour de France cycling titles than anyone in history. Great performers always want to accomplish more, yet many leaders are afraid to ask more of them. Several years ago, I had a chance to chat with baseball's Tony Gwynn, eight-time National League Batting Champion. He practiced at least an hour longer than everyone else each day. I asked him why he worked so hard, he was already a great player. He said, "I want to be a Hall of Famer." Over the years I have come to learn that Tony is not unique in this trait. The best in any field always seem to want to be stretched further.

Retaining Creative Stars

Retaining your most creative talent is a special leadership challenge. Christine Fox, president of The Center for Naval Analyses, the U.S. Navy's independent *think tank*, leads a couple hundred researchers, with over 70 percent holding Ph.D's from MIT, Chicago, Cal Tech, and other elite technical universities. Over the years, Christine has learned much about how to succeed in leading such brilliant and innovative people.

Christine has found that many creative people have difficulty staying focused on one thing long enough to be productive. The leader may have to sift through ten half-baked ideas they present to find one that is truly game-changing. So a leader has to develop patience. If pushed too hard, creative people will leave.

According to Christine, when creative people are working on a project, it often becomes all-consuming to them. They work with great intensity over long periods, routinely to exhaustion. Consequently they need a break before starting their next assignment. The leader needs to give them *space* so they can regenerate.

Another unique factor in dealing with brilliant creative people is in the area of evaluations. These associates are used to getting all A's in school. In the think tank business, not everyone gets all A's. The first time they are told their work is fine, but not excellent, it is the equivalent to them of getting a C. A major role of leadership is to prevent these people from becoming demoralized.

Creative people are best *coached* in one-on-one tutorials. They tend to resist the classroom where there is a perceived challenge to their status, or the implication that their education is less than complete.

Listening is also a challenge for highly intelligent people. Their minds process information faster than others can speak, so their thoughts tend to drift. Many are also hyperactive, as expressed by rapid speech, restlessness, impulsive actions and nervous habits. They are often seen by others as aloof and non-conforming to accept standards of behavior. They can sense they are different.

CHAPTER 4

JEALOUSLY GUARD THE CROWN JEWELS, THEN ACQUIRE MORE:
Poach Their Best Talent

Selecting "A" Players

In austere times with fewer key slots to fill it is critical that an enterprise place its bets on the right new hires or promotions. An important goal is to shore-up your weakest functional areas by filling the void with "A" players.

Perhaps the best executive assessor in the country today, Brad Smart, defines an "A" player as the top 10 percent of talent available at *each* salary level.[1] The thing we should find very appealing in this definition is that an entire organization has the potential to be comprised of nothing but "A" players. To build such an organization should be every leader's goal.

Think of any great team and the two constants you will find are that they had terrific talent across the board and excellent leadership. The Pittsburgh Steelers of the 1970s had a Hall of Fame coach *and* they had nine Hall of Fame players. The great Boston Celtics teams that won nine NBA titles had a Hall of Fame coach *and* four of their starting five are in "The Hall" as well. A U.S. Navy Seal team has an excellent leader and the entire sixteen-person unit is made up of "A" players.

In his landmark book, *Good to Great*, Jim Collins introduced the concept of "First who, then what." Basically, he said you first get the right people "on the bus" (and the wrong people off the bus), and then you decide direction.

Collins' theory was that a lot of good people "get on the bus" specifically because of the quality of people already on the bus. Once onboard, if the bus needs to change direction they can live with it since the reason they got on in the first place was because of the other talented people.

One problem with this argument is that it presupposes that you already have other great people on the bus (not to mention someone talented driving the bus). That would be no problem if your organization has been perpetually stellar like Goldman Sachs or General Electric. But of course, most institutions are not already great.

In any event my main point is — *you can do a much better job in selecting the right people if you have a clear direction in mind, and you know what roles you need great people to fill.* Brad Smart would seem to agree. He said, "A person can be enormously talented, but if those talents are not within the competencies of the job they can be worthless."[2]

Collins' other two points are right on. With the right people, motivation, and supervision, issues are largely non-existent. With the wrong people on the bus it doesn't matter what direction is chosen, the organization won't be great.[3]

In the end, whether you get the "A" players on the bus first or after a direction is set, at some point every enterprise is going to have to stock up on talent and Jettison its sub-standard performers.

The organization most famous for this practice is General Electric. They start by recruiting at the top universities and selecting the best talent from those schools. They systematically develop these people's capabilities all along the way and they methodically weed out the under performers each year. Their CEO is always selected from several capable candidates internally.

So they lose folk all along the way. Sure, but so what? They are able to continually attract the best because these people know they will get terrific development and, if they are good enough can achieve great success within GE. If not, they will top the list of candidates for jobs in other organizations. In fact they take great pride that more former GE executives have gone on to lead more Fortune 1,000 companies than the alumni of any other company. GE's performance over the last several decades speaks for itself as to how well this system can work. Nordstrom is another example of a business that goes to great lengths to hire "A" players. When they opened their first East Coast store in Tysons Corner, VA, the human resources department interviewed 3,000 people to fill 400 *frontline* positions.

Performance — Not Potential

It is important to remember that a person is generally designated as an "A" player on the basis of *performance*, not potential. You could have an entire organization made up of "A" players and still have none that are promotable because of the different skill set that may be required.

Think of a Seal team again. Being an "A" player sniper or demolition expert has little in common with the skills needed to, say, captain an aircraft carrier.

To simplify for the moment, let's assume you are trying to build a team of "A" players without any regard to future promotability. How do you do it?

The Devil You Know

Studies bear out that an institution that starts with the best raw talent from entry level or recent college graduates and invests heavily on developing that talent will most likely be a stellar performer over many years. That certainly is the philosophy of the Pittsburgh Steelers, who have won more games, more division titles, and more Super Bowls than any other NFL team over the span from 1970 to 2009. It is what Google, Proctor and Gamble, Federal Express, Johnson & Johnson, PepsiCo, and a vast majority of the other companies on Fortune Magazine's most admired list each year practice. As one of my clients, the former CEO of Avocent Corp., John Cooper, phrases it, "With inside candidates it's the devil you know versus the devil you don't know with outside candidates." And it makes sense. Because you have data on the insiders over the length of their entire career, you know where their shortcomings really are and you can often mitigate those weaknesses in many ways. With outsiders, it is a bit of a crapshoot.

But at some point every organization must go outside to bring in new blood. How do you get good data to expose "the devil you don't know?"

Assessment Centers and Psychological Profiling

The very best way to evaluate candidates for managerial roles is through the assessment center. An assessment center uses a combination of structured exercises observed by trained assessors, a battery of psychometric profiles, and an in-depth interview by a well-trained interviewer. The major problem with this concept is that unless you lead a really large organization that has a lot of positions to fill, the cost and logistics are prohibitive. So this option is a non-starter for most enterprises.

Despite advances in psychometric profiling, this is not a terrific alternative either. Most competent executives can usually outsmart even the best of psychological tools, thus you are never sure if the candidate's answers are genuine. So for the most part, while such instruments are great for leadership development, as a selection tool their value is debatable.

An excellent way to potentially *eliminate* candidates is by "Googling" them or examining their profiles on *Facebook, MySpace* or other electronic networking sites. But this tactic will seldom result in causing an organization to hire someone, only to reject those who are clearly substandard.

Enhancing the Interview

This leaves the interview with follow-up reference checks as the best available tool to assess a leader's competency. Having said this, my experience has led me to conclude that the way most organizations conduct the interview process is a travesty. Truly illuminating interviews seem to be incredibly rare.

First of all, most people doing interviewing are not properly trained. Second, the typical managerial interview lasts 45 minutes, 60 minutes tops. Of that time, at least 10 minutes is ice breaking and answering questions. So you get 35 to 50 minutes of data *at the most*. And the kicker is: most interviewers ask the candidate virtually *the same questions*. So, even if you have eight people on the interview schedule to assess the candidate, you still only end up with about an hour's worth of insight. Third, it is appalling how few organizations even know what competencies are the most important ones for a candidate to possess to be successful. I had a college professor who said, "If you don't know where you are going, you can't get lost." True, but you won't know when you get there either. No wonder that many human resource executives will tell you that selecting successful managers from the outside, meaning top 25 percent performers, is a coin flip at the very best.

Know What You Should Be Looking For

Fortunately there are some things you can do that don't have to break the bank. First and most important is to take the time to create a list of competencies. Generally for managerial positions competencies fall into six main themes: *technical, leadership, managerial, interpersonal, intellectual, and personal.*

- *Technical competencies* are the bedrock functional knowledge and skills a person will use in the job of, say, controller or design engineering manager. Someone can only really assess these with expertise in that particular functional discipline. I have done a couple thousand assessments over the last 32 years, and while I can assess the other five areas quite easily, I usually have no clue as to whether a corporate controller knows a debit from a credit or how to efficiently reconcile accounts receivable.

- *Leadership competencies* are things such as style, vision, change management and inspiring follower-ship.

- *Managerial competencies* are things like performance management, team building, associate development, empowerment, customer focus, selection, diversity, goal setting, meeting facilitation, and conflict handling.

- *Intellectual competencies* refer to analytical skills, judgment/decision making, conceptual ability, strategic skills, and risk taking.

- *Interpersonal competencies* include approachability, communication skills, presentation skills, negotiation skills, assertiveness, political savvy, and first impression.

• *Personal competencies* are enthusiasm, courage, resilience, initiative, integrity, independence, adaptability, self-awareness, stress management, personal organization, and work/life balance.

Indispensable Tip !

Of all the competencies, the technical competencies are the easiest to develop if a person is deficient.

Once you know which competencies are the most important, questions can be structured around each required area. For a rather detailed list of questions for each competency, you may want to get a copy of *Topgrading*, by Brad Smart. In my opinion it is the best selection-interviewing book ever written. But the real power of the interview process is how well you listen to and interpret the answers.

The Interview Team

Now that you know the most important criteria comes the part where all the interviewers need to work together as a team. If you have eight assessors, each should be assigned a specific set of competencies to explore in-depth. For instance, three people can be assigned to dig deeply into the candidate's technical bandwidth and work history. The five remaining interviewers are assigned one each of the other five competencies. After the interviews are over, all eight assessors gather together to hammer out a comprehensive evaluation of the candidate. If done well, this process will up your batting average in selecting A or B players to around 75 percent.

Indispensable Tip !

You may want to consider hiring a professional in the area of executive candidate assessment to supplement your internal team. A competent professional will use a three-hour structured interview format centered on the five non-technical competencies.

Beware of relying on professional recruiters or executive search firms to perform this type of screening. Often their motivation is primarily to get the position filled, thus they won't do more than a surface scan. Most simply do not have the time or skill to conduct a three-hour assessment.

Because skilled professionals have been well trained in the art and science of interviewing, their accumulated mental database of hundreds of executive interviews, and the sheer amount of time with the candidate, a breathtaking amount and quality of information can be compiled.

Usually professionals will want to get to know the other members of the executive team and the organization's culture so they can make a better determination of "fit" with the position. Upon completion of their assessment, the professional drafts a several-page document detailing the candidate's strengths and potential concerns. This is followed up with a phone debrief with the hiring manager, usually within 24 hours.

Four Important Considerations

1. Select People with Passion for your Product/Service

My evidence is anecdotal, but in 32 years of involvement in selecting people, I have made one near universal observation. People who are passionate about the organization and/or its products/services prior to joining it, tend to exhibit a wide range of positive behaviors once they get the job. Specifically, they seem to be less likely to be tardy, absent, or quit the organization. They are more likely to volunteer for overtime, offer suggestions, and be considered good team players. They file fewer grievances, lawsuits, and score higher on measures of associate satisfaction. Think of Stephen

Spielberg sneaking onto the Universal Studios lot everyday for months when he was a teen to see how films were made. You just had to know that kid would grow up to be a great filmmaker.

2. Hold Out for the Best

If "A" players settle for hiring "B" players, it is almost a given that these same "B" players will end up hiring "C" players to work for them. World class organizations create a culture where all associates are *encouraged* and *rewarded* for hiring people who are even better than themselves in their areas of greatest weakness. They ostracize people who lower their hiring standards just to get a warm body on board that can start cranking out work.

3. Use Common Sense

Often candidates look great on paper but end up to be terrible choices because of the context of the job. During the dot com boom, startup companies were fighting over each other to attract senior vice presidents from Bellsouth, Ph.D's from Motorola and professors from MIT. Most of those "lucky enough" to land one of these gems found out in short order that most lacked the frugal temperament, energy, and scrappy nature necessary for the hand-to-hand combat of the dot com world.

4. Beware the Halo and Conformity Effects

The halo effect is simply the notion that people are attracted to others who seem like themselves and are repelled by folks who seem "different." Research also indicates that good looking and well-dressed applicants tend to get hired over even far better applicants who are not physically attractive. Thus, hiring managers might want to consider holding the initial interview by phone so as to lessen the likelihood of being swayed by the halo.

Also, no one on the interview team should let their feelings about the candidate be known until all the days interviews are complete. Studies confirm that once others have weighed in on a candidate one way or the other most people tend to let this override their own assessment.

Gene Weingarten, a reporter for the Washington Post conducted an interesting experiment. He convinced world-renowned violinist Joshua Bell to perform Johann Sebastian Bach's "Partita in D Minor for Solo Violin," on a priceless Stradivarius violin for forty-five minutes at 8 a.m. in a Washington D.C. metro station. The object was to see how many people would pause to listen and how much money they would toss in his case as tips.

Nearly 1,100 people walked past and Maestro Bell collected less than $33.[4] The lesson, people tend to place a great deal of credence on the opinions of others — be those opinions good, bad or indifferent.

Reference Checking

Extensive reference checking is an essential component to any good selection process. Frankly, this has become something of a lost art. Most executives assume that a person's previous employers will either say nothing at all or at least never provide any damaging information. This in fact was true for many years. However, courts are now determining that companies have a *legal responsibility* to share any negative information they may have on their previous employees. If they don't, and it is later found that they had pertinent facts they did not disclose, they could be held liable for damages suffered. If the hiring manager conducts the reference check rather than going through human resources, the odds of collecting valuable nuggets of information increase dramatically. And if the references don't call you back, that in itself should be a "red flag."

In addition to references, it is always wise to conduct a background check on the individual to corroborate the facts that were presented as well as uncover any criminal history or past substance abuse. With millennial applicants, you might get a lot of insight into them just by checking their profiles on *MySpace* or *Facebook*. Virtually everyone in that cohort seems to have a web page or two these days. And most people can easily be "Googled."

It is critically important that senior leaders make time to fully participate in the interview process. It sends an unmistakable signal of the importance of talent selection. At Four Seasons hotels, *every* prospective hire, regardless of position, goes through a minimum of five interviews, including one with the general manager of the property. Turnover is less than half the industry average.

If you think about all the hoops that someone has to jump through to get permission to buy a $150,000 software package compared to how little thought goes into new hires, it is ridiculous. The right decision on a software package gives no advantage the competition can't duplicate, but a superior hire could have an unbelievable impact on the enterprise.

One of Fortune Magazine's 100 Best Companies to work for, Zappos. com, goes so far as to offer each new recruit $2,000.00 *to leave* the company during their training period. Zappos.com figures this is an inexpensive way to weed out the marginally committed before they do real damage, negatively impact the culture, or cost the company larger sums to terminate down the road.

While all this might sound time consuming and expensive, and it is, consider the alternative. Organizations that don't follow a process like the one outlined in this chapter fail to select "A" and "B" players about half the time. The cost of those failures is astronomical. When you consider search firm fees, relocation, up-front bonuses, severance packages, wasted training and orientation, the costs often total hundreds of thousands of dollars. And this is before taking into account hidden costs like higher associate turnover caused by the poor leader, lower customer satisfaction, or gross incompetence.

Ultimately any coach is only as good as the talent he assembles. Constant turnover in the executive ranks is either a sign of poor hiring decisions or poor leadership. Jill Barad lost a lot of talent at Mattel. Gateway founder Ted Waitt let one bad hire effectively kill his company and cost him a great deal of his personal fortune. It is tough to stay on track without excellent people underneath.

The difficult economic environment we find ourselves in today means we must make every shot we take on a new hire and/or promotion count. The good news is that in these tough times there are some incredibly talented people out there for the taking. You might wonder how in the world you can ever financially afford to go after these suddenly available stars. The important question might be, can you afford not to take advantage of this somewhat rare window of opportunity to load up on superior talent that others have been forced to part with? History tells us that this window will not be open for long.

CHAPTER 5

GAIN TRACTION THROUGH TEAMWORK:
A Model of Team Development

Ensuring that an enterprise's key roles are filled with a phalanx of highly talented INDIVIDUALS should under-gird any organizational strategy. But leaders who want to best position the enterprise to weather stormy seas are advised to spend considerable energy in melding these stars into a team. To gain the most traction in good times, creating a team environment is a worthy goal. In tough times, teamwork is the mother lode that can turn average institutions into champions.

Sports dynasties, world-class symphony orchestras, America's most admired companies, elite military units, the most effective government entities, and prestigious "think tanks" are all built in remarkably similar ways, overcoming a highly predictable series of challenges. Understanding the logic behind the cause and sequence of these challenges is key to plotting the solutions necessary to propel the team through to the next level of effectiveness.

The beauty of this model is that it works at any level of team: project, departmental, functional, or enterprise. It can also serve as a blueprint of how to build a team or as a diagnostic tool to determine the team's current

Challenge Driven Team Building System

PHASE 1	PHASE 2	PHASE 3
Challenge of Direction & Focus	Challenges of Structure, Infrastructure, Alignment, and Resources	Challenges of Stretch, Interface & Execution
Situation Diagnosis Mission/Vision Guiding Principles Goals & Objectives Strategy Tactical Plan Priorities Measures	Organizational Structure Systems Alignment Policy/Procedure Alignment Roles/Responsibility Clarification Individual Priority Alignment Properly Allocate Resources	Lift to Higher Limits Negotiate Interface Issues Monitor & Ensure Execution

MOTIVATION

PERFORMANCE

Held Together By Rigorous Selection, Effective Orientation & Ongoing Training

Challenge of Trust & Commitment	Challenges of Sustainability of Leadership & Team Cohesion	Challenges of Change
Create Comfort & Trust Personal Goals to Team Goals Develop Case for Commitment	Internal Team-Confront Issues • Problem Identification • Problem Prioritization • Problem Solving	Revisit Ineffective Norms Integrate New Team Members Allow Maximum Autonomy Provide Frequent Face to Face Interaction
TEAM BUILDING TYPE 1	TEAM BUILDING TYPE 2	TEAM BUILDING TYPE 3

VALLEY OF DESPAIR

effectiveness in key activities relating to each stage.

The elements that go into the creation of championship caliber teams are pretty basic and so few in number that they can fit onto one page. Of major importance, however, is the sequence that the elements must follow. Like building a house where the foundation precedes the framing and the plumbing is installed before the drywall, the activities of building a team must be laid out in a specific order to maximize the effectiveness of the entire process. This is caused in part by the predictability of people when they are put into a group setting and by the logical building of the more task-related activities upon one another.

In building a team, there are two *types* of challenges that must be overcome. They are people- and task-related. The people oriented issues should be dealt with first, as successful resolution will accelerate the team's ability to navigate its way through the more task-specific areas. The overall model is shown in diagram A.

Phase 1 Challenges
The Challenges of Comfort, Trust and Commitment

When people gather in any type of group setting, may it be a cocktail party or the first meeting of a team, there is the potential for a great deal of anxiety. We all tend to be very protective of our egos and sense of self worth, especially around people we are meeting for the first time. Let's face it, people who are anxious and uncomfortable are not going to perform at their best, whether it be a meeting or in a sporting event.

The first challenge of the leader of a new team is to generate some comfort and begin to establish a climate of trust. This is accomplished through Team Building Type 1 activities. Working with hundreds of teams over the years, I have found that it usually takes about 12 hours of actual time spent together for a totally new group to feel comfortable with one another if the time is properly spent. There are four types of activities that serve to get a group comfortable: exercises, instruments, common content, and social.

Exercises

The idea with exercises is for the scenarios to be difficult so the group struggles a bit. By going through something challenging, and performing badly, the members come to realize if they don't learn when and how to put their personal agendas aside, that the experience will probably be a long and painful one. Later, when they succeed together, members develop a sense of camaraderie with high-fiving and lots of energy.

Instruments

Psychological instruments are a good way to provide the members with some insight into themselves and their teammates. Something like my *Interpersonal Preferences Profile* is perfect in the early phase of a team's development. The idea here is to demonstrate the potential strengths each member of the team brings to the group and to point out that the power of the team is in large part determined by its diversity. A team made up of all wide receivers in football would be a really fast team, but I doubt they would win many games.

Another important feature of instruments is that they create a common language. It seems as if most successful teams like to communicate in shorthand and the commonality of the language serves as a critical "bonding" mechanism.

Shared Content

Another important aspect of this early team-building experience is to make sure everyone has the benefit of the same models and terminology. Not only does everyone come to understand important concepts in the same way, but it too provides the bonding that arises out of common experiences.

Social

Never underestimate the importance of some socializing as part of the team-building process. Sharing drinks or dinner, taking in a sporting event together, or participating in a friendly competition can really jell a team.

Essential Knowledge

If you look at any lasting relationship between people you will learn that the initial bond was created due to the things they had in common. And the greater the commonality, the less the differences seem to matter.

To reiterate, via team building activities you have begun the process of building a base of comfort and some degree of trust. There are, however, two additional people-oriented issues present in Phase 1 that need to be addressed. One is how to get members to subordinate their personal goals to team goals. The other is how to generate a high level of personal commitment to the team.

Sacrificing Personal Goals for Team Goals

Over the years in observing people working in groups I've noticed that *most* people are very willing to help others achieve their goals *after* they have met their own needs. Now you may want to wish it weren't so or stick your head in the sand and pretend that isn't the norm, but I would safely wager you are wrong.

So it is *normal* for people in the early stages of a group to be selfish. But it is also counter-productive to the team and must be dealt with.

Indispensable Tip !

The single best way to get someone to put the team goal ahead of a personal goal is for them to *choose* to do it.

It is amazing how much pain people will tolerate when it is their choice. It is equally amazing how little pain people will tolerate when it is forced upon them. In general, the more involved members are in decisions, the clearer their role on the team and the more connection they feel with the other members of the group, the greater the likelihood they will do what's in the best interest of the team.

Generating Commitment

The leader first has to realize she is competing for members' time and energy against everything else they may choose to devote their effort toward. This is where a compelling vision and guiding principles that resonate with the members own values come into play. Good ones not only serve to *direct* the efforts of the members, but also *inspire* them.

In the battle for the 2008 Democratic Party nomination for president of the United States, Hillary Clinton may have had just as clear of a direction for where she would have taken America as Barack Obama, but he did a better job of creating a "movement." People became so inspired with dreams and hope that they were willing to overlook his shallower experience base. And in difficult times such as we find ourselves in today, hope may be the most important thing a leader can arouse in followers.

In my generation, when President John F. Kennedy said, "It is the goal of this nation to place a man on the moon by the end of the decade and bring him safely back to Earth," it was not only a statement of purpose but also something that mobilized hundreds of thousands of workers in hundreds of companies to get the job done.

The Challenge of Direction and Focus

Before any team becomes a champion it first has to have a clear mission or purpose. However, a productive direction cannot be chosen until a considerable amount is known about where the team is starting from. Even the best map in the world won't do you any good if you don't know where you're at.

Situation Diagnosis

Situation diagnosis is the critical first piece of direction setting.

The most common method of accumulating data on the current state of affairs is to conduct a SWOT analysis. What are the *strengths* this team has that can be built upon? What are the *weaknesses that* must be overcome if the team is to enjoy success? What *opportunities* are present that the team should attempt to capitalize upon? What are the *threats* to the team that must be dealt with? This analysis is pretty basic but it is all too often overooked.

The Mission

Once you know where the team stands, the leader can focus on the process of developing a mission. This is a statement of purpose or why the team exists. I worked with the purchasing group of a manufacturing organization recently whose stated mission was, "To procure high quality materials, goods and services within specified cost parameters."

Now this could easily be the mission of any procurement group, but it was still important that it be articulated. When the team did a personnel analysis against the mission they were shocked to find that 40 percent of the people in the group did not do even one thing a year to procure anything. Instead, they were spending their time on production planning, production scheduling and stores, but not on pure procurement. For years, they had been under-funding purchasing and over-funding the related activities.

Guiding Principles

Once the mission has been agreed upon, a set of guiding principles or values should be developed. These are the fundamental beliefs that underpin all of the team's activities. If these values are well chosen and resonate with the personal beliefs of the team's members, it is another way to generate an uncommon level of commitment to the mission.

In my view, people in the United States are *elitist,* despite our protests to the contrary. Most people who desire to attend college would do anything within reason to attend Harvard, Yale, Princeton, Wharton, Chicago, Stanford, Northwestern, MIT, or Caltech. Soldiers want to be selected as a Navy Seal, Marine Recon, Delta Force, or Army Ranger. Students have a strong desire to be chosen as a Rhodes scholar, actors to win an Oscar or Emmy, and journalists, a Peabody award. And, yes, people even want to win that blue ribbon at the dog show or state fair. So why wouldn't people want to be with a winner at work, where they spend a third of their adult lives?

As to inspiring values, for the exact same pay do you think someone wants to work for the Susan G. Komen cancer foundation or a tobacco company? Similarly most psychologically healthy adults do not want to work in a boiler room telemarketing operation that scams senior citizens out of their retirement nest eggs. Therefore, great leaders spend considerable energy aligning the team's guiding principles with the aspirations of the team's members so they feel as if they are in an elite unit or an organization dedicated to noble pursuits. Sam Palmisano, CEO of IBM, said that in his opinion, IBM would never be considered a truly great institution until it made a major contribution to solving some of the world's most difficult problems.

Core Strategy

The core strategy refers to the fundamental philosophy and direction the team will take in its quest to achieve the mission. It is widely accepted that it is one of the leader's prime responsibilities to decide upon the core strategy and "sell" it to the team.

But here is the rub. There seems to be a relatively low percentage of managers (about 15 percent according to many studies) who are wired mentally to be skilled at complex strategic thinking. So while a leader *must* be the one to set the core strategy, he is often poorly equipped to do so on his own. If he ignores this personal deficiency and develops a strategy anyway, disaster is often the outcome.

In the case where the leader is lacking in the strategic thinking capability, he must enlist others inside or outside the organization to provide the strategic alternatives. It takes an individual with an exceptionally strong sense of self-worth to admit to himself that he is deficient in such an important leadership competency. This is yet another reason why it is so critical to choose leaders for the enterprise, function, department, or project that have the right competencies. Or, at minimum, the insight to realize where they are lacking and surround themselves with others who complement their strengths.

Team Goals and Priorities

Getting agreement on a *coherent* set of *team* goals that will ultimately result in the accomplishment of the mission is essential for several reasons. First, everyone needs to fully understand how the goals will allow the mission to be achieved. Second, by hashing out the team's priorities up front, it will be easier to appropriately allocate resources and should reduce conflicts later on. Finally, the process serves to generate buy-in, whereby the team's members can *choose* to subordinate their personal objectives to those of the team.

 Don't Forget This
The key here is that the goal-setting and prioritization process should be participative instead of legislated by the team leader.

Game Plan and Tactics

Far too many teams jump into random activity without first coming to an agreement on how these activities will lead to the accomplishment of the goals. There are seldom goals that don't have several possible alternatives as to how the objectives might be achieved. By taking the time up front to dissect the merits and liabilities of each path, not only will the team more likely choose tactics with the greatest potential for success but also it will generate more confidence within the team that the goals are achievable.

If a leader is successful in overcoming both the people-oriented and task-oriented challenges in phase one, the performance of the group will begin to increase yet still end the phase below average. Morale, however, is a funny thing. It starts unusually high when a new team comes together. People like new beginnings. I bet you know several people who consider January 1 to be the best day of the year. They tell themselves this is the year they are going to get married, quit smoking, stop drinking, lose weight, etc. The year is full of promise.

It is like this in a new team as well. At the beginning of each baseball season, even the most woeful team from the year before starts 0-0, equal to every other team. Perhaps it is the excitement of pursuing a new mission. Maybe it is having high expectations of being able to put into practice what they have learned from past mistakes. Or it could be the energy created by their new and talented teammates. In any event, the morale starts out at an *unsustainably* high level.

Throughout phase one, morale begins a long slow slide. It begins to be eroded by conflicts and disagreements over mission, vision, core strategy, goals, priorities, and game plans. Then one day the team gets mugged by reality. Members look at performance and see that things are nowhere near where their unrealistically high initial expectations had told them they should be. This coupled with the accumulated struggles over direction causes the team's morale to plummet into the *valley of despair*. This is what leads to the phase two challenges.

Phase Two Challenges
The Challenge of Sustainability of Leadership and Team Cohesion

When a team is underperforming, this is where dissention within the team threatens to tear it apart. Finger pointing, backstabbing, and a lot of "I told you so's" create palpable tension among the members. People especially start to blame the team leader. Many believe they could lead the team better themselves. In the 2008 NFL season, the Detroit Lions had a record of 0-16. They didn't win a single game. Now even if you have never seen an NFL game, couldn't *you* coach the Lions to a record of 0-16?

This is a crisis. This is when a leader must step up and tackle the issues head on. Failure to do so makes it highly likely he will be replaced outright or at best, marginalized to the point of becoming ineffective.

In the valley of despair, team building centers on collecting data as to the location and severity of the problems and then gathering the team together to discuss the issues and plot solutions. I use two surveys: the Organizational Environment Index located in Appendix A, and the Leadership Team Dysfunction Index located in Appendix B of the book. The surveys confidentially assess the effectiveness of the team from the perspective of its members.

Typically during this phase of team development, members are unclear as to their roles and responsibilities. They wonder how their role fits with others on the team. They see problems with structure, systems, policy, and procedures.

During the offsite, members receive the results of the surveys. The goal is to acknowledge any dissatisfaction, understand the problems, prioritize them, and create a plan to overcome the issues one at a time.

> ### Essential Knowledge
>
> Nothing will squelch negativity quicker than to get team issues into the open and create a common focus going forward. This will buy the leader the critical time to put in place the infrastructure necessary to propel the team's performance forward.

Challenges of Structure, Infrastructure, Alignment, and Resources

Dealing with structure and infrastructure represents the tough sledding that has to occur if the team is to achieve championship caliber performance. It is fun to create mission, vision, strategy, and plans. It is real work to get in the trenches and put in place the elements that will allow the mission to be achieved.

Structure

Organization structure issues can really have an impact on the success of a team. At the enterprise level I did some work with a 700-person consulting firm whose competitors were giant firms like SAIC, CAP Gemini, and KPMG, who each had tens of thousands of consultants. It became clear that this organization's biggest hurdle was the way they were structured. They were trying to compete in too many geographical areas and never seemed to be able to generate a critical mass. They perhaps had a dozen consultants each at Air Force bases like Edwards and Wright Patterson, where their competitors each had a thousand. Once they were structured in a way to mass their people in a few concentrated areas, they were able to win larger contracts and fuel their engine of growth.

At the function level, one of my clients was experiencing a civil war between Engineering and Manufacturing. It started at the top. Each of the respective vice presidents hated each other, and that animosity spread down through the ranks. When I suggested they choose the stronger of the two vice presidents and change the structure so that both groups now reported to the same person with the new title of vice president of operations, most of the conflict at all levels instantly went away. (The displaced vice president was reassigned to a different division).

Systems

Also in this stage many systems issues need to be addressed. Systems are things like purchasing, contracting, performance appraisal, compensation, management information system, etc. When coupled with policies and procedures, these all aggregate to form the organization's infrastructure. A key point is that infrastructure will win out over mission, vision, goals, plans and priorities almost 100 percent of the time.

An example would be a company that has a value of internal collaboration yet appraises performance in such a way that people feel pitted against one another and then doubles the damage by compensating people only on individual merit, not contribution to team goals. How much collaboration do you think that organization is likely to get?

One example of the power of unaligned infrastructure comes from an aerospace company that manufactured aircraft fuselages. It had a huge machine break down, costing the company $15,000 a day in downtime. So the manager went to purchasing and explained how they needed to call the vendor and have a replacement part sent out by FedEx. Even though purchasing departments generally hate to do anything verbally, they saw the logic of the request and called the vendor. The part was shipped by FedEx and arrived the next morning in the receiving department. When the manager went to retrieve the part, the receiving clerk said, "Where is your purchase order?" The manager replied, "I don't have a purchase order. This was an emergency shipment to get the machine up and running." The clerk shot back, "I can't release anything without the proper paperwork authorized by purchasing, finance, and operations." The part sat in the receiving bin for five days at a cost of $75,000, waiting for the paperwork to wind its way through the system to authorize this minimum wage clerk to release the part. The system defeated human motivation because that is what systems are designed to do. And again, fixing broken systems is not sexy work. It is often something of a long slog just to figure out how the various processes work in the first place.

Roles and Responsibilities

Next, the whole issue of roles needs to be addressed. One problem is that frequently two or more people each feel responsible for the same thing. This is when turf wars typically erupt. Not only is this inefficient, but it is frustrating for everyone involved.

Potentially more serious is when a key role is not identified or filled by anyone. This is one of those cracks that things have a way of slipping through. As an example, for the past twenty-three years I have conducted roughly forty programs a year at major hotel chains like Westin, Marriott, Hilton, and Hyatt. In each case I have to send several boxes of materials to the hotel in advance of my arrival. You know, in not one of those chains do individual hotels have any one person in charge of client boxes. I have tried everything. I send them to my catering contact, but they get lost because catering is all about food and beverage. I send them to my sales contact, but the boxes get lost because sales are about booking space. I send them to myself as a hotel guest, but if the boxes arrive before I check in (which is always the case), the hotel rejects the shipment because they don't list me as currently staying there. I send the boxes to the bell captain, but they get lost because there are multiple bellmen and usually multiple closets. Besides, they seem to only care about bags where they get an immediate tip. I've sent them to receiving, which is a real nightmare because there are hundreds of boxes there and they see their main job as logging in packages that match a purchase order for the hotel. You see what I mean about the need for role clarification?

Individual Priorities

Priorities eventually need to be synchronized down to the individual level. Everyone's plate is overloaded today. So, if I depend on someone for my highest priority item and it is fiftieth on their list, I am in big trouble.

Using hotels again as an example, many meeting planners book a block of guest rooms when they contract meeting space. Booking the space and rooms is the top priority of the hotel's sales manager. Communicating to the reservations department that they should set up the room block seems to be a task they seldom get to right away. It simply is not their main concern. The result is that people call the hotel to book a room against the block only to be told, "Sorry ma'am, we have no record of the X,Y,Z Corporation having a room block with our hotel." Then the caller asks, "Can you tell me if the X,Y,Z Corporation has a meeting scheduled at your hotel over these dates?" The reservation agent replies, "I'm sorry sir, my system doesn't tell me about meetings, only guest rooms." Ouch!

Resources

At this point, you are finally ready to allocate budget, facilities, equipment, and the like. Resources should always be allocated with the greatest likelihood of achieving the mission in mind. Too many organizations operate resource constrained. They start out looking at their resources and then decide what they can do with them.

In Operation Desert Storm, President Bush didn't tell General Schwarzkopf, "General, here are one heavy and two mechanized divisions. What can you do with them?" Schwarzkopf would have naturally replied, "What the hell do you want me to do with them?" Instead, the commander in chief issued a mission. "General, you are to knock the Iraqi Army out of Kuwait and drive them back to their homeland. What will it take to accomplish the mission?"

I have worked with many entrepreneurs over the years, and one advantage they typically tell me they have over larger organizations is that they are "mission driven." When I press them, they say some version of, "Sure our competitors have much more in the way of resources than we do, but I can always count on them being stingy and inefficient on how they allocate them." The entrepreneurs go on to tell me that if they have the proper mission, strategy, goals, and priorities, they can always find the resources. They could take out a bank loan, run up their credit cards, issue stock or bonds, or even choose to sell the company to get the funds necessary to accomplish the mission. Large corporations seldom think that way. And, outside of the federal level, where funds are much easier to come by, almost no government agency *ever* operates mission driven.

> ### Essential Knowledge
> Mission-driven organizations almost always outperform those that simply dictate a budget to a group based upon last year's expenditures.

If the leader survives phase two and the team does not get bogged down, the team will move into the third and final phase on its way to greatness. In the third phase, productivity rises dramatically as infrastructure aligned with the grand design will really start to generate big-time results.

Once the dissatisfaction about being in the "valley of despair" is resolved, members start to see that their hard work in laying the proper infrastructure is paying off. They can see the results improving, and this gets them excited again. Morale pops back up and, with a slight lag time, moves up at about the same level as productivity.

Phase Three Challenges
The Challenges of Stretch, Interface, and Execution

During this last phase of a team's progression, the goal is to make sure it is hitting on all cylinders. Stretching the team a bit out of its comfort zone will be well received by the members at this time because they know they are at the cusp of excellence.

Problems that often arise center around *interface issues* and *execution errors.* The interface between sales and marketing, finance and accounting, operations and quality, or research and advanced development are examples of groups that usually have a certain degree of friction.

Role Negotiation

Through a technique known as role negotiation, representatives from the functions having interface issues sit down with one another and do some good old-fashioned horse-trading. For example, Operations would say to Quality, "We love what you do for us here, please continue to do it. However, these things you are doing are getting in our way. Please consider stopping these activities as soon as possible. And here are some things your group does not currently do, but if you did, it would make our lives so much better. Please consider starting to do these things as soon as possible."

Quality then gets its turn to make requests of Operations and the bargaining begins. In the end, Quality agrees to do, let's say, item A & B in exchange for Operations doing items D & E. Sometimes you have to give people some additional incentive to do the job they are already being paid good money to do. You shouldn't *have* to do this, but sometimes to be effective, leaders need to bite the bullet and do what's necessary to take their team to the next level.

The Challenge of Execution

Thirty-two years ago, when I first entered the business world, few people were talking about execution. Everyone was enamored with strategy. Today, most successful leaders put the ability to execute on an equal level with strategy.

Carly Fiorina at Hewlett Packard got the strategy right when she fought to acquire Compaq, but was tripped up by failure to execute. Her successor, Mark Hurd, concentrated on execution and was widely seen as a corporate savior. Nearly every week these days, you read in the business press that a CEO was sacked due to "a failure to execute."

This step in the evolution of the team means a dedication to monitoring, feedback, and follow-up. It is where "lean" and "six sigma" come into play in a big way at the enterprise level. It is where leaving time at the end of meetings to confirm accountabilities and managers' following up on delegated tasks is important at the individual level.

The Challenge of Change

At about this point in a team's development, certain norms, values, or activities that may have made sense at one time now turn to being ineffective if not downright dysfunctional. These have got to be revisited. When things are going well, teams often begin to get a little lax or sloppy.

Many years ago I conducted seminars on a regular basis for a major telecommunications company with hubs in Virginia, Georgia, Texas, and Colorado. I am one of those people who feel so strongly about people being on time that I almost consider it corporate theft when people are chronically late.

I usually start the program at 8 a.m. on the dot, whether everyone is there or not. But in this company I was shocked to find that in a class of twenty-four people the *first* person did not arrive until 8:05 a.m. with the other twenty-three dribbling in at 8:10, 8:20, 8:30, 9:00 and 10:15. It didn't even seem to matter which location — this was institution-wide.

Of course I would go on a rant about the general irresponsibility of such behavior. In one particular group in Atlanta I had the division general manager and his staff (they, by the way, were in fact punctual). As people rolled in late I did my customary blast when the general manager said, "You know John, that has always upset me as well." I literally stopped in my tracks, looked him in the eye and said, "Well, when the hell are you going to fix it?" As I am sure you have heard by now, a definition of insanity is to continue to do the same things and expect a different result. This organization's leaders preferred to bitch about the ineffective behavior rather than take the steps to change the norm.

Critical Elements In All Phases of Team Development

Selection

It should go without saying that something that pervades all phases of a team's development is selecting the *right* people for the unit in the first place. Do this and everything will be accelerated. Fail in choosing the *right* members and you will spend the majority of your time cleaning up after messes.

Perhaps the prototypical example of this approach would be the 1980 men's Olympic hockey team, which defied all odds and defeated the powerful Soviet Union juggernaut. The Soviets were by all standards a *professional* team. The United States was forced by USOC rules to play with *amateurs*. Coach Herb Brooks methodically set out to find the *right* players to execute his *team first, role player strategy*. Many of the men that made the squad were not necessarily the best overall athletes, but they were the *best fit* with his vision.

Orientation

Orienting new members to the team as they join is much more important than most organizations realize. Without getting new people up to speed quickly, you not only waste money but also risk them making mistakes that could have been avoided. Perhaps most importantly, enough new people who are not properly oriented threaten to pull the team back to phase one. In the business world, Disney is the best I've ever seen at new employee orientation. In the NFL, it is currently the Pittsburgh Steelers. These organizations just keep successfully chugging along virtually every year despite the influx of new talent.

A good orientation program will last several days and include knowledge of products, services, customers, suppliers, philosophy, strategy, flow of information, chain of command, values, structure, and location, among the usual benefits and compensation pieces.

Training

As to training, it is unbelievable how little of it is done in a typical organization in business or government. In professional sports, training happens every day. Ditto for the military. In business, people are lucky if they get a couple days of training a year. I can't tell you how often people come to my seminars and say, "Yeah, I had some leadership training about five years ago." As if this one inoculation was all they would ever need.

It should be mandatory that all associates get at least one week of training each year in something, whether it is technical, interpersonal, personal or leadership/management. Since nearly everyone agrees we are in a "knowledge economy," shouldn't we continually be investing in our associate's knowledge?

CHAPTER 6

GAIN TRACTION THROUGH TEAMWORK:
Unselfish Play —
Some Can, Some Can't, Some Won't

Super Bowl winning coach Brian Billick said, "Self-interest is as much a law of nature as is gravity. Keep in mind that you can't defy the laws of nature. You can however, suspend them temporarily. It is this suspension of self-interest that is at the heart of building any team."[1]

Team Norms

There are many productive norms that successful teams develop and several dysfunctional ones that must be eliminated if the team is to maximize its potential. Great leaders learn they must quickly point out and extinguish selfish behavior while looking for ways to reward the unselfish acts of others as a critical early norm.

Diagram A shows common productive and negative norms of behavior. Those at the top are productive norms any team might consider adopting. Those at the bottom are the ones any team should seek to minimize. Appendix B in the back of the book is an instrument that will allow you to

LEADERSHIP TEAM DYSFUNCTION INDEX

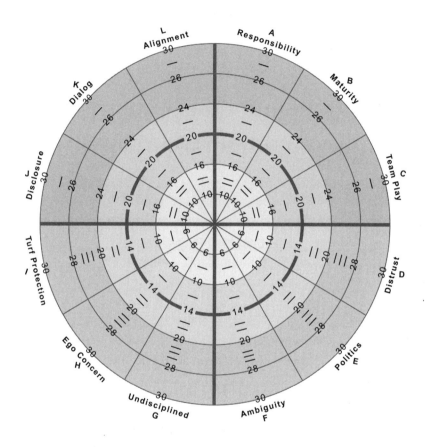

Very Low Scores = At or Below the 25th percentile
Low Scores = Between the 25th and 50th percentiles
Moderate Scores = Between the 50th and 75th percentiles
High Scores = At or Above the 75th percentile

	Percentiles
	91 - 100
	76 - 90
	51 - 75
	26 - 50
	11 - 25
	1 - 10

assess the current effectiveness of your norms.

A team should strive to achieve scores above the 75th percentile in the positive norms while holding all the negative norms below the 25th percentile.

Positive Norm – Team Play

Hall of Fame basketball coach Dean Smith was often cited as having the most unselfish players despite the fact that his entire roster was made up of previous high school All Staters or All Americans, each accustomed to being the center of attention. Part of it was selecting players who were capable of playing within the framework of a team concept. But it was far more than that. He made it an early priority to establish the norm of "team play."

Coach Smith tells the story of a practice where a new player shot the ball every single time he touched it. Exasperated from watching him, Coach Smith pulled his other four teammates off the floor. The new player asked, "Who is going to inbound the ball to me?" Coach shot back, "You need to understand that you can't do a thing without at least one other player."[2] Point made.

As to establishing a positive norm, Coach Smith went to great lengths to capture statistics and provide recognition for unselfish acts that benefited the team, such as setting effective screens, diving on the floor in pursuit of the ball, assists, blocked shots, aggressive defense, and deflected passes.[3]

Also, Coach Smith was the father of the concept of having a player who scores a basket as a result of a good pass point to the player who made the pass on his way back down the floor.

Essential Knowledge

To encourage team play in a business setting,
try the following:

• Do not penalize anyone who temporarily sacrifices headcount or budget in favor of more important team priorities. People are smart. If they permanently lose budget, headcount, or status they will be loath to give for the greater good.

• Acknowledge publicly the unselfish acts of others.

• Create collective team measures and review them regularly. Pass out rewards each time a team milestone is met.

• Punish quickly, harshly, and publicly the selfish acts of others. When people see self-centered behavior as a ticket to failure, they will adjust. Sometimes fear is a more powerful motivator than the benefits of success.

• Do not hesitate to remove members who are not team players. On June 10, 2008, Jerry Angelo, general manager of the Chicago Bears, placed running back Cedric Benson, the number four player selected overall in the 2005 NFL draft, on waivers. Benson had lax workout habits and after his second alcohol-related incident in a month, he was cut unceremoniously from the team. Angelo said, "When individual priorities overshadow team goals, we suffer the consequences as a team. Those who fail to understand the importance of 'team' will not play for the Chicago Bears."[4] You can imagine the message this act must have sent through the rest of the team.

Negative Norm — Turf Protection

The easiest way to reduce turf protection is to create a mix of team incentives such as stock options, outright gifts of stock, 401k programs, gain sharing, or joint performance appraisals.

When people hoard resources or focus on their own goals to the detriment of the larger team, the entire organization must spend more money than would otherwise be required to accomplish the same level of productivity. Members caught doing these things need to be banished for a time to the corporate equivalent of Siberia.

Leadership Tales from the Workplace

Robert Sutton in *The No Asshole Rule* tells of George Zimmer, CEO of the Men's Wearhouse, firing one of the company's most successful sales associates. The man routinely stole customers from other sales reps, made disparaging remarks about the company culture and openly refused to help other employees. Despite losing the top salesperson, the store revenue went up 30 percent. Though none of the remaining associates matched the departed salesperson's individual productivity, collectively they did better. The fellow had caused others to adopt poor work habits.[5] A leader often can gain addition through subtraction.

Positive Norm — Disclosure

Pat Summitt, the winningest basketball coach of all time, leads the University of Tennessee Lady Vols. By her own admission, she is a pretty tough woman. One of the lessons she learned *after* she had already spent 14 years in coaching, was the importance of closeness through disclosure.

When she first started coaching she set up very strict player-coach boundaries. She felt she couldn't do her job if she was too open with them or let them get too close. In 1997 she finally admitted, "I got it wrong. It was 14 years before Tennessee won its first National Championship. I was so busy being tough, I didn't understand the value of getting to know the players on a deeper level, their real strengths and vulnerabilities."[6]

She now holds a "family night" where everyone would bring pictures of their families and talk about where they are from. Pat learned that "small intimacies make a team."[7]

Essential Knowledge To Increase Disclosure

- Hold a meeting where each team member is asked to share with the group his/her greatest strength or contribution along with their greatest weakness. Make sure everyone goes beyond the typical stated weaknesses, like "impatience."

- Going public with the results of their scores on 360-degree evaluations is another way to open up the group.

- Having everyone on the team share their scores on profiles, such as the "Interpersonal Preference Profile," will go a long way to promote mutual understanding.

- You might want to encourage team members who have been disrespectful of one or more of their peers in the past to take the opportunity to seek those people out and apologize. Most people will accept a sincere apology.

Negative Norm — Distrust

One of the biggest causes of distrust stems from a lack of knowledge of the other members of the team. What are their backgrounds? What kind of family life and activities do they pursue outside of work? What are their goals for the future? Leaders should take regular opportunities to spend one-on-one time and group time with the members of the team. Familiarity breeds trust.

When people in the team make decisions or ask questions, it might be helpful to let everyone know the intention behind the behavior. It helps for everyone in the team to give each other the benefit of the doubt if they aren't quite sure of the intentions behind their words or actions. Most of the time they mean well, not ill.

A leader should try to make himself vulnerable on occasion by sharing a personal failure or weakness in front of the group. Not only will it show people you are strong enough to admit you are not perfect, but you will be amazed at how others will follow your lead and open themselves up. Starbucks CEO Howard Schultz once said, "The hardest thing about being a leader is demonstrating vulnerability."[8]

If someone in the team offends you, point it out to the person, then drop it. Don't hold grudges. More often than not, the person holding the grudge gets penalized more than the other person. It is usually a complete waste of time, and often at the root of the grudge is something rather petty in the larger scheme of things. If you, as the leader, are currently holding poisonous feelings against someone, make the first move to acknowledge it and call for a truce or ask for a fresh start. Most people will accept the olive branch once it is sincerely offered.

Positive Norm — Dialog

The strength of any team is in the diversity of its members. However, this power is diluted if there is limited dialog among the members. At Zappos.com, managers are supposed to try and spend a minimum of 10 percent of their free time outside the office doing things with their team members. These members invariably report that communication and trust increase by 20 to 100 percent after these informal get-togethers. Every year the company publishes an *unedited* associate blog about life at Zappos and distributes a copy to all 1,600 employees.

With newly formed teams, try brainstorming or other forced techniques to get everyone in the team involved. Make meetings more exciting by occasionally holding them offsite. When you hold regular onsite team meetings, vary the location, length, style and even the places where people usually sit around the table. This will both enhance creativity and break up cliques. Try to spend at least a few minutes of every session on something that will build better teamwork. Once the team has "jelled," tackle at least one controversial topic each meeting to get members comfortable with constructive debate.

Indispensable Tip !

A critical take away of most participants in my seminars is that after seeing the diversity of views regarding how to tackle each of the challenges presented in the program is that they should seldom make a decision of consequence without asking others what they think.

Negative Norm — Ambiguity

Team members can do a lot to come together themselves as a team even in the absence of a strong leader. The area of ambiguity, however, needs to be corrected by the leader.

Make sure everyone on the team is clear about their own objectives and priorities. Then make sure these are shared with the other members of the team. Be sure and post key metrics where anyone on the team can see them.

Positive Norm — Alignment

Create a team vision/mission statement. Get everyone to participate in its development. Briefly review it with the team regularly. Have members create and agree on a set of guiding principles and key norms of interaction.

Another excellent idea is to have each member of the team to publicly commit in front of their peers to support team decisions. This is especially important where a decision was not the unanimous choice of the team. Eliminate the common practice of saying, "I was outvoted by the team." This undercuts the power of the decision and the alignment of the group.

Negative Norm — Politics

Let's face it; every team has a bit of politicking and posturing going on. If it gets out of control, however, the team can be in big trouble.

It is critical that members do not talk behind each other's backs. A terrific norm to adopt is for members to agree that if someone starts talking disparagingly about another member of the team, politely interrupt them and suggest that they deal with the person directly. When each person agrees to live by that code, it can make a powerful and immediate difference.

Try not to "hitchhike." This occurs when members say the politically correct thing or what other people want to hear, rather than what they truly believe. This creates a false sense of consensus and will, ironically in the end, not really show you to be an independent thinker. If there are frequent "meetings after the meeting," where participants share their "real" views among themselves, this is a major red flag signaling dysfunction.

Members should also agree to not attack another member of the team personally. If members disagree, they should argue with the idea, not put down the person. Emotion-producing language like idiotic, stupid, lame, or moronic must be avoided.

Everyone should realize that their peers on the team can see through "posturing." No one likes "brown-nosers." Let performance generate the respect you seek.

Positive Norm — Maturity

One thing that aids dramatically in developing maturity is for the membership of the team to be kept relatively stable. Research indicates that teams whose composition remains the same perform better than those that constantly have to adjust to the arrival of new members and the departure of old ones (the exception being R&D teams).

Members develop familiarity with each other and their collective tasks and priorities. Members can settle in and focus on the work instead of getting to know their new colleagues.[9]

Mature team members welcome constructive insight, which will help them grow personally or help in achieving a successful outcome. They also quickly let others know when they are at fault. It is highly unlikely people will continue to pile on more criticism once someone has said, "That was my mistake. Here is why it happened and this is what I am going to do to prevent it in the future."

Mature teams conduct "postmortems" after major failures so they can learn from their mistakes. Successful teams view setbacks as an inevitable part of achieving excellence. Going through difficult times together forges a bond that is difficult to break later on when times get better.

Negative Norm — Negativity

A team's collective belief that it can be effective is one of the best predictors of the team's ultimate performance.[10] Cynicism and sarcasm are two things that can quickly erode a team's confidence. People, regardless of organizational level, have egos to protect and usually do not react favorably to cynical barbs tossed their way. Instead of negativity, find things to praise others for and the practice will feed off itself.

It is also a good idea for members to withhold the urge to reject an idea until they fully understand it. Ask lots of questions. Seek to find the pros and cons, not just the cons. Focus on listening first, then adding your perspective after everyone has spoken.

Blame shifting is another type of behavior guaranteed to produce negativity in a team. Ultimately the more members try to dodge responsibility, the more blame typically ends up in their own lap.

Arrogance, self-centered actions, and defensiveness are also behaviors that can lead to others becoming negative. It doesn't take more than a couple toxic members of a group to deplete the energy of the whole team.

Positive Norm — Responsibility

Members of any team want the others in the group to pull their own weight. It should be totally acceptable to non-emotionally confront people who are not living up to their commitments. The approval of or desire to not disappoint one's teammates is important to almost every human being.

To develop collective responsibility, most successful sports coaches use peer pressure. In Pat Summitt's system, if a player dogged it in a drill, the whole team needed to repeat the drill. Outside practice, if a player skipped class, the whole team had to spend time together in the study hall.[11]

The more tightly connected team members are compensation-wise to each other, the more likely they will live up to their commitments. Also, when a team has a purpose it believes in you see other members willingly pick up the slack when teammates are temporarily unable to perform their roles.

Responsible team members pledge to each other that they will deliver on their commitments. They also don't bite off more than they can chew. They are honest when they need help.

Essential Knowledge

Keeping posters in conference rooms that list the team's agreed-upon norms of behavior will significantly increase the quality of the team's interactions.

• Immature teams have a tendency to make decisions too quickly. They seem to want to "play nice" and make some progress rather than risk being seen as disruptive. Teams should guard against this tendency.

• Public recognition of unselfish team play is one of the most effective ways to incentivize the continuation of collaborative acts.

• Forty percent of the time, poor performing teams say their problems are caused by personality conflicts.[12]

• Teams of volunteers are significantly easier to lead than when members had no choice as to their participation.

• It is important to set norms as to how decisions will be made. The options are: 1) leader decides after input from the group; 2) team decides after input from the leader; 3) decision is delegated to an appropriately qualified member or subgroup of the team. You have to realize you've got trouble on your hands if the outcome of a meeting is to schedule another meeting.

• Championship teams are built around the individual talents of the members. The first thing every member notices in any type of team is the perceived abilities of the other members of the group. As any great Hollywood director will tell you, the key to a great performing team starts with the casting.

CHAPTER 7

USE TRUST AS THE GLUE THAT CEMENTS RELATIONSHIPS

We see it all the time. Wealthy, powerful, educated or sophisticated people in leadership positions crashing and burning in spectacular fashion after years of success. Some are breathtaking in their stupidity, such as the overnight demise of Rev. Ted Haggard, New Jersey Governor Jim McGreevey, or Illinois Governor Rod Blagojevich, due to betrayal of trust.

The self-proclaimed "Sheriff of Wall Street," former New York Governor Eliot Spitzer was busted paying a prostitute. He said, "I failed to live up to the standard I expected of myself. I have acted in a way that violates my obligations to my family ... my sense of right and wrong." Dennis Kozlowski at Tyco, Kun-Hee Lee of Samsung, and hotel queen Leona Hemsley got nabbed in tax evasion schemes. Harry Stonecipher was forced to resign as CEO of Boeing after an alleged affair with a subordinate. Andrew Fastow and Bernard Ebbers were convicted of cooking the books at Enron and WorldCom respectively. Henry Nicholas at Broadcom and William McGuire at United Health Group got caught up in allegedly backdating stock options. Former NASDAQ Chief Bernard Madoff plead guilty to bilking thousands of investors out of billions of dollars in one of the largest Ponzi schemes in history. Former ImClone CEO Sam Waksal served jail time for securities fraud. Religious leader Jim Bakker of the PTL ministry fleeced his own flock. The world is filled with people of questionable character who somehow ascend, at least for a time, to positions of power.

Just the perception of a betrayal of trust can tarnish a leader's legacy, even if it cannot be proven. Opinion polls in 2006 showed that upwards of 70 percent of American citizens had come to believe that George W. Bush knew there were no weapons of mass destruction or serious ties to Al Queda when he used these as justifications for going to war with Iraq.

The blizzard of breach of trust scandals over the past few years has caused many people to simply *expect* their leaders to lie, cheat, steal, act immorally, or otherwise abuse the power of their positions. As a result, most people tend to place their trust in others more grudgingly than ever before. A Time Magazine/CNN poll found in 2003 that 71 percent of people believe "the typical CEO is less honest and ethical than the average person."[1] Imagine how much higher the figure would be today given the greed of Wall Street and the great sham perpetrated by many major commercial banks.

Taking the time to establish a basis of trust with followers would seem to be common sense, but sadly it is not common practice. Some leaders are simply too busy. Others think that their associates will trust them because of their position or until they do something untrustworthy. A few come across as inauthentic, failing to realize how they are perceived. Yet, if a level of trust can be established, it can serve as currency that will allow the leader to pursue his agenda of change more aggressively and effectively.

Twelve Habits of Trustworthy Leaders

Habit One — Act With Authenticity

All leaders have two selves — the inner self and the outer self. Authenticity can best be defined as consistency between the two selves. The notion of a person being "for real" means that phoniness is virtually eliminated.

Leaders often mistakenly believe that leadership is about playing out a scripted role, adopting a persona or delivering well-written speeches. Many are tempted to think their power to move people in the desired direction derives from the size and location of their office, the impressive-sounding title they have been given or the tricks they can learn about Machiavellian manipulation.

Aspiring leaders search for what they believe will be the holy grail of leadership, a checklist of traits they can develop and cross off the list on their way to the Ivory Tower. After a lifetime of studying, working with, consulting to, and coaching executives, I believe the strongest leaders are all about authenticity. It starts with knowing yourself and developing into the best self that your natural gifts and hard work will allow you to become. It is about character and lasting relationships.

Indispensable Tip !

Respected news anchor Tom Brokaw's most important advice to David Gregory, the young man chosen to succeed the late and beloved Tim Russert on "Meet the Press," was, "Don't try to be someone else. There is only one Tim Russert.²"

Many leaders do know themselves but fail to appropriately disclose their shortcomings to others. Over the years I have advised thousands of leaders at all levels to go public with the results of the 360-degree feedback they receive in my seminars. By my estimation, about one in five actually follow through and do this when they return to work. What makes this shocking, is the leaders' direct reports are the ones who gave these people the insight about their weaknesses in the first place — they already know. All they are looking for is an admission from the leader.

Now, as you might expect, weaknesses are best disclosed *after* leaders have demonstrated their competence, skill, and developed something of a positive track record. This disclosure doesn't need to be a bare-your-soul issue of "true confessions." No one wants to work for a self-flagellating loser. And, it would be a huge mistake to dwell on one's weaknesses in the midst of a crisis.

Dave Schlotterbeck, then CEO of Alaris Medical Systems went public with the results of his 360-degree evaluation in front of his top 130 managers at their annual Global Leadership Forum in Palm Springs. Up until then Dave was generally regarded as a bottom line, take no prisoners executive. As he spoke you could have heard a pin drop. The people in the room were both mesmerized and inspired. Then one by one, each of his direct reports, none of whom had planned to share their results with the group, stood and followed Dave's lead. It was a seminal event in the organization's history, creating a collective bond that remained for years. It led to the company adopting a core value of transparency and began Dave's emergence as a *leader*. Michael Dell did the same thing via a worldwide video conference to all Dell managers and received hundreds of e-mails praising his courage and honesty.

We forgave Princess Diana and Bill Clinton's human weaknesses, Southwest Airlines founder Herb Kelleher's sometimes unpolished style and Dallas Mavericks owner Mark Cuban's outlandish tirades because we sensed they were genuine people, passionate about something they cared deeply about.

There is something disarming about a leader who is not afraid to speak candidly. There is a magnetic attractiveness to someone who possesses conviction. Combine the two and a leader can light up a room despite underwhelming platform-speaking skills.

Far too few leaders are willing to take the risk of opening themselves up around their people. They have yet to learn the secret that making an emotional connection is often more important than their exact choice of words. They simply don't "get" the contagious nature of personal passion. Senator Hillary Clinton saw a major shift in people's perception of her during the New Hampshire presidential primary when, in a rare moment of dropping her guard in discussing her disappointing showing in the Iowa Caucuses, she "humanized" herself.

Habit Two — Be Visible and Available

It's unlikely that we will trust someone we do not know. It is difficult to know someone we seldom see. Plenty of executives give lip service to "leading by example" or the importance of being "visible," but most let more pressing events keep them from actually doing it. It has been my experience that associates at all organizational levels want to judge for themselves the capabilities and compassion of their leaders. They want to know that their leader can be trusted and that there is a firm hand guiding the enterprise. None of this can be accomplished if a leader hides behind closed-door meetings, reports or a massive desk and manages remotely through e-mail, cell phones, and faxes.

From the leader's side, not being on the scene often causes them to be cut off from critical insights and perspective, which can often only be gleaned from "being there." It has been documented many times that the "charge of the Light Brigade" was ordered by an officer far removed from the battlefield.[3]

Where a leader spends his/her time sends an unmistakable signal that the activity is highly valued. When Bill Marriott Jr. visits more than 300 of his company's hotels a year, he is shouting out loud and clear that there is no substitute for being out in the field where the action is. When Gordon Bethune took Continental Airlines from the worst ratings of any legacy carrier in such things as on-time arrivals, baggage handling, and customer satisfaction to the best, he did it largely by placing himself on the frontlines. He had meals with the mechanics, ramp personnel, reservation agents, and flight attendants, which made up the bulk of his airline. He visited every major airport as often as he could and provided the example to his staff that it would be a good idea for them to do it too. He listened, he watched, he coached, and he inspired. He gave an important face internally to the enterprise.[4]

When Sam Walton was alive he made it a habit to drop into Wal-Mart stores unannounced and sit with associates in the back of the store during early mornings. He said on numerous occasions that some of the best ideas he ever heard percolated up from those impromptu get-togethers. Bethune, Walton and Marriott were among the most trusted business leaders of their generation.

Leadership Tales from the Workplace

I was asked to conduct a strategic planning retreat with the top twelve executives of one of the nation's largest and best-known theme parks. One by one they presented volumes of studies and statistics on everything from the average wait time at each major attraction in the park to the sales-per-hour of every restaurant or hotdog cart on the property. Yet, when questioned, most of these executives seemed to have very limited depth of understanding of the fundamentals of their part of the operation. They knew *what* was going on, but they seemed to have no clue as to *why*. Worse, they had only vague ideas about what to do in the future to solve a problem or capitalize on an opportunity. They did however seem surprised when the results of the companywide employee opinion survey indicated that they scored low on trustworthiness. Finally it dawned on me to ask them how much time they spent each day walking the park. To my astonishment, the largest amount of time *any* of these executives committed to this activity was 10 minutes, and even he admitted that was only because that was the time it took him to walk to his office from the parking lot and back. How on earth can you successfully develop trust or run a business where virtually all of your associates touch the customer in some way and never spend time with them?

At the minimum, a leader has a responsibility to be available to his/her followers. But so much can be gained from being out in the nooks and crannies of the operation and so much can be lost if one is not visible.

Former Secretary of State Colin Powell would deliberately walk the same route at the same time every afternoon, setting himself up to get "ambushed." His associates knew they had access to his ear if they had an issue. Powell made it clear to his direct reports that in no way would he use this information as a way to undermine the chain of command.[5] This is an extremely important nuance to avoid creating undue anxiety among your staff. And, if you are out and about and happen to make a decision in one of your people's areas of responsibility, you should immediately inform your subordinate as to what occurred and why.

A Tale of Two Leaders

Some years ago, a 2,500-person manufacturing company hired a new president from outside the industry to run the company. He had one of the most impressive resumes a 32-year-old fast track superstar could have ever assembled. PhD in nuclear engineering from one of the finest universities in the country, White House Fellow in his mid-twenties, division vice president of a major company at 28, and a Mensa-level IQ of nearly 170 — the whole nine yards. This company had a strained relationship with its union for years, which did not get much better during his tenure.

During the next five years he became seen as aloof, uncaring and unapproachable. He seldom set foot in any of the numerous manufacturing cells in his company. In fact, most could recall only his initial orientation tour and a few times when he wanted to videotape a presentation with machinery running in the background as a backdrop. Grievances and turnover went up, and the number of employee suggestions went down.

After a few years of mostly large losses he was replaced by a leader with a style 180 degrees different. The new leader's IQ was probably significantly lower, and he possessed a bachelor's degree instead of a PhD. Yet within a matter of months he was able to generate incredible rapport with the rank and file of the union.

Each Monday morning the new leader would begin his day by getting onto a flatbed electric cart that had a massive coffee urn on the back. He filled the remaining space on the cart with 10 dozen doughnuts that he would purchase on his way to work. For the next couple of hours he would drive through the manufacturing facility, inviting the hourly associates to stop work for a few minutes and join him by the cart.

The first time this fellow would hit an area he would require each person to shake his hand and tell him his/her name before they could get the free coffee and doughnut. As you might imagine, given the previous president's style, they thought this was some sort of publicity stunt, and surely they would never see him again. To their amazement, he not only reappeared the next week, but also remembered most of their names. He then proceeded to ask them about their families, hobbies and life outside of work. When he showed up the third straight week, he would ask how their daughters were doing in Little League or whether their sons had recovered from the flu.

After several weeks of generating comfort and building trust, the new leader began to probe into more substantive issues. He would get their thoughts on problems they were experiencing, quality or equipment issues or simply any ideas they thought might be worth pursuing. In addition, it became known that he and his wife had a standing tailgate party in section J-5 of the stadium parking lot during the local NFL team's home games. *Anyone* from any part of the company was invited to stop by to share some refreshments.

Perhaps not coincidently, there were very few labor issues, the contracts that came up for negotiation during his tenure were resolved amicably, and there were a record number of associate suggestions each year. A few years later, the new leader leapfrogged over the former to become CEO of their Fortune top 50 company, where he went on to lead them to record profitability. The sad part is that the former leader exhibits one of the highest levels of honesty and ethical conduct of any executive I have ever gotten to know. But, because of his invisibility, few others ever got to see that side of him. Garnering trust, it seems, takes much more than simply being of high character.

Habit Three — Using E-mail Properly

Watching a typical manager work today you would think you were looking at the control room operator of a nuclear power plant. Hours upon hours spent staring at a plasma screen display sending and responding to e-mails seems to be derigueur for today's techno-savvy managerial class.

Management by e-mail is a fact of life, but it seems the pendulum has swung too far regarding its place in a manager's repertoire of tools. E-mail was designed to complement face-to-face interactions, not as a substitute for it. Today it is not that unusual to see a manager holed up the entire day in his or her office pounding out an endless stream of e-mails. I once had a participant in my seminar that admitted to sending a record 500 e-mails in one day, and averaging a thousand a week. Not coincidently he received some of the lowest trust ratings I have ever seen on his 360-degree feedback survey.

E-mail is absolutely game-changing for sharing data between here and a location thousands of miles away. It is perfect for sending those odd-hour missives and directives when a visit or phone call would be out of the question. But I have to agree with Super Bowl winning coach Mike Ditka, who said that inside an office, "Sending e-mails is the worst thing you can do. If you need something, walk down the hall and tell someone so you are sure that what you want gets communicated fully and there is not misunderstanding. You cannot recover the wasted time that comes with someone later saying, 'Oh, *that's* what you wanted.'" Former U.S. Secretary of State Madeleine Albright feels that despite all kinds of instant communication today, face-to-face contact is absolutely essential. It is a better way to deliver tough messages and allows you to take the measure of the other person.

Essential Knowledge

When you do choose to use e-mail, here are a few things to keep in mind.

1. People using e-mail tend to be less inhibited by social niceties and quicker to resort to extreme language and invective "flaming." It does not take many "shots" fired by e-mail to taint the whole relationship.

2. You lose the flexibility present in a face-to-face interaction. In a live encounter, the speaker can alter his communication in midstream if in reading the body language of the other person it becomes apparent that the message is off base. Face-to-face encounters allow for real-time interruption, feedback, education, and damage control. In essence, you can prevent possible mistrust from happening in real time when you are in front of another person. By the time you find out about the mistrust down

---

the road through other e-mails, the damage has been done.

3. Associates who deal with each other primarily through electronic means find it harder to reach consensus and feel less empathy and compassion for one another. They simply don't have the same feelings of trust.

4. When you have a disagreement with one of your peers, resist the urge to copy your or their boss on the e-mail string. This is childish, guaranteed to incense your peer, and invites retaliation. It also burdens already busy higher-level executives with things they expect you to resolve at your level. This puts you in a bad light even if you turn out to be "right" in the battle.

5. Don't send e-mails to anyone while you are in a state of anger. Go ahead and write what you want to say but place it in the "send later" file. In a few hours, when you have calmed down, look at the e-mail again. Most often you will be glad you didn't send it. Always remember that anything you write negatively in an e-mail can be forwarded to the universe and often is.

6. Avoid terse one- or two-word answers devoid of any tact. The ideal length of an e-mail is five sentences containing a single thought.

7. Answer *all* non-spam e-mails within 24 hours at the very least. Even if you just acknowledge receipt of the e-mail you will be doing yourself a favor. It is absolutely unbelievable how many managers let hundreds of e-mails pile up in their system. It is the height of rudeness and incredibly arrogant to fail to respond to the legitimate requests of your colleagues and associates, not to mention the loss of productivity when people are waiting around for a response. If you really want to piss people off, don't

respond at all. Unless you are Marcel Marceau, silence is not a good idea.

8. Don't send e-mail with a long distribution list if you are looking for a decision or response. The more people you send the e-mail to, the less likely any one person will respond or take action.

9. Remember that e-mails can be considered legally binding and used in suits and litigations.

Habit Four – Accountability

Some leaders choose to moan about the lack of the organization's vision instead of creating one for their area.

Some leaders choose to compromise who they are by doing something they feel is unethical instead of taking a stand.

Some leaders choose to perpetuate a culture where people feel smothered instead of creating a model environment for others to emulate.

Some leaders choose to let poor performance slide instead of confronting it head on.

Some leaders choose to play the victim instead of making a difference in the things they can control.

Some leaders choose to expect their bosses to read their minds and know they don't have the understanding, data, tools, or materials they need to perform effectively.

The point is, in every case, *leaders* are accountable for the choices they make and the results they create.

It has been my experience that members of Generation X and Millennial's in particular have developed something of an entitlement mentality. They seem to act as if the world exists to cater to their every need. As a society we have made it too easy for people to duck personal responsibility. Lawyers can find loopholes in any contract. Bankruptcy laws almost beg people to file. People can annul a marriage years after the fact as though it never happened. It seems someone is always urging us to file a lawsuit when we feel aggrieved in even the slightest way. It is important that leaders stand up and be accountable for their actions.

When Tom Peters coined the phrase, "It is often easier to seek forgiveness rather than permission," he was sounding a call for executives to step out and take charge of their areas of responsibility. I see reluctance to take action in the majority of managers who are sent to my seminars. Yet I seldom, if ever, hear the senior executives who sent these people say they wish their direct reports would take less initiative.

At Ritz Carlton Hotels, they have built accountability into their "Twenty Basics," which are down to earth guiding principles of associate behavior. For example, basic Number Ten states, "Each employee is empowered. When a guest has a problem or needs something special, you should break away from your regular duties and address and resolve the issue." Basic Number Sixteen says, "Escort guests rather than point out directions to another area of the hotel." They back these principles by giving every associate a large discretionary spending amount that can be used to solve guest problems on the spot.

This philosophy runs counter to what typical organizations do when they compensate only for individual performance, provide no discretionary spending authority, and write tight job descriptions, which punish people for going outside their area of responsibility.

Job descriptions are necessary to create a set of hiring criteria. They also might work okay for low-level administrative or factory positions. But they create negative unintended consequences when used for knowledge workers. These jobs require a lot of judgment and the requirements for success change frequently. Skilled associates should be encouraged to roam and spend, within reason, to accomplish the task.

Accountability erodes when one or more of the following takes place on a regular basis:

1. "Head in the Sand," where leaders pretend there really is no problem or that it will simply solve itself.

2. "Skapegoating," where leaders try to shift blame away from themselves.

3. "Duck and Cover," where the norm is to document excuses.

Eva Chen, CTO and co-founder of computer security firm Trend Micro, is an example of a no excuses leader who did whatever it took to succeed. In her firm, she would often pretend to be a secretary when she attended engineering meetings. She believed she wouldn't be taken seriously as a woman CTO so she would make occasional suggestions from a position less threatening. Eva went so far as to have two sets of business cards made up; one as the CTO and the other as an engineering secretary. While it is appalling someone would have to do this, that's a leader doing what she thought it took to get the job done.[6]

💡 Don't Forget This 💡

The central premise of a culture of accountability is that it is a leader's job to eliminate things associates might use as excuses, reward accountable acts and correct or eliminate members who behave in an irresponsible manner.

To create such accountability there needs to be a shared purpose, trust, group recognition/rewards, and clear roles with both fixed and flexible boundaries.

Habit Five — Transparency In All Encounters

Dr. Michael Burns, president and COO of Ferndale Pharma Group, has one of the best relationships with his board and associates of anyone that I have ever met. He is so beloved that even after Mike left the company to become the CEO of ReproMedix, a decision Mike later deemed to have been a mistake, the board chose to re-hire him as president of Ferndale Pharma Group. The organizations associates applauded the decision.

Mike says, "I was totally open with everyone that my decision to leave was a mistake. I wasn't embarrassed that things didn't work out. And, because of the loss of face I suffered, it made people think twice about the possibility that the grass may not be greener somewhere else."

Mike believes in the concept of transparency with people. He attempts to ensure that associates understand as much as possible about the business. He goes to great lengths to explain to them why things are important to the enterprise and to them personally. He not only shares the organization's goals and plans with everyone but frequently asks associates in small round-table discussions if these things are appropriate and realistic. He has learned when the company's demands of people are impossible, that's when people cut ethical corners.

Mike's most fervent belief is that forcing people to do things is never as helpful as getting them to embrace whatever needs to be done. And, the foundation of embracing change is candor. He goes to great lengths to declare his motives and clarify his intent when he makes decisions or requests something from his staff.[7] It is unlikely that people will trust a leader if the leader's motives are not known, misunderstood, or misinterpreted.

Habit Six — Respect the Boss' Needs

Every year a few otherwise successful CEOs lose their jobs in large part for ignoring the care and feeding of their bosses, the board of directors. Perhaps it is the hubris that accompanies success. Maybe it is the fierce independent streak that high control personalities exhibit. Sometimes it is over-reliance on a personal relationship. Or it might simply be the failure to place communication with the board as a high time management priority.

Ed Zander at Motorola, Stanley O'Neal at Merrill Lynch, and Carly Fiorina at Hewlett Packard are examples of smart people making mistakes with their boards. In Fiorina's case, by her own admission in her memoir, "Tough Choices," she had disdain for the operational capabilities of her board and was continually "surprised" by the advice and requests from its members.[8]

Ed Zander apparently viewed perhaps his most powerful board member as an activist and a "distraction," while Stanley O'Neal reportedly was attempting to merge Merrill Lynch with Wachovia without even bothering to inform the board.[9] No wonder the directors lost faith in these leaders.

In pre-Sarbanes-Oxley days, boards of directors were made up of cronies of the CEO and, honestly, were not expected to know much about the inner workings of the company. They were for the most part expected to be a rubber stamp for the decisions of the CEO. Many did not even attempt to know enough about the organization to be tempted to offer meaningful advice. Consequently it was probably dangerous to act on whatever suggestions they did make.

My, how times have changed. Now that members of the board can be held personally liable for failing to exercise diligence and shareholder lawsuits have become common, both the composition of the board and how members view their responsibilities are dramatically different.

Tips for Transparency with the Board of Directors (or any other boss)

1. Get to know each member's personality, strengths, weaknesses, fears, and aspirations. Don't try to change your bosses; adapt.

2. Always communicate *major* ideas and plans before taking action. Most bosses hate surprises.

3. Respond quickly and courteously to requests for information, even though it may not be your highest priority at the moment. The people who can terminate your employment should always be a high priority.

4. Attempt to build a relationship on a personal level, but don't rely too heavily upon it.

5. When you disagree with a recommendation or suggestion, don't just ignore it or drag your feet. Provide the rationale behind your disagreement. Make sure the discussion ends with both parties stating their understanding of the actions to be taken. When possible, follow-up in writing or by e-mail to confirm the decision.

Despite the merits of your arguments, avoid getting so angry that you publicly criticize the boss. You will only make matters worse and burn a bridge that may come back later to haunt you. Focus instead on the leader's plusses. This is difficult as it is not normal for us to look at the strengths of someone who is making us miserable. At the minimum, learning to adjust to a boss of a different style builds tolerance and demonstrates how not to act when we get into a position of power. Colin Powell said in a speech I attended a few years ago that the two years he spent working for a commander he considered to be morally bankrupt were instrumental in convincing him of the kind of leader he didn't want to be.

6. Get in the habit of regular communication via e-mail, phone calls, or personal visits at a frequency level to their liking.

7. Be truly open to advice from the board. Presumably board members have enjoyed some modicum of success in their lives and careers. Perhaps there are critical pieces of insight that they are offering, but you have to be receptive.

8. If members of the board begin to roam around the organization taking your staff's precious time or changing staff priorities, you have to step in. You must make it clear that you run the business and that their violating the chain of command cannot be tolerated. Do this politely, but firmly, and tell them that you will be happy to provide them with any information they seek. It is amazing how disruptive it

is when board members wander the halls and drop by the offices of your staff. It puts your people in a real dilemma as to how to respond.

9. For the most part your job is to present solutions to problems you are encountering when dealing with the board. In a meeting it is not a good idea to just toss a problem out to the board to get their reaction. They will most likely get the impression they hired the wrong person if you do this too often. Don't lose control of the meeting.

10. Tell them what *you* need to be successful.

One of a leader's highest priorities should be to create an environment of openness and trust with the people who are in a position to terminate their employment.

Habit Seven — Display Humility, Not Arrogance

One quality that seems almost universally present in failed executive careers is arrogance. It is a major cause of insensitivity ("I am better than you"), unwillingness to delegate ("I am smarter and more capable than you"), betrayal of trust ("I can get away with it"), blind ambition ("I deserve it"), inability to work for a boss with a different style ("Can you believe I have to work for this idiot"), poor staffing decisions ("It doesn't matter who I hire as long as I am around to direct them"), and downward only communication ("If people at lower pay grades were better than me, they would have my job and I would have theirs"). It seems arrogant people always need other people to look down on.

 Don't Forget This

Feelings of low self-esteem (disliking oneself and feeling unworthy of good things) are at the root of arrogance. The arrogant person is desperately trying to mask internal feelings of unworthiness by projecting false bravado.

It is difficult to stay grounded when everyone is falling all over themselves to tell you how great you are. But somehow effective leaders manage to keep their true priorities in life straight. Jim Collins in his research for the breakthrough work, *Good to Great,* found that level-five leaders (the type at the helm of every great company he studied) "channel their ego needs away from themselves and into the larger goal of building a great company."[10] They seem to embody the biblical notion of humility by thinking, "But for the grace of God go I."

Humility involves respect for others but it should not be confused with weakness. American Express head man Ken Chenault, Intel's Paul Otellini and Anne Mulcahay of Xerox are CEO's who are as mentally tough as any you will find. Yet they conduct themselves in a respectful and quietly assured manner.

Humble leaders see no task as being "beneath them," avoid seeming like a "know it all," treat everyone they encounter with respect, readily admit mistakes and use self-deprecating humor. They go out of their way to mention and thank the people who contributed to their success.

In comparison, uttering racial slurs, telling ethnic jokes, demeaning someone's physical disability, sexual innuendo, and using a condescending tone are but a few of the things insensitive leaders sometimes do that get them into hot water. What Eliot Spitzer *did* in soliciting a prostitute was bad enough. The fact that he was also seen as brash throughout his career caused a "deafening silence" as almost no one stood by him or came to his defense.

Insensitivity factored into the black eyes suffered by the likes of Bob Nardelli when he was let go at Home Depot, Rubbermaid's Wolfgang Schmitt, Daimler Chrysler's Jurgen Schrempp and countless other leaders in all walks of life. As Dave Schlotterbeck, CEO of CareFusion, said, "It took me far too many years to realize that I seldom have to raise my voice to get my staff to know that I want something done."

Habit Eight — Promote Ownership

It is much easier for followers to place their trust in something if they have been involved early in the process and been kept informed all along the way. In developing plans, selecting priorities, making decisions and seeing to it that tasks are properly executed, few things are as important as "buy-in." But trust is reciprocal and involvement alone will not ensure your people will fulfill their end of the trust bargain. There are several reasons why employees fail to take ownership of their part in the process.

A common explanation is that they simply disagree with a leader's course of action all together. These people can create real trouble because their inclination is to openly resist anything related to the action expected of them. Worse, they may even go so far as to enlist others who share their views in their "resistance movement." People like this will look to bail out of the process at the earliest opportunity. *The best approach to take with someone who disagrees with a decision is to first try and educate them on the merits of the decision or reasons behind the course of action.* If, however, the person fails to "get it," then he must be moved into a position where he cannot block the actions of others.

A second cause of failure to take ownership is because associates see themselves as being overloaded by other tasks. People like this might even agree that the action required of them by the leader is a good thing; it's just that they feel "swamped." Periodically taking things off people's plates will work best here. Failing that, it is imperative that the leader clarify to the employee and all others who may be affected that the work he is requesting is of the highest priority.

Indispensable Tip !

Everyone is overloaded with work these days. So many things people are asked to do add very little value. At least once a quarter every associate should be allowed to suggest items to be taken off their plates. You will get far more buy-in to the tasks that remain.

A third type of situation leaders encounter is where people put forth a token effort to comply with the tasks expected, either out of loyalty to the leader or a sense of professionalism. *Attempting to win the "hearts and minds" of these people through inspiration is the key.* Three of the best ways to accomplish this are showing associates that they play a key role, creating as much involvement for people as possible, and allowing some flexibility in terms of the latitude they are given to structure the tasks in ways they find desirable.

Tales from the Workplace

In *The Art of Possibility*, Benjamin Zander, conductor of the Boston Philharmonic, says that he came to a startling realization one day after he had been conducting for nearly twenty years. It dawned on him that while the conductor graces the cover of the orchestra's program, he does not personally produce a sound. His success derives solely from enabling the musicians to play each phrase as beautifully as possible.

Even though an orchestra is one of the last bastions of truly autocratic leadership, Zander thought it best to break tradition and give his players a voice. He initiated a ritual of placing a blank sheet of paper on each musician's stand before every rehearsal. They were invited to write down any observation that might allow them to play the piece more beautifully. When he would adopt a player's suggestion, he would make eye contact and nod at the proper moment to the musician responsible for the improvement, thus turning it into *their* moment. Needless to say, both the performance and the buy-in were enhanced.

One of my favorite phrases is, "Change done to you is stressful and debilitating, while change you choose is liberating and growth producing." It is truly amazing how much pain people will tolerate if it is their choice and equally amazing how little pain they will tolerate if it is forced upon them.

Too many managers make the mistake of planning everything for their people down to the smallest detail, thus disenfranchising them in the process.

A fourth reason people resist taking ownership is that they fear the consequences of failure more than they value the benefits of success.

Dr. Denis Waitley tells the story of placing a two-foot-wide piece of wood on the ground and asking a person to walk across the beam. If they are successful, they get $20. Of course no one balks at taking that challenge, as there is very little likelihood they will fall off the beam, and even if they do, the consequences are not very severe. However, when that same beam is placed on top of a multi-story building, very few people choose to walk across for the same payoff. They now are driven almost entirely by fear. *For these types of situations the leader either needs to greatly increase the reward for success or reduce the penalty of failure.*

The final reason people passively or aggressively resist doing what is expected of them is that there is no real penalty for failing to comply. In an oft-told story about parachute packers, supposedly they felt great about achieving a quality level of 99.9 percent. Of course one paratrooper out of a thousand didn't think that number was too impressive. So the commander changed the system. Once a week the packers would make a jump with the parachute they wore picked at random from those packed the week before. The error rate promptly went to zero. This is what happens when "buy-in" is taken to heart instead of merely being a slogan.

What "buy-in" does is increase the overall *effectiveness* of decisions. The quality of a decision times peoples commitment to implementing it determines the overall effectiveness of the decision. Suppose that you make a perfect ten decision on a ten-point quality scale, but the commitment of the people to implement it is a two. The effectiveness factor is twenty. But, suppose the quality of the decision is an eight and people's commitment to implement it is also an eight. You get a score of sixty-four or triple the effectiveness of the so-called perfect decision. The biggest way to up that commitment part of the equation is through involvement.[11] As they say in the military, soldiers who are active in planning the battle seldom battle the plan.

Habit Nine — Trust Others In Order to Become Trusted In Return

One executive I worked with years ago used to stand at his office window each morning taking notes as to what time various people arrived. Yet he never bothered to see what these people were accomplishing. In his mind, if they weren't in the office at least an hour before the official starting time, they weren't dedicated.

There are so many occasions when salaried associates work late into the evening, travel for the organization on their own time or work weekends that it is a frustrating waste just to put in *face time*. Essentially, we need to show our people that we trust their judgment as to how they allocate their time to accomplish their key tasks.

Cali Ressler, Jody Thompson, and Brad Anderson of Best Buy have gone one step further. In the book *Why Work Sucks,* they describe the "results-only work environment" they created together at Best Buy.

A key premise of their system is that results against expectations should be the thing that counts most in the organization. They advocate a radical overhaul of the culture of enterprises as it relates to things like time spent on tasks and physical presence at work. Their approach goes well beyond alternative work arrangements like telecommuting. It attempts to put to rest cherished but wrong-headed notions that organizations should reward effort or how many hours a person works. Amen! In a knowledge economy, it should be all about results against expectations.

In the "results-only work environment," people can generally work from whatever location they want and put in the hours they desire, as long as they meet all their objectives. The culture does not ostracize people for coming in late or leaving early. There is no attempt to pile on more work if an associate finishes early and wants to leave.[12] You can imagine the sense of being trusted that people working in such a system feel.

Habit Ten — Deliver Consistent Performance

A leader's credibility derives in part from her ability to deliver consistently superior results — past and present. This regularity of performance is what gives followers the impetus to trust that the leader will produce similar results in the future. Most people have come to realize that the best predictor of future performance is past performance.

The ability of anyone to routinely perform at high levels is due in large part to possessing the *requisite capabilities.* These are the knowledge, skills, attitudes and style to do the job at hand. The *perception* of a leader's capabilities will be enhanced if she also possesses the degrees, certifications, and other credentials that serve to give independent testimonial to the leader's presumed capability.

When it comes to trust, track record matters. Warren Buffet gets the benefit of the doubt in trust-related disagreements because he has demonstrated ethical performance over time. Colin Powell's track record guarantees him the underlying credibility to establish a basis of trust with people quickly in new situations. Opinion polls showed that most people believed he was not trying to deceive the United Nations when he gave his impassioned plea that Iraq was stockpiling weapons of mass destruction. People believed that Powell truly thought Saddamm Hussein was a threat that needed to be stopped. Not so for former President George W. Bush.

Consistent performers live up to their commitments even when it hurts. In *Winners Never Cheat,* John Huntsman, chairman of Huntsman Chemical, tells of a handshake deal he made with Emerson Kampen to sell a stake in one of his divisions to Great Lakes Chemical. The agreed-upon price was $54 million. For whatever reason, Great Lakes Chemical took over half a year to get the formal paperwork in order. During that time the value of the stake rose by almost $200 million. Right before the papers were to be signed, Kampen called Huntsman and offered to pay half of the increase or $100 million more than what was agreed upon. To his amazement, Huntsman said no; they had a handshake agreement at the $54-million price and that is the way the deal would stay. Now that is living up to a commitment!

To build trust through performance, credible leaders keep at jobs until they are complete. There are a lot of "starters" in this world. But there are precious few "finishers." Credible leaders seldom make the same mistake twice, are able to ignore distractions that derail others, and they take charge of situations starting to go poorly, well before the "eleventh hour." These types of leaders let their results be their calling card, not their words. They realize that their trustworthiness is diminished if they don't deliver the things they promised. So they are extremely careful in the promises they make. The "average wait time" signs you see at Universal Studios while you are in line for an attraction, deliberately state a longer wait time than will actually occur. They want you to feel good that you had a shorter wait than expected.

Habit Eleven — Exude Ethical Honesty

We live in a world where it is difficult to hide anything from anyone for long. The proliferation of data available on the Internet has rendered futile most attempts to protect all but the most sensitive organizational secrets. Thus, adherence to the notion that it is best to tell the truth has probably never been more critical.

Star Pitcher Andy Pettitte of the New York Yankees came clean as soon as he was confronted with others' testimony that he had used performance enhancing drugs. In terms of any lasting damage, the whole affair is pretty much a non-issue.

By contrast, Olympian Marion Jones denied for years that she had used performance-enhancing drugs, evidently including at least once under oath. Her prison sentence was due to the cover-up, not the crime. She learned the hard way that you can't talk your way out of something you behaved your way into.[13] Ditto for Martha Stewart and more recently, former Detroit Mayor Kwame Kilpatrick.

Tales From the Workplace

A truly bizarre story of, *"You Get the Leadership You Deserve,"* appeared in the February 16, 2009 issue of the Orange County Business Journal. It pretty much sums up the sad state of affairs in corporate America today.

An investor in a company with an $800 million market cap, himself the former head of a company who spent years in prison for fraud, embezzlement and other financial crimes, alleges that the company CEO didn't hold degrees from a prestigious university as claimed on his official biography. The investor brings this to light because his own unseemly strategy is to dig up dirt on companies, short their stock, go public with his scandalous information and profit when the stock falls. His strategy works brilliantly as this company's stock falls 45 percent from December to February.

Meanwhile, the CEO when confronted with the charge

initially "categorically denies" misrepresenting the degrees. Two separate investigations conclude he does not hold degrees from the university. The CEO then recants his previous denial. So, this CEO has now been caught in major lies twice, the stock has cratered and the prospect of sharehold lawsuits looms large. To add insult to injury, the CEO evidently despite being in the job for eight years has failed to develop a successor.

Now in most companies an employee at any level caught falsifying documents is usually unceremoniously terminated. Perhaps because of their own failure to ensure adequate CEO succession the Board of Directors decides to keep the CEO with what many would perceive to be a slap on the wrist. Astonishingly an analyst who tracks the company in a note to his clients said, "We wholeheartedly acknowledge and applaud this CEO's invaluable leadership." Have we gone completely mad in this country?

Drastic times often tempt leaders to consider cutting ethical corners they would never have dreamed of cutting under more normal circumstances. A small business owner in my community was faced with the prospect of bankruptcy. Instead of engaging her associates to help her come up with innovative ways to save the enterprise she chose to get illegally creative. She asked each associate to file for unemployment claiming they were laid off. In actuality, her proposition was to have them continue to work full time. She would pay them the difference between unemployment and their full pay, thus cutting the businesses out of pocket expenses for the same work. This is different than California's "Work Share" program where partial unemployment benefits may be paid to workers who have their hours significantly reduced. Even if the business did survive, how could associates trust her again? How could she look herself in the mirror each morning with any kind of respect? Just imagine the stress she would have each day wondering if she would get caught defrauding a governmental entity. And, unethical leaders give associates an excuse to rationalize their own dishonest acts.

Somewhere along the way many leaders seem to have lost their conscience, this moral compass that provides insight into what is right versus wrong. The penalty for straying from one's conscience is guilt. There are only two types of people who are free from guilt. The first are those that follow their moral compass. And the second are those devoid of moral grounding. Given the steady stream of stories detailing the ethical lapses of leaders in all walks of life, it appears that many leaders have no shame — no moral compass.

Unfortunately, there is no simple, universal formula that details what is ethical. A leader's ethical system is his personal set of *ground rules* for making what he considers to be the *right* decision. Generally there are four separate and competing ethical frameworks:

1. conscience based ethics as described by Martin Buber;
2. social contract ethics of Jean Jacques Rousseau;
3. rule ethics as popularized by Immanuel Kant;
4. the end result ethics of John Stuart Mill.

In Buber's view, ethics is defined by one's conscience. In effect, we can sense when we do something that is wrong and we experience a surge of guilt. By contrast, Rousseau would say the rightness of an action is determined by the customs and norms of a particular community. For instance, if it is common practice in a country that bribes be paid to facilitate business, then it is acceptable to pay them. Kant believed the propriety of an action is determined by laws and standards. In Kant's view, if it is legal then it is also ethical. Mill purported that the morality of an action is determined by considering its consequences.[14] Obviously, there are plenty of times when one or more of these sets of *ground rules* will be in conflict. In a simple example, while I began this discussion with the idea that it is best to tell the truth (a conscience based ethical framework), this might fly in the face of a *consequences* ethical framework that says that we should not unnecessarily hurt people's feelings.

My point is that a person of integrity is defined as one who makes an effort to use all four ethical frameworks. In practice it implies that an effective leader, when faced with a consequential decision consider the expected consequences, rules and laws, customs and norms of the community, and one's personal convictions, with the whole process grounded in common sense.

Perhaps the simplest test of all would be for a leader to ask, "How would I feel if my parents, spouse, and children were to read a story in the newspaper about the decision I made or the behaviors I engaged in?"

Habit Twelve — Pay Attention to Perceptions

In difficult times everything a leader says or does becomes more closely scrutinized. In an instant, a leader's reputation can be enhanced or tarnished. Executive pay is one area that has never been put under a more powerful microscope than it is today. At a time when millions of people are losing their jobs, leaders need to make a choice — to become a role model of shared sacrifice or be vilified as one who arrogantly exhibits greed.

University of Connecticut men's basketball coach, Jim Calhoun unwittingly became the poster child for the latter, sullying an otherwise fine career of leadership. In February 2009 after his 799th career victory, Coach Calhoun was ambushed by a tactless reporter during the post-game news conference. The reporter asked, "Being the state's highest salaried employee at $1.6 million, given the states $1 billion deficit, do you feel you should give back any of the money to the state?"

Before the question was fully asked Coach Calhoun defiantly said, "Not a dime back." The reporter began to ask again, and Calhoun repeated, "Not a dime back." Coach Calhoun then proceeded to launch into an angry tirade directed at the reporter. Now most people feel Coach Calhoun has every right to keep his money as he does bring in far more profit to the university than he is paid. But, his actions were hardly ones to emulate.

Within days Connecticut state legislators fired off a letter to the university president demanding that Calhoun be reprimanded. They wrote, "With increased success comes increased responsibility. Coach Calhoun's actions were not in keeping with the highest ethical standards that we expect from a representative of the University of Connecticut."[15] His historic 800th win later that week went largely unnoticed while the video clip of the incident ran endlessly on every media outlet from ESPN to CNN.

NFL Commissioner, Roger Goodell, and GE CEO, Jeff Imelt chose a better path. Goodell voluntarily took the largest pay cut at 20 percent of anyone else in the organization. Imelt refused a $12 million bonus that was due to him by contract. Both men exhibited the highest form of ethical leadership by becoming role models of shared sacrifice.

Trust is not built in a day, but it is built daily. And, one misstep can destroy all the goodwill the leader has painstakingly worked to generate. But making these twelve habits the foundation of your daily work life will greatly increase the odds of success.

CHAPTER 8

CHANGE THE PLAYING FIELD THROUGH CULTURE:
Understanding the Effects of Culture

Organization culture was once described by Marvin Bower, the longtime legendary head of McKinsey and Company, as "the way we do things around here."[1] It consists of the norms of behavior and codes of conduct practiced by the mainstream of any group of people. Edgar Schein of MIT views creating and managing culture as perhaps the most important thing leaders do.[2] Dave Schlotterbeck, CEO of CareFusion, the sixth largest medical technology company in the world with over $5 billion in revenue, believes that shaping culture is the most powerful tool for influencing the performance of an organization that management has at its disposal.

Dave confided that one of his most important learnings was that a senior team could actually choose the culture they want to have, that this culture can truly be customized to meet an organization's needs. In difficult economic times culture can act as an all-important anchor to provide stability for associates in an increasingly tumultuous world. For leaders it can provide a homing beacon that provides direction for decisions that need to be made before the full script is written.

Don't Forget This

It is an inescapable fact that the behavior of the senior-most managers or the most influential people in a unit creates the cultural environment within which everyone must work.

In essence, associates follow the lead of influential people by adapting their own behaviors to fit in with the expectation of their leaders.

Some behaviors create a positive work culture while others make it more difficult for people to perform effectively. As with personality types, organizational behaviors tend to cluster around a relatively few themes. By understanding these cultural clusters of behavior we can objectively look at certain managerial behaviors and determine whether performance will likely be enhanced or hindered by the various elements present in each culture theme.

Diagram 1 shows sixteen distinct organization cultures. The eight at the top of the graph are the productive cultures a unit might consider adopting. The eight at the bottom are the ones that every organizational unit should try to minimize. Appendix A in the back of the book is an instrument that will allow you to assess the current effectiveness of your unit. Most parts of an organization should strive for scores above the 75th percentile on at least four productive scales while holding all eight dysfunctional scales below the 25th percentile.

Productive Work Cultures

There are cultures that tend to produce important organizational outcomes such as member satisfaction, trust, teamwork, motivation, positive relationships, customer satisfaction, productivity, shared values, accuracy, timeliness, role clarity, authenticity, increased number of suggestions, mission clarity, reduced number of grievances, and fewer lawsuits. Following are eight qualities that often result in a productive culture.

DIAGRAM 1

ORGANIZATION ENVIRONMENT INDEX™

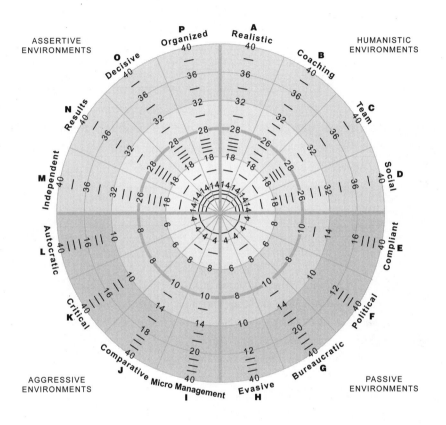

Low Scores = At or Below 25th percentile
Moderate Scores = Between the 25th and 75th percentiles
High Scores = At or Above the 75th percentile

91 - 100
76 - 90
51 - 75
26 - 50
11 - 25
1 - 10
Percentiles

Independent

The independent culture is one characterized by members who are encouraged to, and capable of, operating independently of close supervision. In such a setting the outcomes are usually high motivation and low turnover, high creativity, and a strong sense of ethics. Generally the leadership in such a culture respects members who are candid and passionate. This type of atmosphere can obviously be beneficial anywhere, but is most often found in universities, think tanks, law firms, consulting firms and the R&D functions.

To increase the strength of this culture, teach managers to respect candor in their associates and educate the members to be constructively candid. Allow people with passion and personal conviction the freedom to pursue items of interest to them as long as it does not result in a major loss. Reward the independent actions taken by your superior performers. Rely heavily upon guidance through values while minimizing onerous amounts of bureaucracy.

Indispensable Tip !

At software maker Intuit, engineers are allowed four hours per week to pursue things they think have value without any guidelines from marketing as to their economic viability. At NetApp, voted the best company to work for in America in 2008 by Fortune Magazine, they dumped a dozen-page travel policy in favor of simple guidance. "We are a frugal company. But don't show up dog tired to save a few bucks. Use your common sense."

Results

In this culture, the focus is on bottom line achievement within the parameters of ethics and humanistic treatment of associates. In such a setting, a premium is placed on ensuring good ideas get implemented. Roadblocks and barriers to people's performance are identified and overcome. Members compete against standards of excellence instead of against each other so there can be many winners. Substandard performance is identified early and constructively confronted. While this atmosphere would be valued in any enterprise, it is most often found in professional sports, hedge funds, venture capital firms and manufacturing or operations units of larger organizations. General Electric and Redwood City, CA-based Basic Chemical Solutions are examples of organizations that foster this type of culture.

Essential Knowledge

In organization opinion surveys, nearly 70 percent of employees typically say that management is not doing enough to get rid of deficient performers.

To strengthen this culture, quickly and constructively confront poor performance. Celebrate successful implementation of effective processes and the completion of projects. Make sure everyone is working against things they have a reasonable degree of control over. Use Kaizen teams (a group of associates specifically chosen to spend a week mapping out a process and suggesting more effective alternatives) to break through ineffective processes.

Decisive

In this culture speed is essential. There is a bias for action and members are encouraged to make tough choices. Generally there is a tolerance for ambiguity and comfort in making decisions without waiting for 100-percent data. Members are encouraged to think for themselves and take appropriate action without excessive checking with the boss. Both Google and Qualcomm work hard at developing this type of environment.

This atmosphere is most often found in manufacturing, fast-growing high-tech companies and military units during battle. To strengthen this area, praise and reward members who do their best in making tough choices. Get data on the critical elements of a situation and then make a decision. Trust your experts' opinions, even if they cannot fully explain them to you. That's why they are experts and you are not. It is impossible to teach you everything they know that went into their recommendations.

Organized

An organized culture should exist where there is a lot of interaction required for success or where capital equipment requirements are so high that a mistake could be fatal to the enterprise. Alternatives are developed and analyzed before decisions are made so the best path is chosen first. It is usually characterized by highly effective work processes, scenario planning, risk management, and thinking several moves in advance. This atmosphere would obviously be beneficial anywhere but, is most often found in capital intensive industries such as aerospace/defense, oil and gas, heavy equipment, automotive manufacturing, and the engineering and IT functions. Boeing and Shell are the archetypes of this culture.

To strengthen the organized culture, budget money and time for up-front planning in important projects. Do not criticize those managers who take their team offsite to do planning. Reward sound risk assessment, risk management, and scenario thinking. Encourage everyone to think several moves in advance.

Realistic

A realistic culture is characterized by optimism, energy, three-way feedback, and members stepping up to take personal accountability. Moderate stretch goals are set and achieved and people are non-defensive when criticized.

This type of atmosphere would be appropriate almost anywhere, but is most often found in advertising agencies, hospitals, think tanks and consulting firms. To foster such an environment it is important that members are trained in giving and receiving feedback and that credit is shared widely for success. Members who are realistic in their schedule, sales, and budget estimates should be singled out for praise. San Diego based Scripps Health gives every associate a substantial bonus after patient satisfaction scores improve significantly.

Coaching

This type of culture is not always necessary, but is usually quite beneficial. If there were a lot of veterans and low turnover, perhaps other environments would be more appropriate. However, if the organization is characterized by lots of young or relatively inexperienced associates, this focus is probably essential.

Coaching implies lots of attention to support, encouragement and motivation. You want people to try new things and know they will not be punished for reasonable mistakes. There should be frequent communication and people development must be both emphasized and funded.

You often find this culture necessary in a sales or customer service department or organizations with high turnover like restaurants or banks.

Select managers who are interested in coaching. Reward managers for developing their associates. It should become an accepted norm to correct rather than punish deficient performance. The organization must make a financial commitment to invest heavily in people development programs for all organizational levels and set a goal for each associate to receive a certain number of hours of training per year. At Accenture, every associate is assigned a career counselor. Training averages close to two weeks per year for each associate.

Team

Virtually everything is done in teams today. R&D no longer employs researchers who work in isolation on a backbench thinking up new products. Manufacturing associates work in "cell" teams and jointly with others in "Kaizen" projects. Even sales representatives often team up with technical experts and designated "closers."

In a team culture, anything that creates friction or gets in the way of speed must be minimized.

Fostering an informal collegial way of working together with few status differentials is a terrific way to reduce friction. Conflicts need to be quickly and effectively mediated. Members should feel informed, listened to, and involved. There should be lots of credit sharing.

To create this culture, leaders need to break down silos and walls and encourage information exchange between units. Joint goal setting, team-based appraisal, and pay structures should be established. An online knowledge management system that all associates can tap into should be a high priority.

Examples of equalitarian cultures are Dallas-based TD Industries and Kansas City-based Burns & McDonnell, where all associates are shareholders, and consulting firm MITRE, where the CEO is paid only eighteen times what the lowest paid associate earns.

Social

Constructive interpersonal relations, tact, consideration, and friendliness are high priorities in a social culture. People in the organization are treated with the same importance as results. The leaders are visible, available, and approachable. There is extensive orientation of new employees, lots of informal get-togethers, and organization-sponsored events.

A strong social culture is vital in customer service or sales departments as well as any organization geared to dealing with the public like retail merchants and airlines. The theory is that abused employees become customer abusers, while satisfied employees go out of their way to create positive customer experiences. It may not be so important in backroom operations where there is infrequent customer interface.

To strengthen a social culture there should be member-centered human resource policies. Events like birthdays, employment anniversaries and special occasions should be celebrated. Managers should wander the halls, have informal meetings and team-building sessions, and eat some meals with their employees. Whole Foods Market and REI go to great lengths to try and instill a social culture.

Dysfunctional Work Cultures

There are cultures that tend to produce negative outcomes such as member dissatisfaction, grievances, role confusion, lawsuits, theft, turnover of talented associates, hoarding, distrust, turf protection, infighting, fewer suggestions, and low productivity. Here are eight qualities that often result in such a culture.

Compliant

Members in a compliant culture are expected to subvert their own judgment and obey directives without question. In such a setting, everyone tends to be reactive instead of proactive. Risk avoidance is a high priority. There is limited upward flow of information, and challenging of senior managers is discouraged.

This type of dysfunctional culture is typical of some aerospace companies, the military, quick serve restaurants and some sporting teams. To create a better environment, vehicles need to be created where members have an opportunity for dialog and feedback with senior leaders. People who take a reasonable risk and fail should not be unduly punished. Members should be given greater latitude to use their own judgment.

Political

In a highly politicized setting, the *appearance* of competence is more important than the actual results. Members switch priorities in "knee-jerk" fashion to please their bosses. Everyone seems afraid to make waves or deal with conflict. Leaders are wishy-washy, which causes a lack of respect. Indecisiveness reigns. Performance management is based more upon friendships with the boss than real accomplishment.

This culture is often found in highly regulated industries. To reduce the ill effects of this culture, make sure poor performance is confronted regardless of a member's connection to the boss. Find a few maverick associates and publicly reward them. Let everyone know that disagreement before a decision is made is not a sign of disloyalty. Try to give associates stability by minimizing changes to their schedule.

Bureaucratic

In this setting, systems, procedures, and rules take precedence over common sense, empowerment, and judgment. Change innovation and new ideas are difficult to implement. Anyone the least bit unconventional is driven out of the organization. There is expected to be blind obedience to the system.

This is often characteristic of slow moving industries like banks, accounting firms, insurance companies, or government agencies. To reduce the negative impact of this culture, find members who take reasonable risks and then publicize their actions. Frequently review standard operating procedures. Get rid of or fix processes that are causing dysfunction. Change the dress code to allow for more individuality; poll your clients to see how they are reacting to doing business with you. Hire "mystery shoppers" to provide an objective evaluation of the ease of interacting with your organization.

Evasive

The emphasis in this culture is for associates to do as little as possible that might come back to haunt them in some way. Leaders seldom communicate with each other, engage in blame shifting, and pretend that problems don't exist. Everyone seems evasive, indecisive, and overwhelmed with their own responsibilities.

This type of culture is found wherever elected officials have significant influence or where the unit has fewer resources than it needs to accomplish its mission. To remove the ill effects of this climate make it clear that it is unacceptable to ignore problems or shift blame. Severely punish anyone who does. Try to provide a reasonable resource allocation that gives associates a fighting chance of successfully delivering on their accountabilities. Do not severely punish mistakes that come from taking reasonable risks.

Micromanagement

The micromanagement culture places emphasis on overkill analysis, scrubbing and re-scrubbing even routine reports to be error free, and avoidance of risk. This works well if the leaders are extremely bright and talented and everyone else is a dolt. The danger is that the drive for perfection squeezes out creativity, the best performers leave, and the main messages are lost in the details. Leaders tend to be overly critical of mistakes and documents are looked at by numerous people for any little error before submission to upper management. It is very costly and would only make sense if the matters were critical.

This climate is often found in engineering departments or in backroom operations. To reduce the dysfunctional aspects of this culture, set time limits for making decisions. Only micromanage substandard performers. Recognize how costly and frustrating it is when everyone is afraid to submit a routine document with a typo in it. Work hard to develop some creative approaches to important situations.

Comparative

An organization dominated by a comparative culture is wrought with unhealthy internal competition. Members tend to look for ways to undercut one another. In meetings, there is an air of condescension. There is very poor cooperation, trust, or teamwork. Sandbagging, hoarding information, and outright sabotage is practiced by the overly competitive.

This culture is often caused by forcing people into a bell-shaped distribution of performance and lopping off the bottom performers, even if they are meeting expectations. To overcome the more detrimental aspects of this climate, you should start by having people compete against standards instead of against each other. Go out of your way to reward acts of cooperation and teamwork and punish overly self-serving behavior.

Critical

Of all the dysfunctional cultures, the critical one is often the most destructive. Here, negativity, sarcasm, and cynicism prevail, leading to constant conflict and hard feelings. Members hold grudges and look to even the score with their peers. Leaders seem suspicious and distrusting. They focus on assigning blame for mistakes instead of helping people learn to avoid making them in the first place. A win/lose adversarial climate pervades the organization.

It is important to turn this environment around quickly as it is defeatist and zaps energy. Ground rules need to be put in place to stop the negativity, rumors, innuendos, and back stabbing that goes on. Praise and reward consensus and look to praise people who perform well.

Autocratic

The autocratic culture is the classic old school way of running an organization. The thought behind it is that people are basically lazy or incompetent and need to have their every move directed from above. This works well in a crisis or when the leadership is far more knowledgeable than the members. Long-term, this is a disaster waiting to happen. The use of intimidation and coercion causes regular backlashes or drives dissent underground. With little delegation and empowerment, the talents of associates are squandered. The rigidity involved reduces innovation. There is usually high turnover of talented associates. The biggest problem is that with no information flowing upward, the senior leaders get so cut off from reality that they make catastrophic decisions that could have been easily avoided if they were more connected to frontline associates.

The autocratic culture is found in some areas of the military, many government agencies, and quite a few family-owned enterprises. To reduce the adverse effects of this culture, train leaders on alternative decision styles like collaboration and consensus. Coach managers who are too heavy-handed with their people. Invest effort to determine who can safely be empowered. Train senior leaders in the use of more sophisticated bases of influence.

CHAPTER 9

CHANGE THE PLAYING FIELD THROUGH CULTURE:
Changing an Organization's Culture

The quickest way to upend a dysfunctional culture is to make wholesale changes in key leadership slots and replace the departed with executives who already embody the approach you are looking to promote. If this is the method chosen, then attention should be focused on ten key elements of positive culture.

1. Guiding Principles

Crafting a coherent set of norms of behavior or principles should be the new leadership's first order of business once the new team is in place. The best ones are not pie in the sky platitudes but crisp, memorable, and descriptive bullet items. For example, Yum Brands CEO David Novak articulated a number of principles for "Taking People With You."[1] To list two as an example:

Wipe out "not invented here." Listen and involve others; learn from the best.

Create a vision and personalize it. People need to say, "I understand it, I'm excited about it, and I can make it happen."

Once the principles are outlined, they must be introduced with a splash and then followed up with small meetings where a dialog of how to put the key behaviors into practice can be hashed out.

Dave Schlotterbeck advises that the senior team has got to be in alignment in just about everything relating to the culture. He believes that it casts a much larger shadow throughout the organization if everyone at the top is saying the same things about major decisions. He spends most of the time in his senior staff meetings getting alignment. When the team makes decisions they are very careful to try and assess how the organization at large will interpret these decisions. This can be difficult to achieve since some may not be interested in total alignment.

Indispensable Tip !

If an organization is experiencing hyper-growth, it is difficult to resist the temptation to just fill slots with the first available body that can be thrown into the fray. A solid set of guiding principles will often be the only thing that keeps an organization from making compromises in the hiring process.

---

2. New Employee Orientation

Once the right people are on the team, the new employee orientation process is key to inculcating the values. People's minds are the most receptive when they first join a new organization.

Great orientation gets everyone off on the proper footing. It serves to show each new member exactly how to behave to be successful in the new venture. Limited orientation, or if it is done poorly, not only scuttles a golden opportunity, but eventually the haphazard behaviors of the new people will create great confusion as to what is expected from everyone.

At Stanley Steemer, each new associate is handed a "passport" that lists eight top executives with whom the employee must meet. At the end of the meeting, the executive signs the passport. It signals the newcomers that they are indeed important and serves to remind the senior staff that every single associate should be made to feel special.[2]

3. Manufacture Symbols

Make key values visible with wallet cards, signs, lapel pins, flags, or logos. People have notoriously short memories of what they are not regularly reminded of. These symbols can be a fun way to bring focus to a principle until it becomes totally ingrained in the collective psyche of the unit. Mary Kay Ash used a diamond broach in the shape of a bumblebee. Experts in aerodynamics to this day can't understand how a bumblebee is able to fly because their wings are too weak to support the body, but they do. Her message was that persistent people can accomplish what many people think is impossible.

At Nucor Steel, they have a long tradition of putting every associate's name on the front and back covers of their annual report.

4. Create Unique Language

There are unique words or phrases that capture attention and become associated with the values in people's minds. Barack Obama's "Change you can believe in" or Wieden & Kennedy Advertising's "Foster Ignorance" leave an indelible impression.

5. Tell Stories

The re-telling of stories, which provide examples of the values in practice, is a great way to imprint them throughout the organization. Studies show that people view as more truthful, and tend to remember longer information that comes in story form.

I remember when Hugh Chare was president of a major division of Morton Thiokol way back in 1986. We were at the Cliff Lodge at Snowbird creating a statement of values and his staff was arguing about the order the principles should be listed. Now Hugh is normally a mild mannered guy, but he slammed his fist onto the conference table and said, "I refuse to sign any document that does not have safety as our highest priority. I will put a padlock on the doors and hang an 'out of business' sign on it before I will see a person badly injured or killed on my watch." That story made the rounds for several years and forever endeared Hugh to the frontline workers who had seen a number of their fellow employees killed and injured a few months prior when a rocket motor blew up during a test.

6. Offer Role Models

The importance of a role model is to make the values human and seem within the grasp of everyone on the team. When Dick Vermeil took over as head coach of the dreadful Philadelphia Eagles in 1974, he needed a role model to show the team that in his eyes, hard work, grit, and determination were just as important as raw talent. He held open tryouts and took a chance on Vince Papale, a 30-year-old bartender who was substitute teaching at a local high school. Vince not only made the team, but his work ethic on special teams inspired even the most cynical veteran to look in the mirror.

7. Create Rituals

Military recruits enduring "boot camp." Rookies having to sing their college fight song and wait tables for the veterans of sports teams. The conferring of nicknames. All these serve to pull a team together and cement the new principles.

A daily ritual at Ritz Carlton Hotels is "The Lineup." At the beginning of each day at every Ritz Carlton facility in the world, all employees meet by department for twenty minutes. They review "the credo" (Ritz's set of guiding principles), they share a story of exceptional customer service from another Ritz property, discuss how it reflects a core value, and make comments about how they might apply it that day in their own property. This daily reflection on the values is the strongest I have ever seen and creates a connection among all Ritz associates throughout the world.[3]

8. Value Celebrations and Ceremonies

Elite organizations always make certain that achievements are celebrated and everyone knows why something is being honored. Mary Kay Ash may have been the best that ever lived at making the weeklong "seminar" at the Dallas Convention Center a true extravaganza. Solar Turbines rings a giant bell when a sale is made. The late Indiana University football coach Terry Hoeppner instituted "The Walk" and "Defend the Rock" ceremonies at Indiana University to begin to build a football tradition at a school dominated by basketball. The Bakken Award ceremony honors scientific achievement at Medtronic. These serve to instill pride in living the values at a high level.

9. Change Routines

Changing the routines of the workplace can go a long way to instilling a new atmosphere. When Willie Randolph managed the New York Mets, his approach was certainly old school. Hair had to be a certain length; facial hair was to be neatly groomed; no loud music in the clubhouse or on flights. Despite having one of the highest payrolls in baseball the Mets were not quite a .500 team. Interim manager Jerry

Manuel dumped the strict rules and within days, the players were singing together on the flights, going out together, and blasting music before the game. Mets broadcaster Wayne Hagin said, "This team's personality has changed overnight. I've never seen anything like it."[4] The Mets played the rest of the season at a level seventeen games above .500 with the same players, and Coach Manuel was rewarded with a new two-year contract.

10. Measure Performance

It is crucial that behavior consistent with the values be measured in a visible way. When Pat Riley was coaching the Lakers to five NBA Championships, he created a new statistic called the plus/minus number. For the first time each player was judged against his own career-best averages in things like rebounds, points scored, shooting percentage, minutes played, and the like. He tracked effort statistics for things few other teams chart, like taking charges, jumping for rebounds, and diving for loose balls. It was a way of having players compete against their own standards, which was critical in Riley's "team first" concept.[5]

Indispensable Tip !

Allow your direct reports to have a say in the specific types of metrics they will be judged against.

It is a bit more difficult to quickly change the environment where you have no intention of changing out the key players. The strategy can embody the previously outlined ten elements, but it must include five visible actions from the new leader.

Cultural Change at Disney

Bob Iger was able to overhaul the culture of the Walt Disney Company in just over a year while retaining essentially the same key executives that his predecessor Michael Eisner had put in place.[6]

Under Eisner, Disney executives were reportedly micro-managed, un-empowered, frequently second-guessed, often lectured to, and seldom consulted. The result was a culture of compliance with limited risk-taking, a huge bureaucracy and slow decision-making.

Where You Spend Your Time

Eisner spent his time with his finger deeply in everyone else's pie. Iger is almost totally hands free. He empowers his staff to negotiate contracts, do the deals, tinker with the movies and design the marketing. Iger visits the troops at the gaming division's brainstorming sessions, spent time healing the wounds of the Disney Pixar dustup, getting suggestions from industry heavyweights like Jeffrey Katzenburg, and smoothing over some rough spots with the board.

Where You Invest the Organization's Resources

Eisner spent money on action films. Iger wanted to take the company back to its roots of animation, so he cut the number of action movies in half and doubled the animation budget. Eisner failed to articulate or properly resource a digital strategy. Iger has moved big time into funding that area. Eisner was into a large bureaucracy, Iger prefers decentralization.

The Questions You Ask and the Statements You Make

Eisner dissed lower level staffers by reportedly writing nasty notes on less than impressive proposals. Iger asks about the roadblocks his people are running into and how he can help. With Eisner, statements mostly seemed to start with "I." Iger usually refers to "we."

What You Reward and Punish

To paraphrase Dr. Michael LeBoeuf, the Greatest Management Principle in the World is, "What gets rewarded gets done, what gets punished gets avoided, and what we pay attention to and measure gets done in priority to what we don't pay attention to or measure."[7] In my mind there has never been a truer concept regarding management effectiveness. No matter what changes a leader may try to implement, if the rewards, punishments and measures are not aligned properly with what's wanted, the leader has very little likelihood of success.

Eisner evidently rewarded people who waited for direction and did as they were told. It was well known that he punished people who attempted to steal the spotlight. Iger rewards independent action and team play and punishes heavy handedness.

How You React to Critical Accidents

Eisner all but told Pixar to kiss off. Iger knew repairing the relationship with Steve Jobs and getting Pixar back into the fold was critical to his long-term vision.

To be fair, in earlier years Disney had a good run under Eisner's direction. Perhaps it was that the organization had bumped up against the limits of what can be gained under the autocratic style, or it could simply have been that different times and different challenges required a change Eisner had not been able to make.

Leaders must be diligent in identifying and weeding out dysfunctional behaviors while clearly communicating the new set of desired actions. Deciding whether wholesale changes in key slots are needed is perhaps the diciest decision of them all.

CHAPTER 10

GROW YOUR SEED CORN, DON'T EAT IT

Generation X and Millennial workers routinely cite the opportunity for personal development as one of the top three reasons why they join and decide to stay with an organization. Add to the mix the impending retirement of a huge number of baby-boomers currently in leadership positions and you can clearly see why organizations should be desperate to develop a new cadre of leaders. Yet ironically, in tough times people-development activities are usually the first things to be eliminated. This is shortsighted and usually ends up costing firms who do this many multiples of the money they think they are saving. It is the equivalent of a farmer eating his seed corn.

By building a reputation for leadership development, organizations will position themselves to attract these generations' best and brightest when the recession passes. As word spreads that an institution invests heavily in the development of its people even during down periods, it will become a magnet attracting even more of the most talented young people. [1]

In the challenging economic environment we find ourselves in today, it may not be possible for organizations to give the kind of bonus payments and merit increases employees have come to expect. But if associates feel they are honing their skills and learning new things this "psychic capital" may be enough to at minimum prevent dissatisfaction and cause the best to choose to stay.

In helping organizations develop thousands of their most promising associates over the last 32 years, it is abundantly clear that certain experiences stand above the rest in producing well-rounded leaders. Many of the best of these experiences might not even hit the associates' radar screen as being "developmental" unless you go out of your way to tell them.

In the movie *The Karate Kid,* a young man (Daniel) desperately wants to learn karate from an old master, Mr. Miyagi. In exchange for teaching Daniel, Mr. Miyagi has him perform chores around the house, such as scraping a wooden deck, painting the house, and endlessly polishing Mr. Miyagi's car in a very specific circular "wax on, wax off" motion.

After many weeks of chores and no formal karate lessons, a frustrated Daniel confronts Mr. Miyagi and says, "For weeks I have done all these favors for you and you have yet to teach me a thing about karate." Mr. Miyagi then shows Daniel that the "wax on, wax off" and "paintbrush up, paintbrush down" motions are the exact same moves necessary to block an opponent's punches or kicks. In effect, Daniel had developed muscle motor memory and the discipline of karate without being the least bit aware of it.[2] The best developmental experiences seem to be a lot like Daniel's; growth and skill building, which may not register in one's mind as such at the time.

Indispensable Tip !

Michelangelo felt that inside every block of stone dwells a beautiful statue. He focused his efforts on chipping away at the stone to get rid of what was preventing the statue from appearing. So too should we chip away at the things preventing our people from growing into their full potential.

Many organizations narrowly visualize associate development as consisting only of classroom training, mentoring and promotions. The following are a wide range of options you can choose from as developmental experiences with the typical competencies learned listed after each experience. The idea is to develop a customized plan for each "high poten-tial" and every star associate that best fits with their needs and goals.

The Process of Developing Your People

Leaders who desire to grow into a senior executive position should endeavor to chart a regular progression through as many of the following developmental assignments as possible. Often *lateral* moves can be just as instrumental in a leader's development as *promotions*.

Promotion From Individual Contributor To First-Level Supervisor

As an individual contributor, an associate is primarily responsible for her own work. Often she develops some bad habits or ineffective behaviors in the process. Thinking too highly of one's self, competing with peers, hoarding information and seeing management as the enemy are among those that are common. Despite these behaviors, if she is technically good enough and has some degree of respect from her peers, she might eventually get promoted into a position of supervising others.

When first promoted she might have a tendency to adopt a new set of ineffective behaviors. She may attempt to overwhelm her people with her own expertise. Or she might be tempted to give herself the "plum" assign-ments, unilaterally make decisions, view requests from her people as an in-trusion on her work, fixing others mistakes instead of coaching them to do it correctly, or failing to take responsibility for their miscues.

Associates who can overcome these common mistakes and eventually be promoted again learn many things from this experience, including:
- budget, project and human resource planning
- selection of team members
- delegation and succeeding through others
- interpersonal effectiveness
- coaching
- acquiring resources and building relationships on behalf of the team
- communication skills with more diverse audiences[3]

Increase In Scope To Lead First-Level Supervisors

This type of assignment is all about handling more people, a bigger budget and greater pressure. It usually occurs within the same function that the person was in as a first-level supervisor, but not always. The decisions become more consequential in this type of role.

An associate typically learns many things from this type of assignment, including:

- holding the supervisors accountable for doing the supervising
- effective delegation
- creating an environment where both supervisors and individual contributors will be motivated
- responsibility and handling pressure
- coaching
- deploying resources among units
- building a team of supervisors

Move From a "Staff" Role to a "Line" Role

Every business has core functions deemed critical to the enterprise. In Proctor and Gamble it would be brand management, in Nike or Target a marketing assignment, and in Turner Construction a project manager role. Generally there is considerable pressure to perform quickly and a very clear bottom line to hit.

The types of things associates learn from these assignments are:

- how the heart of the business works
- profit and loss responsibility
- broad knowledge
- working under pressure

Move From a "Line" Assignment To a "Staff" Role

Key organizational support roles would include finance, human re-sources, IT, purchasing or legal. Usually these functions allow a relatively junior associate to interact with senior level executives frequently, and very early in their careers. In a sense, the associate becomes a technical expert in a deep slice of knowledge.

Typical developmental skills learned are:
- influence without formal authority
- an enterprise-wide view of the business
- working with a more nebulous bottom line
- how high-level executives think and act

Start Up Assignment

This challenge involves creating a new department, facility or business from the ground up. The associate cannot rely on existing structures, processes or procedures to guide his early days in the assignment. The sky is the limit on what can be tried or accomplished.

Typical things learned include:
- understand something in minute detail from beginning to end
- confidence in new situations
- the level of creativity/innovation they possess
- a broad perspective
- embracing risk
- handling the pressure of a "go live" date

Turnaround Situation

A turnaround assignment involves stepping into a poor performing unit, attempting to halt the slide and create excellent performance going forward. Typically there is a tight time window where the operation will be closed or disbanded if it cannot be saved. This is often incredibly difficult since the organization the associate is taking over is starting below zero and often has lots of unresolved issues. Usually poor performers are still in the unit and must be quickly identified and dealt with.

Typical competencies developed include:
- making tough personnel decisions quickly
- situation diagnosis skills
- problem solving
- rapid-fire decision-making
- working under pressure

High Visibility Project Team Leader

Julie Gilbert, vice president Women's Leadership Forum (WOLF) at Best Buy, believes people learn to lead by attacking actual business issues and solving problems that benefit the business. She oversees "WOLF Packs," which are teams that choose a project that benefits Best Buy and are charged with getting their ideas into stores within three months.[4]

Leading a project usually is a relatively short duration assignment. It might be given as a task in addition to the associate's normal workload or it can be a temporary full-time assignment. These are projects that report very high up in the organization and usually involve either an executive's "pet" idea or an initiative deemed critical to the enterprise. Therefore there is a lot of scrutiny and a high-pressure environment. The project team is often comprised of peers or in some cases, people even higher in formal rank than the leader.[5]

Typical competencies associates learned include:
- lateral influence skills
- conflict resolution tactics
- conceptual and organizational skills
- how executives think
- working under intense pressure

Increase In Scope to Functional Vice President

This type of promotion is when, let's say, a manager or director of staffing is now tapped to head the entire human resources function. The manager is all of a sudden responsible for wide ranging areas such as compensation and benefits, employee relations, labor negotiations, training, organization development, safety, and security, in addition to all the staffing-related activities.

In this type of role it is easy to become overwhelmed and isolated. There may be a temptation to create a fiefdom, avoid areas that are unfamiliar, play favorites with former peers or a failure to link the function's strategy to that of the larger organization.

Typical competencies developed at this level include:
- effectively leading large communication meetings
- a willingness to learn from other "expert" people in the function

- leading strategic planning sessions
- communicating with people in field locations
- developing a strong network
- managing upwards and sideways

Promotion to Head an Entire Business Unit

This developmental opportunity consists of leading an entire multi-functional entity, usually involving overall profit and loss responsibility. Some traps that executives can fall into include an inability to grasp how the unit makes money, failing to properly utilize support people, sacrificing the long term for short term expediency, and poor time management. In such a role, the needs of wide-ranging constituencies such as customers, suppliers, board of directors, and governmental agencies must be balanced against one another.

Major competencies developed at this level include:
- the value of every function of the organization
- balancing revenue growth with profitability
- effectively using support people
- balancing the short and long term
- culture, structure, systems, and processes enterprise wide

Peer Networking

Taking a leadership role in an outside trade organization, attending a two-week summer university program, or sitting in on cross-organizational meetings would be examples of this type of developmental opportunity.

The value of such opportunities include:
- learning of issues in other organizations
- sharpening technical or leadership knowledge
- comparing perspectives cross organizationally
- developing an internal and external network of resources
- career strategy comparison

Classroom Training

This would entail attending internal and external seminars and workshops. Though these activities involve very few days in the life of one's career, they are critical components of a leader's development. It is like Tabasco in the ingredient list for a Bloody Mary. Compared to the tomato juice and vodka, it is not much in volume, but it provides the critical flavor to the mix.

Typical benefits of classroom training include:
- business, leadership, interpersonal and technical knowledge
- state of the art tools, ideas and thinking.
- feedback on style
- confidence
- networking
- finding out how you compare to others
- the realization that most leaders face similar challenges

International Assignment

In today's world even relatively small organizations have something of a global presence. American managers tend to be very "USA Centric" in their approach to the rest of the world. Often this type of assignment will also include the lessons from a startup or turnaround situation as well.

Competencies gleaned from international assignments include:
- the United States does not lead the world in quite a few things
- developing alliances in a strange land
- figuring out how to get things done without a network to rely on
- how another part of the world lives and works
- a foreign language
- how U.S. executives are perceived

Shadow Cabinet

At Anheuser-Busch, eighteen high potential director-level associates from a cross section of the business are selected to form a "shadow cabinet." The goal is to expose the group to strategic issues of which they would otherwise be unaware.

Prior to the meeting of the actual strategy committee, the shadow cabinet members receive the agenda and conduct their own strategy session as though they were the real committee. The group generates a list of strategic recommendations that a subgroup of their members actually present to the real strategy committee. They then brief the rest of the shadow cabinet as to the decisions made at the meeting.

Through this process the cabinet not only is forced to think strategically about important business issues, but they are able to observe high-level executives in action and become "visible" to senior management.

Non-Profit Board of Directors Assignment

This would involve rising to the board of directors level in a non-profit or governmental organization like the United Way, local public utilities board, planning commission, or the like. Since relatively few associates are ever chosen to serve on the boards of public companies, this is a terrific way to get that perspective.

Typical lessons learned include:
- lateral influence skills
- social and interpersonal skills
- working under a regulatory microscope
- meeting facilitation and decorum
- how to represent the enterprise in the larger community

Mentors

Most high-level leaders I've encountered had the benefit of multiple people who took them under their wings as a formal or informal mentor. Indra Nooyi, chairman and CEO of PepsiCo, Inc., believes that mentors ought to be the one to select mentees because they must see some potential in a mentee and will therefore be interested in grooming the person for success. She benefited from the mentoring of Steve Reinemund, her predecessor as CEO at PepsiCo.

Medtronic has a highly successful company-wide mentor program that they rely heavily upon as a vehicle for associate retention. They believe the program pays for itself many times over.

Having a mentor provides the following:
- the opportunity to learn from someone who has traveled the path before
- building relationships across and upwards in an organization
- honest feedback from someone who cares

The future of mentoring may well be electronic. IBM is pioneering an internet based system called "Blue Pages." Associates fill out a questionnaire similar to a "LinkedIn" profile on steroids. Using a web search tool they can pose questions to everyone in the system or direct them specifically to people who are likely to offer the advice they seek.

Executive Coach

If you are at the vice presidential level or above and you want to maximize your effectiveness, you really need to add an executive coach or two to your posse. A decade ago a leader admitting that he needed the help of a coach may have been seen as a sign of weakness. These days the job of senior executives is so complex that to attempt to learn everything you need to know without help is not only impossible, but also inefficient.

It is often lonely at the top. At the minimum a personal coach can be a trusted sounding board for your ideas and frustrations. Having someone to vent to without having to worry about reading about it on the front page of the business section of your local paper is quite valuable.

There are two basic types of executive coaches. One provides leadership advice and the other helps with strategy or technical ideas. An extremely important role of a leadership coach is to make sure you have frequent insight into how you are perceived by your boss, direct reports and key peers. Once you know where you stand, a good coach will provide you with tools, techniques, ideas, and models, which can help you solve problems from style to strategy.

In an oft-told story, a man is standing in line at the supermarket talking on his cell phone. "Hello, a while back you had an opening for a purchasing manager. Is the job still available?" After a brief pause, he continued, "Oh you have, six months ago. How's he working out? I see, thank you, goodbye." The person behind the checkout stand having overheard the conversation says, "I'm sorry the job is no longer available." The man replies, "Oh, I'm not looking for a job. That was my own company. I was just calling to see how I was doing." Everyone wants to know how they are perceived though most are not as creative as this guy was in how they go about it.

In professional sports, not one hour of practice goes by without a member of the team getting feedback or, as I prefer to call it, "insight" from the coach. Yet in business, team members tell me these coaching insights are nearly non-existent. I believe it is the most under-appreciated and under-utilized tool in a leader's developmental bag. When done correctly, it can be a game-changing performance multiplier. If you are not getting feedback from your boss, take the initiative and seek it out.

I am not talking about formal reviews or things that take extensive amounts of time. Perhaps 30 seconds of insight after a team member has given a presentation to point out the one best thing you noticed or the most important thing to improve in the future.

Providing insight is the process of describing to another person how his or her behavior affects you, others and the accomplishment of a task. Helpful insight is motivating while poorly given insight can be de-motivating. Most associates desire insight so much that in the absence of knowing how they are doing, they will attempt to develop their own scoreboard. For insight to be helpful, an associate must understand the data, accept the insight and be able to do something about it. Most managers withhold insight, because they fear hurting the other, making him or her angry, or being rejected.

💡 Don't Forget This 💡

The difference between being a coach and a critic is that while neither may like the current behavior, usually the coach has other ideas or options for the person to consider.

Books/Movies/The Internet

A relatively inexpensive developmental tool is an internal Book of the Month club. Each month the organization pays for a book on leadership, teamwork, or interpersonal effectiveness for each associate in the club. The group meets after hours once a month to discuss how to apply the key lessons prescribed in the book. Not only will this improve the knowledge base of the workforce, but also it is a great exercise in team building. The same concept can be used with movies. Associates might also benefit from having the organization's learning and development department lay out a self-paced instruction e-learning curriculum. If someone in the organization reviews associate progress on a monthly basis, there is a high likelihood the associate will stick with the program.

Some Advice and Cautions

Here are some final words of advice about developing your people.

1. Associate development at all levels requires an enormous commitment of both time and money. Many CEOs claim that up to half their time is spent on talent identification and development. Seminars, mentor programs, daily coaching, and shifting people around every few years costs a lot of money.

2. Identify your "high potentials" early in their careers. The ones who have a good work ethic, seem to be quick studies, and possess maturity beyond their years are easy to spot even in their first assignments. Put together a long-term developmental plan for the talent you would least like to lose.

3. Be careful not to move managers around too quickly. It often takes going through a couple of complete cycles in an operation to see which decisions are really good ones and which turn out to be mistakes. People learn more from the poor decisions, which didn't work out, than from what initially may appear to be a success. General Electric liked to move managers around every two years. Now it is closer to four.

4. Provide a proper mix of the experiences detailed earlier in this chapter. Be strategic on the timing of certain assignments. It is often easier to give associates lateral assignments into all areas of the organization earlier in their careers when the consequences of a failure would not be catastrophic.

CHAPTER 11

ENERGIZE THE WORKFORCE:
Create a Smorgasbord of Things That Motivate

It was a scene that could easily have been part of a Hollywood movie, which is a bit ironic since it was unfolding live just a few miles from that cinematic capital of the world. In the Los Angeles Coliseum the fans had just settled into their seats for the opening game of the USC Trojans 2007 football season. The players were of course excited to begin their quest for another National Championship, but there was also a feeling of emptiness. Moments before kickoff their beloved place kicker, Mario Danelo, who had died a few months earlier falling off a cliff, was honored in an emotional ceremony followed by a moment of silence.

Early in the first quarter USC scored its first touchdown of the season and Coach Pete Carroll sent only ten men onto the field for the extra point. One player was obviously missing, their kicker.

Slowly the crowd began to recognize what was taking place. They saw the holder kneeling in an empty backfield, a football version of the Air Force's missing man formation to honor Danelo. A thunderous ovation rose up from the stands. USC was penalized for delay of the game and the ball was moved back five yards. There are chills all around the Coliseum and at that instant a permanent bond was formed between the coach and his play-ers.[1]

There are dozens of things that can motivate people, but the most powerful ones are always genuine and come from the heart. One of the most important duties of a change-focused leader is to find the keys to unlocking the spirit and energy of each and every member of the team and employ those keys at the proper times and places.

Through the groundbreaking work of Dr. Frederick Herzberg[2] it is clear that motivation is a two-sided coin. There are behaviors, activities, processes, and things that get in the way of a person's motivation. These must be identified and fixed of course. But even if all these "hygiene items," as Herzberg called them, are taken care of, a person will not exhibit even an ounce of motivation. He simply won't be de-motivated.

The other side of the coin is "motivators." These are the behaviors, activities, processes, and things that cause a person to be burning with desire. If both sides of the coin are paid attention to it would not be a stretch to say that an organization's effectiveness could be increased by a couple orders of magnitude.

Don't Forget This

One of the most common motivational mistakes leaders make is assuming that everyone is motivated or frustrated by the same things they are.

The Best Ways to Excite Your Workforce

Show Respect

Mary Kay Ash was kind enough to meet with me several times in the late 80s when I was conducting my seminars for her company. She probably understood human motivation at a practical level better than any CEO who ever lived. Mary Kay Cosmetics would spend tens of millions of dollars each year on some of the most imaginative motivational programs ever designed. Yet, in her view, there was nothing more important than showing each person she met that she respected them as a person. She did this by taking a few seconds with each individual who was called onstage (and each multi-day event had thousands of associates) to look them in the eyes, shake their hand or give them a hug, and tell them how thankful she was for their efforts. Mary Kay told me about one of the biggest motivating factors in starting her company. She once traveled for several days by bus to attend an awards banquet and was not even looked in the eye, let alone congratulated by the CEO for winning her award. She vowed at that time that if she ever had a chance to be in a similar position, that she would never leave anyone feeling as empty as she felt that day.

Once mutual respect is established, virtually any slight by either person will be seen more empathetically. Studies show that associates who are treated with respect are at least twice as likely than others to report being very satisfied with their jobs.

Work For a Cause

For Patagonia founder Yvon Chouinard, the cause is environmental protection. For Jim Goodnight of SAS Software, it is re-inventing education. Ben and Jerry's has donated a significant share of its profits to important causes through its own foundation since 1994. To engage associates, Umpqua Bank of Portland, Oregon, gives *everyone* 40 paid hours per year to volunteer for the cause of their choice. People have more dedication to organizations that support something they strongly believe in.

Seek Meaning

Shortly after President Reagan awarded the prestigious National Medal of Science to the famed heart surgeon Dr. Michael DeBakey in 1987 I had a chance to visit with him at the Texas Medical Center in Houston. Dr. DeBakey was 79 years old at the time but still making his rounds. Of course everyone in the complex knew who he was but surprisingly, Dr. DeBakey also seemed to know virtually everyone he encountered.

A legendary story at the Texas Medical Center involved a janitor that Dr. DeBakey had befriended. When asked what his job was the janitor would proudly reply, "I am Dr. DeBakey's partner in saving lives." When pressed as to how a janitor could make such a claim he responded, "Until six months ago I didn't think I counted for much around here. But one day Dr. DeBakey addressed our department and said that more patients die at the center due to complications *after* surgery than ever die *during* surgery. It doesn't do the doctors any good to perform perfect surgery only to see the patient die a week later from a staph infection. The doctors cannot control the environment the patient enters after leaving the sterile O.R., but the janitors can. Therefore we are all partners in saving lives."

Now I haven't met the janitor in your building but do you think Dr. DeBakey's janitor is more or less likely to be absent tomorrow? More or less likely to be tardy? More or less likely to file a grievance, lawsuit, steal, sabotage or quit tomorrow? Be more or less predisposed to offer a suggestion? Yet the tasks are the same as any janitor — cleaning floors and rest rooms or picking up trash. One janitor is looking at his watch counting the hours to quitting time while the other is saving lives. Creating meaning in a person's mind is the most transformational thing a leader can do. And, as rates of change accelerate, people are even more attracted to things that provide a sense of purpose and direction.

Every quarter, Medtronic beams by satellite to all locations a series of inspirational speeches delivered by recipients of Medtronic products such as pacemakers or spinal implants. These people would not have the same quality of life and many probably would not be alive without Medtronic. This ritual serves to keep associates centered on the important work everyone there does.

Have High Expectations

People want to work where they will be tested to their limits to see how much they can truly accomplish. Members of the armed forces accept the draconian measures employed during "hell week" to become a U.S. Navy Seal precisely because the expectations are so high. The philosopher Goethe put it this way: "Treat a man as he is, and he will remain as he is; treat a man as he can and should be, and he will become as he can and should be."

Generate Involvement

Future Hall of Fame NFL Coach Mike Holmgren would form a players committee made up of the teams' leaders each season. He met with them on a regular basis to seek their advice and ask their opinions on team rules, the design of training camp, practice schedules, and the like. A real sense of ownership was created when the players saw their suggestions implemented.

Offer Personal Significance

On the battlefield in wartime, the officers eat last because it is the soldiers who are doing the actual fighting. The troops are the truly important factors that will win or lose the battle. Since its inception, Nordstrom has portrayed its structure in the form of an upside-down pyramid. Customers are at the top and each descending level of management supporting the frontline employee is pictured with a pair of hands propping up those closest to the customer (see diagram A). Yum Brands calls its headquarters building the Customer Support Center. Expensive artwork has been replaced with gallery after gallery of photos of frontline workers.

In business, government and even the peacetime military, this concept of support of those doing the actual work seems to have become lost. Executives pull down ever more gluttonous pay packages while they squeeze their "soldiers" for every penny. Some "lead" their organizations off a cliff and then pull the ripcord on their golden parachutes. And despite all the studies on the virtues of the empowered workforce, micromanagement seems as prevalent as ever. The Work In America Institute claims that only one in ten workers work in an empowered setting. Associates just don't feel a sense of being seen as important in the larger scheme of things. No wonder books like *Why Work Sucks* and *The No Asshole Rule* are so popular.

Nordstrom Organization Chart

CUSTOMERS

Sales and Support People

Department Managers

Store Managers, Buyers,
Merchandise Managers,
Regional Managers,
General Managers

Board of Directors

Create a Break in Routine

It is important to sense when morale is lagging and create a break in routine with something fun. Take the team out to Dave & Buster's Arcades. Go bowling. Play laser tag or paintball together. Rent out a movie theater and let everyone get their fill of popcorn. In the afternoon, bring in ice cream. You will be amazed at the motivational lift this type of thing will give the team.

Focus On a Critical Issue

I have advised several clients over the years to close their operation for all but emergency business for a day to make a point of some kind to associates. Blue Ox in Pender, Nebraska, closed its whole facility on Jan. 2, 2005, to get everyone to see the importance of quality. With one person manning the switchboard, everyone else spent the entire day in meetings and problem-solving sessions trying to put together a plan to improve the quality of everything they did from answering phones to producing product. The U.S. Air Force has done a similar thing by grounding all planes to focus on safety. On Feb. 26, 2008, Howard Schultz closed all 7,100 Starbucks locations nationwide for three hours to re-train all employees in making their exotic coffee drinks to the highest standards.

There is no doubt these are moves to be taken to bring attention to serious issues. But, every time I have recommended this my clients tell me it made the impact they wanted and produced results that exceeded the costs.

Be Generous With the Trappings of Success

Winners function best in first-class surroundings. The lobby should make an immediate and positive impression. The facilities must always be clean and neat. The walls should be freshly painted; carpet clean, and the place should have good lighting and furnishings. If there are break rooms, lounges, or cafeterias, they should be comfortable and well stocked with things like game tables, refrigerators, microwaves, and vending machines. A key is that these types of things are available to all associates, not a select few. Otherwise it doesn't take long for jealousy to raise its ugly head.

There should be pictures and awards displayed in the lobby, hallways, and other public areas. Conference rooms should have all the proper equipment so there is no wasted time hunting down the things needed to run successful meetings. Onsite conference meeting rooms should be stocked like a hotel conference facility. Make sure fresh markers, pencils, pens, pushpins, tape, scissors, Post-it notes, calculators, and other assorted amenities that might be needed are readily available.

At SAS Software, most associates have their own offices. Founder Jim Goodnight believes "people are so much more productive in their own offices than when they are being distracted by people on either side." This flies in the face of the accepted notion that an "open office" is more collaborative.

At SAS they have free snacks, subsidized cafes, magnificent sports facilities, on-site childcare, and its own primary healthcare center free to associates. Turnover is 4 percent per year against an industry average of 20 percent.[3]

In tough economic times leaders are faced with a mighty temptation to dramatically scale back or eliminate the trappings of success. Doing so normally saves little as productivity often suffers and turnover often increases. If it absolutely has to be done, let the associates decide what things should be cut.

That being said, leaders must be especially cognizant of perceptions during a downturn. Firms that are laying off associates are ill advised to continue with lavish holiday parties or expensive junkets to top-of-the-line resorts. And, it should go without saying that if your organization is one of the many receiving taxpayer assistance, then all things which might raise the ire of lawmakers should be cancelled. The vision of Big Three automaker CEOs traveling to Washington in private jets, AIG's $400,000-plus bill for executive spa treatments, and Wells Fargo's planned twelve-day extravaganza at the Wynn & Encore Resorts in Las Vegas were like begging for a public backlash.

Permit Freedom

Being trusted to perform work without excess supervision is a real motivator for many people. Talk to most successful entrepreneurs who once worked inside someone else's organization and they will tell you that the ability to work with relative freedom is one of the main reasons they went into their own business.

Tales from the Workplace

Patrick Mahoney, president of West Coast Arborists (WCA), one of the largest and most successful tree care companies in the Western United States, really knows how to rev up and retain a workforce. WCA provides GPS-based tree inventory and total arbor care services to 191 cities through a team of more than 600 dedicated professionals. In an industry that can have upwards of 100 percent annual turnover, WCA has almost no unwanted defections after the first ninety days. Many associates have been with the company for more than twenty years.

A core philosophy of WCA is that motivated field associates keep city residents happy, who in turn sing the company's praises to the government leaders responsible for future contracts. In short, this creates a virtuous cycle where all parties win.

Pat has created a deceptively simple system to ensure workforce engagement. All area associates are given an *identical, clear* and *unchanging* goal for the amount of revenue they are responsible for generating each day. *Every evening* the thirteen area manager's tally the figures for each associate's billings and do an e-mail *call in* to headquarters. This *call in* details the total revenue generated in the area, lists any associates who failed to reach the target and reflects the *heavy hitter* who produced the most money that day. Upon receiving the *call in* reports, *all members of senior management* personally telephone each *heavy hitter* to congratulate them on their accomplishment. The *heavy hitters* each receive a monetary bonus while those who failed to make their quota are asked what kind of help they may need to ensure they make their goal the next day.

Frequent Feedback is also an important part of the process. All associates can see how they did each day in comparison to everyone else by looking on a plasma screen television in each area office or tapping into the results online. Pat says this is hugely motivational as everyone wants to be the *heavy hitter* and no one wants to see their name at the bottom of the list.

To promote customer satisfaction, associates work is routinely audited for quality. They also receive a monetary bonus for each letter of commendation that a customer writes to the city. They are placed on a *watch list* if the work is deemed to be substandard. Associates all know they will be immediately terminated if they are found to have falsified even a single document of work performed.

Pat believes "people tend to hang out with people who are much like themselves." So, he gives a large bonus to any associate who refers another worker to the company that passes the ninety-day probation period. He figures 80 percent of his employees were hired through this vehicle.

For office workers, Pat is a practitioner of *open book* management. All associates are given access to the companies' financial performance. He also believes in sharing the wealth. Bonuses are paid when quarterly targets are met. Pat is a humble, self-effacing leader who believes the heart of any business is positive relationships with others. You would be hard-pressed to find one of his associates who does not revere him or a customer who does not value him as a partner.[4]

Have Plenty of Celebrations/Recognition

In every team effectiveness survey I have ever done, one of the five lowest scoring items is, "We regularly celebrate our teams successes."

Celebrations are not merely ways to have fun during working hours, but also can be instrumental in reinforcing key values.

The City of Anaheim values loyalty and promotes a sense of family. They celebrate years of service, birthdays, and even throw baby and bridal showers. Blue Ox, the premier provider of RV aftermarket products, has a company-wide steak dinner in the parking lot to celebrate no lost-time accidents. Solar Turbines rings a giant bell when they receive a turbo machinery order and has an annual quality awards banquet where dozens of teams who have saved the company money through quality are honored. Medtronic has the Bakken Award, an internal Nobel Prize for innovative work. Southwest Airlines celebrates awards like being number one in customer satisfaction, on time performance, or baggage handling. Organizations located in cities that have professional sports franchises often have huge pep rallies when one of their teams makes it to the playoffs, giving away all sorts of team playoff logo apparel. Gordon Bethune at Continental Airlines had a celebration in the parking lot where they tossed the company's procedure manuals in a bonfire.

The Michigan Wolverines football team awards maize-colored football stickers to players who make exceptional plays. Ohio State University does the same with Buckeye stickers. It is amazing the pride players feel when their helmets are full of stickers and the lengths they will go to get more. The military awards medals, and non-profits tend to give a lot of certificates and plaques.

Associates seem to love company picnics or dinners where the organizations leaders serve the food or dunk tanks where each employee can take a shot at the boss. Open houses, bring your child to work days — the list is endless.

The point is, people love celebrations and they love to be recognized for a legitimate contribution.

Indispensable Tip !

Figure out what your organization values most, then develop some fun and frequent ways to reward and celebrate those things.

Don't be afraid to open the wallet on this stuff. It pays for itself many times over in the form of lower turnover, decreased tardiness and absentee- ism, less grievances, fewer lawsuits, reduced theft, and more employee sug- gestions.

Encourage Camaraderie

Creating closeness to others increases everyone's sense of connection and esprit de corps. The many soldiers stationed in Iraq and Afghanistan will tell you that while they are fighting for their country, they really are afraid of letting down their comrades in arms. Pro athletes in team sports will tell you they miss most the connection to their teammates when they retire.

The Orange County, California, Deputy Sheriff's Academy trainees decided to run a half marathon as a group. It is difficult enough to run 13.1 miles at any pace and in silence. These trainees ran the entire course at a constant pace with a drill instructor calling out a cadence they had to repeat: "I wanna – Be a dep-u-t sheriff, I wanna wear the five-point star. I wanna-be a po-lice officer, I wanna put the bad guys away."

Talking to several of the officer candidates afterwards, they all said the peer pressure and camaraderie of the group was all that kept them go- ing during the difficult stage of the race.

Cardinal Health sponsors a *Biggest Loser* contest. Modeled after the hit TV show of the same name, the associates compete for prizes to see who can lose the most weight. The good spirited competition among friends has been highly motivational for all involved.

Build Pride

Years ago a manager at AT&T called me and said he was finding it impossible to motivate one of his older, longer service supervisors to do more than the minimum necessary to get by. He asked if I could help. I talked to the service supervisor at length and came to find that he was the father of two young women who had just entered the workforce. You could just tell that these young ladies were the center of this guy's universe. So I said to him, "How would you feel if your daughters came home one night and told you that they were really discouraged? You asked why and they said, 'My boss could care less about the company. He is doing nothing to help me succeed and just seems to be there to get a paycheck and slide into retirement barely getting by. How would you feel?" He answered, "I would be mad as hell and feel awful and very disappointed." I said, "Well, each of these people you supervise are someone else's son or daughter. I am pretty sure that's how they would describe you to their parents."

The blood drained from the man's face and he put his head in his hands. "Oh my god, you are so right," he said. "I never thought of it that way at all until just now." Appealing to a person's sense of pride, if done tactfully, can be a powerful motivator.

Lavish Praise

Best-selling author Ken Blanchard became a multi-millionaire largely with one simple phrase, "Catch people doing something right." What a simple yet powerful concept. Whenever I give legitimate compliments to people, they physically seem to straighten up. A smile breaks out on their faces and they seem to find new energy. This is critical for relationship focused personality types, but seems to work well with everyone to some degree or another. The father of American psychology, William James, said, "The deepest principle of human nature is a craving to be appreciated." Mary Kay Ash said the two things people want more than money are recognition and praise. How many people do you know that are sick and tired of all the recognition they are getting?

Allow Authenticity

Being an authentic leader means endeavoring to express a point of view honestly and openly on important matters. There are so few truly authentic leaders that people find it terribly refreshing when they do find one. I believe a great deal of Barack Obama's appeal as a leader stems from the fact that he doesn't seem like your ordinary run-of-the-mill politician who will say whatever is necessary to get elected, regardless of his true convictions.

Essential Knowledge

At some point even money-driven people want more than a paycheck. They want to know their lives had some kind of purpose or meaning that made all their sacrifices worthwhile.

Inspire with a Vision

Jason McElwain was an autistic 17-year-old senior at Greece Athena High School in New York. His vision was simply to be a part of the school's basketball team as a manager. For several years he had worked every practice and never missed a game. In the last game of the season Coach Jim Johnson had a different vision. What if he could find a way to actually get Jason into the action as a player? On Feb. 28, 2006, in the last contest of the season, Coach Johnson put Jason into the game with four minutes left to play. What happened next defies all explanation. Jason hit six three-point shots and one two-pointer for a total of twenty points in four minutes, perhaps the greatest number of points amassed in that amount of time in the history of high school basketball. With each shot the crowd became more delirious and was jumping up and down in the stands so hard it is a wonder they didn't collapse.[5] Coach Johnson's values of fairness, compassion, and finding a way to reward someone who had helped the team for so long would have been inspirational even if Jason hadn't scored a point. Those values resonated with all the players on that team, and will for all future teams Jim Johnson will ever coach.

Pay Well

We all like money but some like it more. Bottom-line, task-oriented personality types see money as a way of keeping score. For these people it is truly motivational, if only for a short time. Tying compensation to performance will cause many people to expend extraordinary effort to get the prize. Make sure you are compensating the things you truly value. Having said this, suppose you were offered a quarter million dollars a year to spend eight hours a day, five days a week all year long, moving a pile of rocks from one side of a building and back. Would you do it? Most people would find the work so tedious that they would want to quit after just a few months on the job. By contrast, Olympic athletes receive no pay. Though they have very little chance of winning a medal, they nonetheless pour their heart and soul into training for hours on end over several years, for a few minutes of glory.

Use Fear, but Sparingly

Alexander the Great would land his troops by ship on the shore of territory he wished to conquer and then in full view of the men, he would burn the ships. Because there would be no escape by sea, they were highly motivated to take some ground.

Fear motivation is a last resort option of desperation. It should be employed sparingly, if ever, and the leader must be prepared to follow through on the threats. It helps to have the ability to coerce people to do what you want, but coercion is a very fragile and dangerous base of influence. But it is an option.

Set Firm Deadlines

Visit the warehouses where the Rose Parade floats are assembled on New Year's Eve and you will see an unbelievable amount of activity. People are frantically rushing around hammering nails, attaching roses, spray painting. You can sense their excitement. If you ask them why all the fuss, they will simply say, "The Rose Parade is tomorrow," as if there couldn't be a better explanation. They all know what they are working toward. If someone was having a problem, everyone automatically pitches in to help without anyone telling them to. They have been transformed by the dream and energized by the deadline.

People like a sense of closure. It is highly motivational for some of us to simply cross things off our "to do" list each day. Allowing associates to see the end result of their efforts is always a smart thing to do. If the outcome is good, it serves as a sense of accomplishment. If not, it might provide the resolve needed to have a better outcome the next time around.

New Beginnings

Having a defined season in sports not only provides for a sense of completion, but also serves to give the team a periodic new beginning. In business, "kickoff events" can provide the initial jolt necessary to get a team moving in the right direction.

CHAPTER 12

ENERGIZE THE WORKFORCE: Eliminate Things
That Decrease Motivation

Some things leaders permit to happen turn people off and reduce their motivation to excel. Here are a few examples of things that should be minimized or eliminated.

Uncertainty as to Job Security

Even successful people and high-level executives don't give their best efforts when they are looking over their shoulders wondering whether they will still have a job next week. Just like an NFL quarterback needs assurance from the head coach that a few bad passes or an interception won't cause him to be benched, associates in business organizations need to have clear communication that their jobs are not in jeopardy.

This is especially true when the economy is poor or the organization is experiencing difficulty in the marketplace. You might be tempted to think that your best performers would know that their jobs are safe. Ironically they are often the ones who get unnecessarily concerned. It is always a good idea to provide as much assurance to your stars as you legally can that they are valued.

Poor Working Conditions

If the workspace is too hot, freezing cold, dusty, noisy, or too cramped, this causes frustration. When a chair causes chronic backache, the computer setup strains eyes or might lead to carpal tunnel syndrome, these are problems. An aerospace client of mine had a roof that leaked so badly that the workers were soaking wet by the end of the shift. In their conference rooms, the heat became so unbearable in the summer that people routinely passed out in meetings. It is hard to get excited about working for a place that has so little regard for its associates.

Bureaucracy

Few things can be as irritating as idiotic rules. Need some supplies? Fill out a form that takes purchasing a week to process. Having a problem? Don't dare talk to someone in senior management or another department without going through your boss. The policy says you can't have people stay in a hotel unless it is over 100 miles from the facility. So, just pay airfare to fly everyone to a place more than 100 miles away so you can have everyone stay overnight as part of your teambuilding.

In a large metropolitan area that I visited some years back, there was a particular bus stop where everyday hundreds of people would line up waiting for a bus. Day after day, dozens of half-empty buses would blow past the stop on their way to who knows where. After months of frustration, hundreds of angry patrons descended upon the Transit Authority Board demanding an explanation. After hearing their complaints, the chair of the board said, "You have to understand that if those buses paused to pick up the passengers at your stop, they wouldn't be able to stay on schedule." Say what? Unassailable logic for sure, but the larger point of why they are in business seems to have been missed, don't you think?

Contrast this with the California Department of Motor Vehicles office in Escondido. The general manager has a Wal-Mart type greeter installed in the entryway who politely says, "Welcome to the DMV, do you speak English or Spanish?" The *guest* is directed to the proper area where he is met with, "How may I help you?" No employee can take lunch between 11:30 a.m. and 2 p.m., as it is the busiest time in the office. All associates have been cross-trained to do any job. The general manager envisions his job as *reorganizing* the department on a moment-to-moment basis, depending on customer needs.[1] Now that's a civil servant that is leading for change!

Dr. Russell Ackoff tells the story of Madge, a housewife who would often stop to cash a check at a store located near her home. One day when Madge stopped at the store to cash her check, she was informed of a new policy: no check cashing. She was irate, but not for long. She went into the dress department and bought a dress priced at around the amount of the check she wanted to cash. The store accepted her check. She then took the dress to the return desk and asked for a refund. They gave it to her in cash.[2] No system can be as smart as some of the people it serves.

According to Gordon Binder, former CEO of Amgen, "Many organizations unwittingly undermine their personnel by cluttering the path to progress with roadblocks, whether it's superfluous paperwork or a labyrinthian corporate structure that makes accomplishing even the simplest task an exercise in head-banging frustration."[3] Amen!

Bureaucracies tend to standardize procedures, thereby taking judgment completely out of the equation. The goal sounds good — to eliminate variation. To accomplish this, the procedure attempts to specify exactly what should be done under the mistaken assumption that the people writing it can predict every possible situation. Exceptions to the rules, no matter how much sense they make, are non-starters. Many bureaucrats are seduced by the idea that there is "one best way" and that it can be taught. "The one best way is doomed to fail. It is inefficient, since it works against some people's natural talents. Second, it is demeaning — by providing all the answers it prevents each individual from perfecting and taking responsibility for his own style. Third, it destroys learning. Every time you make a rule, you take away choice, and choice with all of its illuminating repercussions is the fuel for learning."[4] Fourth, it takes too much time. "I'll have to get my boss' approval just doesn't cut it anymore."

Rules and procedures start out innocently enough. They are usually established for very specific reasons and generally because someone did something wrong that the organization wants to prevent from happening again. Sometimes litigious paranoia is the cause. Over time, the original rationale and spirit of the rule becomes lost on everyone. Rules are usually created to either stop someone from doing something or cause something to be done in a very specific way. Because both of these things can be a hassle, employees or customers seem to be constantly on the lookout for ways to get around the rule so they can do what they want.

Sure enough, a creative individual finds a way to get around the rule. The organization's response: create an addendum to close the loophole. At this point the disease becomes degenerative. People are then forced to get even more inventive, creating a downward spiral that ends with organizational hardening of the arteries. Ninety-nine percent of the people are forced to comply with a system designed to prevent the 1 percent of bad apples from doing something. Despite all the effort to prevent it, most of the 1 percent still manage to find a way to beat the system.

At the Manhattan headquarters of Merrill Lynch the internal mail system was so broken it took days to get internal documents properly routed. So, enterprising employees started sending packages of data from one floor to another via Federal Express because it was quicker than its own mailroom. Apparently the culture did not encourage identifying and fixing the root problem. Instead, they created a rule that said an associate needs a boss' approval to send a FedEx package. They could have really benefited from a boss who simply decided to improve the mailroom.

General Electric looked at a random sample of the major mistakes made by its businesses. They were surprised to learn that *none* of the major errors would have been prevented by one more approval up the chain of command.[5]

Bill George, the former highly successful CEO of Medtronic, said, "It is impossible to legislate integrity, stewardship, and sound governance."[6] He went on to say, "As organizations get larger, the natural tendency of managers is to control the enterprise with rules, processes and procedures. An insatiable bureaucracy is a huge barrier to innovative ideas and dampens creativity no matter how much the company spends in R&D."

Bureaucracies are also inefficient and create obstructions. Thus they invite and encourage corruption. Bribes are required to make them operate more nimbly and less obstructively.[7]

Too much bureaucracy can actually obscure what is really going on in an organization. A study by Hackett Benchmarking found that an average performing organization has 372 line items of budget detail; world-class organizations have only twenty-one. If an objective is not being met, it is much more easily spotted among twenty-one items than 372. Don't get me wrong; I am not advocating that we do away with rules and procedures. But the pendulum has swung too far in the bureaucratic direction. As Herb Kelleher, founder of Southwest Airlines says, "Policies should be followed but people should use their brains in interpreting them!"

The solution — create hard and fast rules only for the things that if done incorrectly will lead to a breach of safety, the law, ethics, or a difficult to recover from act. Everything else should be handled through creating a culture of values based self-governance.

Shared values bind people together. Understanding *what* they are trying to accomplish reduces comprehension errors. Understanding *why* they are being asked to do things within certain parameters inspires creativity.

Dan Widen of Widen and Kennedy Advertising once told me that one of his core values was to make sure that the people he hired had more influence on results than the system had in trying to contain that influence.[8] Widen and Kennedy has been one of the most innovative and successful ad agencies for well over twenty years, despite a relative absence of rules.

Nordstrom has very few written procedures and even fewer cast-in-concrete rules. They use self-governance centered on the organization's core values to *guide* their associates' behavior. As Jim and Bruce Nordstrom said to me many years ago, "We want our thousands of associates, most of whom we will never personally meet, to do what we would do if we were in their shoes. We could do this by trying to think through every possible permutation of situations they might face and write a bookshelf full of manuals, most of which will never be read. We choose to be diligent in hiring good people, explain what we value and are trying to accomplish, and coach or eliminate people who go beyond what a reasonable person would consider acceptable behavior."[9] Research has proved that organizations earn a 4 percent higher return on sales when associates are given more responsibility and discretion.[10]

Once a month, Gordon Binder at Amgen would ask scientists in various areas of the company, "Is there anything getting in the way of your work?" He believed they felt as good about being asked that question as they would if they got a raise. Most talented people hate red tape.[11] Jimmy Blanchard, chairman of Synovus Financial, constantly asks people to list the twenty-five dumbest things management does in the company. Andrea Jung CEO of Avon meets regularly with the top twenty sales people in each region to get their ideas on how to minimize bureaucracy.

Key Question ?

How often do you ask your people to see what is getting in their way?

If people truly understand and buy into what the organization is trying to do, then they don't need to be tightly controlled. They will know what needs to be done and all but a very small handful will do it. As Brad Anderson, CEO of Best Buy, puts it, "We've created a distinctly human culture that lets people have fun while working hard, that lets them be themselves and trusts them to do their jobs."[12]

Only values based on self-governance can simultaneously control behavior and inspire people to live up to the spirit of the rule. People do the right thing because to not do the right thing betrays not only the organization, but also the individual's own values. Betraying oneself brings internal conflict, those disturbing little voices in one's head.[13] Most people truly do want to do the right thing, especially when they are treated with respect in the first place.

Breaking down silos is also a critical step in busting bureaucracy. James Dyson, inventor of the fabulous Dyson vacuum cleaner, insisted on memos being banned in favor of cross-departmental conversation.[14] Silos dampen enthusiasm. We seem to find a way to work around them in a crisis. Why not just make internal barriers less obstructive once and for all time?

Key Question ?

What are you doing to make things flow more fluidly within your organization?

Lack of Appropriate Guidance on Delegated Tasks

Analytical, detail-oriented personalities in particular need a lot of structure. They actually will often freeze and do nothing in the absence of specific guidance. They want to know what procedures apply, the type of report format you want and the frequency, the people they can ask for help, and a dozen other things. For efficiency sake alone, everyone on the team should have a pretty good idea of guidelines and expectations.

Conflict

Most people hate conflict at work. Relationship oriented personalities in particular will often be so uncomfortable with unresolved conflicts with peers that they will leave the organization entirely. Those that remain are often far less productive when there is too much tension in the team.

Disrespect

Associates at any level want to feel important. When they are kept in the dark about important things relating to their job, barred from participating in decisions, talked down to in a condescending manner or referred to as "grunts, pawns, or the little people," they rightly feel disrespected.

A clear sign of disrespect is failure to listen to people. Being half ignored causes people to feel unimportant. Managers that take phone calls, bang away on their laptops, or fiddle with their blackberry devices in meetings or when others are in their office, are courting a backlash.

Another indicator of disrespect is *perceived* unfairness. When associates feel they have been treated unfairly it is almost always couched in terms of a comparison with others. Be sure that all associates are given an equal opportunity to excel, and that their total compensation package reflects their true contributions. The furor over the outrageous bonus payments made to executives of AIG was caused in large part by the perception they were being rewarded for dishonesty, greed and driving their business into the ground.

Don't Forget This

Most people I've talked to over the years who quit a job in frustration quit because of a disrespectful boss, not a disrespectful organization.

My assistant, Marlene Pegler, said to me, "I believe the true measure of a person's character can be seen by how they treat people they don't necessarily care for. It takes nothing — no work at all, to treat someone you like with dignity, respect, and courtesy. But if you can treat someone you don't care for with the same dignity, respect, and courtesy, then that tests your mettle. And while sometimes it takes work, it's those little challenges that build character."

Tales from the Workplace

I was asked to conduct a week-long training session on teamwork with senior executives of a large company in Ohio. The training took place at a rustic state park in the middle of the state. In the same facility some first-level supervisory training was taking place from the same company a couple of rooms down the hall. The senior executives had lavish catered lunches while the first-level supervisors had boxed lunches. Even worse, dinner was held in the same dining hall, but the senior executives were allowed to order off the menu while the first-level supervisors all had to eat the same thing. No one from the senior group seemed the least bit concerned that a bad message was being sent, while the first-level supervisors to a person felt dissed by the obvious slap in the face they received. Needless to say, teamwork went nowhere in that company.

Stagnation

Jerry Colangelo, the highly successful former owner of the Phoenix Suns and Arizona Diamond Backs, said that in his view, "Stagnation is always an issue. The leader of the organization must be cognizant of the problem. There is nothing more ruinous than a workforce that is bored, uninterested and restless."[16] My former doctoral classmates, Kevin and Jackie Freiberg, refer to these people as "Dead People Working." In repetitive jobs it is terribly de-motivating to do the same thing day-after-day. Effective leaders have got to interject frequent changes in routine to keep everyone alert at the very least.

Humiliation

It is simply amazing that bosses still regularly humiliate their associates in public. Jokes, public reprimands, singling out certain associates for regular ridicule are just a few things that fall under this category. Real leaders recognize that people need encouragement the most when the results are poor. Floggings in the town square are just not the way to motivate winners. Usually the people responsible for the failure are feeling much worse than anyone else about it. As John Cooper, the former CEO of Avocent Corp., always said to his staff, "Did you give your best effort? Did your people give their best effort? If so, let's get them fired-up for the next quarter instead of having them feel defeated because of last quarter's results."

It is apparent that keeping associates energized is a complex task. It cannot be done solely with structured programs or inspiring speeches. It is an ongoing and never-ending process, and must be tailored to the needs of each individual. It requires unrelenting effort, imagination, and a deep respect for each associate.

Don't Forget This

One of the most important duties of a leader is to find the keys to unlocking the spirit and energy of each and every member of the team, and employing those keys at the proper times and places.

CHAPTER 13

PLAN AHEAD OR PLAN TO FAIL

Imagine some not so very trustworthy relatives coming to you with a three-page document asking you to give them a ridiculously large sum of money. They can't really describe what they are going to do with the cash, but they tell you it involves buying up a whole lot of property that no one else seems to think is worth very much. You ask them what they plan to do with the property once they own it, and they mumble something to the effect that they will gradually try and unload it to other people for a profit. When you request a repayment schedule they say it will take years and you may never get your money back at all. Of course you turn them down in an instant.

A few days later they return with a 400-page document requesting 20 percent more money than you turned down a few days earlier, saying only that it will be catastrophic to the family if they don't get the money. Not only do they still not have a clear goal for the funds, but also they essentially tell you that the additional 20 percent will be frivolously spent. What would you do? Well, as taxpayers we somehow thought it was a good idea to give them the money. It was of course the great federal government Wall Street bailout of 2008 through the Troubled Asset Relief Program (TARP). Now to be sure, this is a gross over-simplification of the crisis we found ourselves in at the time. And, because we felt backed into a corner perhaps it was the only option. But ill conceived plans driven by expediency also happen in the business world everyday, just not of the same magnitude.

Talk to frontline associates and they will tell you categorically that a major frustration they have with leadership is the start-stop-start-change direction approach that is often taken in organizations. After repeated fits, starts and changes, people throw up their hands in disgust and figure, "Why bother, whatever we do is likely to be wasted efforts when they change their minds again."

Errors In Planning

Every organization seems to realize that having clear goals is a vital first step around which plans can be developed. Creating a target that serves as a basis for sound decision-making would seem to be so obvious it shouldn't need mentioning. However, it has been my experience that organizations continually make fundamental errors when it comes to goals.

1. Leaders set the goal too high or too low.

2. Leaders fail to create incremental sub-goals that will lead to accomplishing the larger goal.

3. Leaders set several objectives, which are so counter to each other that they sub-optimize.

4. Leaders constantly change their minds as to the objectives they seek to meet.

5. Leaders fail to measure progress toward the goal.

6. Leaders skip the step of creating a master plan to achieve the goals.

7. Leaders plan to the point of overkill.

8. Leaders let expediency drive their decisions.

9. Leaders let themselves become consumed by fire-fighting activities.

10. Leaders don't plan for things that can go wrong.

11. Leaders allow events to escalate out of control.

One — The leader sets the goal too high or too low

Several CEOs I've met claim that setting impossible goals causes their people to achieve more than they would have if the goals were more realistic. Extensive research, common sense, and my 32 years of personal experience would suggest otherwise.

Figure 1 lists the strength of a person's motivation on one axis with the perceived probability of success on the other axis. If people believe there is little or no hope of achieving a goal, then most will have limited, if any, motivation to try. Instead, political behaviors will increase as everyone becomes concerned with who will end up taking the fall for the failure they believe will most certainly occur.

FIGURE 1

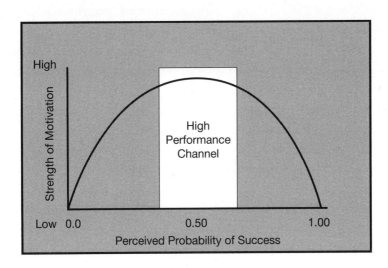

On the other hand, if people feel all they have to do is to show up and the goal will likely be easily achieved, then there is no strong motivation likely there either. When individuals come to believe they can turn on their talents at will at the last minute if necessary, they often wait to do just that. This is one reason why the best teams in any sport often struggle with opponents whose objective rankings would suggest are far below their class.

A change-focused leader should strive to keep people in the "performance channel" where the goals are a *major stretch* but still considered achievable with hard work, ingenuity, and a little luck. Sometimes the leader's challenge will be to get into the trenches with people to help them see that with proper planning, above average effort, and a little creativity, the goal is more reasonable than it first appeared. At other times the leader may need to "shock the system" to shake people out of their complacency.

Two — Leaders fail to create incremental sub-goals that will lead to achieving the higher goal

While our end objective must be set well ahead of where we are today for it to be motivating, incremental sub-goals must also be developed leading to successive approximations of the end result. Smaller goals clarify the path and build up the self-confidence necessary for the attainment of the more distant goal.

Let's look at this in practice. Suppose I am a salesperson who desires to earn at a level 50 percent higher than my current income within six months. An increase of that magnitude is likely to be difficult at best, since we may be attempting something well outside our preset limits of self-confidence.

In many types of sales there is a direct relationship between the number of sales calls made and the volume of business produced. Incremental sub-goals might then be thought of in terms of making 10 percent more sales calls next week. The following week I might then want to make 10 percent more calls than the week before, and so on. By starting small and working up to a higher level, we stay within our comfortable zone of self-confidence and increase our chances of meeting the major performance stretch of a 50 percent increase in earnings.

Sub-goals, which take us successively closer to our desired end result, also serve another important purpose. Every goal we fail to achieve diminishes our self-confidence. There are obviously better odds on meeting small sub-goals than there are in meeting one monster goal. But we must assure each of our sub-goals is being met along the way. To accomplish this, we are advised to set up a small payoff or reward for each sub-goal achieved. The reward should be something really pleasing and it should not be accepted unless the sub-goal has been met.

Three — Leaders set several objectives which are so counter to each other that they sub-optimize

When people "buy into" stretch goals, they tend to become obsessed with hitting these targets. It is therefore vitally important to make sure departmental goals are in alignment throughout the organization. When they are not aligned, sub-optimization is the result.

Tales from the Workplace

A medical instrument company that sells hundred-thousand-dollar-plus machines was organized into profit centers, with their engineering group set up as one such unit. Part of the group's mission was to generate 7 percent profit on all internal or external work performed. They were free to accept or reject internal or external projects as they saw fit.

Due to several unforeseen events, including an unexpectedly large unfavorable legal judgment, the company faced a cash flow crisis. If they could not generate a sizable amount of cash quickly they were likely to default on their loans. In panic mode the CFO went to the sales group and said, "Go push as much product into the pipeline as possible. The only thing I am concerned about is that we get immediate payment and at least break even on price."

To a sales organization, this type of thing rarely happens — the opportunity to meet quota without having to worry much about margin. The next day a top producer convinced a customer who had not been able to afford new equipment for some time to buy 100 machines at 2 percent over cost,

---

as long as they could come up with the cash immediately. The customer was thrilled with the deal as this was seen as the break they had been looking for to jump-start their own business into profitability.

The sales executive went to engineering and said, "We need you to customize these units, but we can only give you 2 percent profit on the job." Engineering declined to sign off on the order. The exasperated sales executive persisted, "But this will bring us profitable parts sales, service business, some profit on a very large order, keep a good customer in the fold for future higher margin sales, and help us solve our cash flow problem." The engineering manager replied, "I would love to help, but I don't get credit for parts or service, I am not sure if this customer will survive long enough for us to get higher margins down the road, and I'm not responsible for cash flow, that's the CFO's job. Besides, if I accept 100 units at 2 percent, the next hundred units we work on would have to generate 13 percent just to get us back on our plan. It would be smarter for me to only take outside work at the normal 7 percent margin rather than work on your discounted order. So, I'm afraid I can't sign off on the job." The shocker was that the CEO believed so strongly in the profit center concept that he was initially against intervening in the dispute. In his thinking, to force the engineering group to accept the low margin job would give them an excuse if they didn't meet their year-end targets. It literally took the threat of the CFO resigning to bring the CEO to his senses and save the business. The goals had been set so narrowly as to work against the greater good.

Four — Leaders constantly change their minds as to the objectives they seek to meet

The world moves fast and favors those who can shift to meet new demands on a moment's notice. That being said, if strategic planning is done properly then the need to change goals should be an unusual exception, not standard practice. It is appalling how much inefficiency and morale loss is created by organizations that have the habit of pulling the rug out from under their associates' feet by *constantly* changing their minds as to the goals. People naturally begin to adopt the attitude, "Why bust my ass, I'll just get halfway through the project and they will change their minds again." If you find yourself attempting to run your organization this way, it is likely a symptom of ineffective planning.

Indispensable Tip !

If you feel you have to change direction it helps to take great pains to explain to people why the change was made and to express your appreciation for the difficulties this will cause them. Like other areas of leadership, communication, empathy, and a sincere apology will go a long way.

Five — Leaders do not regularly measure progress toward the goal

We achieve goals that are clear, measured, and result in rewards we highly value. This is a law of life as old as prehistoric man. One shot before and after a performance assessment is no good. Appraisal of results against plan must be continual.

Ongoing appraisal of results implies measurability. All goals, be they the end goal of a 50 percent improvement in income level within six months, or the sub-goal of 10 percent more sales calls next week, must be stated in an appraisable manner. In other words, we need to know how we will be able to recognize success when it comes along. The best goals specify what is to be done, when, and by whom.

Placing timeframes on goals creates multiple effects, not all of which may be positive. Therefore, a great deal of care must be taken in setting timelines. Time schedules that require too much of a stretch cause pressure to build up if it appears that we are going to miss the target. A certain amount of pressure is highly positive. Moderate degrees of pressure motivate us to achieve results. Extreme pressure, however, can be debilitating. In addition, there is the problem of missed deadlines causing lower self-esteem.

The timelines we set on our goals just cannot be missed. If we set a goal of making twenty sales calls this week and we only make fifteen, we are five behind. Assuming our timeframe was a stretch to begin with, it is unlikely the five missed calls will ever be made up.

Top salespeople seldom make their annual goal when they miss the first quarter's quota. Harold Geneen, the former CEO of ITT, had nearly seventeen straight years where ITT made its target.[1] Herb Kelleher and Southwest Airlines did it every year from 1973 to his retirement in 2006.[2] During this period *they never missed making a quarterly target.* They insisted upon achieving the sub-goals, since they knew they were a critical prelude to making the end goal. They understood achieving the latter end goal was highly unlikely unless they made the former sub-goals.

It is easy to underestimate the importance of meeting early commitments. After all, why get upset when there is so much time left to "make up the difference?" Well, the answer is life seldom bestows good things upon people who mortgage the future. *People who don't make their incremental sub-goals just flat don't make their larger goals.*

Timelines set too loosely are equally ineffective. They cause us to procrastinate far into the future. For most of us it is just human nature to wait until the last minute to get things done. A further problem is mentally we tend to lock out data on opportunities that may allow us to reach our goals sooner.

Six — Leaders skip the step
of creating a master plan to achieve the goals

A planned course of action forces us to think several moves into the future. Pool hustlers, poker players, football coaches and chess masters excel because they plan several moves in advance and can play out their strategy accordingly. Shots, plays, and moves become part of a series of events tied together to reach a defined end.

It is neither possible nor feasible to create an *exact* path that will lead us to our overall goals. The world is just not that predictable. Nevertheless, having a process consisting of steps with built-in flexibility dramatically increases the likelihood we will reach our objectives.

Most people simply do not live long enough to count on trial-and-error learning to see them through. Mickey Drexler, ousted CEO of GAP, repeatedly made decisions on gut feelings and was known for impulsively flip-flopping on decisions others thought were *done deals*. This culture of uncertainty was the final nail in his coffin as profits went from $877 million in 2000 to a $7.7 million loss in 2001.[3]

Bill Walsh, the legendary Hall of Fame coach of the San Francisco 49ers, believed in "scripting" the first fifteen plays of the game in advance. He found this eliminated the player's pre-game anxiety because they knew ahead of time what they would be asked to do. He saw the value of allowing critical decisions to be made in an atmosphere where there was time to properly concentrate.[4] We get exactly the same benefit in the business world when we plan effectively.

You may have heard the tailor's adage, "Measure twice, cut once." I did some work with an aircraft fuselage manufacturer, and they were all set to begin assembly in a new building. The director asked the production manager, "Are you sure this thing will fit out the door when we get it done?" The manager replied, "Sure, no problem." The director said, "Did you measure the width and height of the doors?" The manager said no he hadn't. The director of course, ordered the man to measure and sure enough the fuselage had no way of fitting through the door. It may at times feel like you are being a pest, but asking tough questions is part of effective planning.

A master plan makes it possible to develop periodic checkpoints where progress can be compared to plan. In some areas of society this is literally a life or death matter. Think of an airline pilot. Long before the passengers arrive, the cockpit crew has been hard at work. Even though the captain may have made the run a hundred times before, he has filed a flight plan and has checked the instruments, fuel and weather. The computer could tell him where the plane would be at any given time during the flight.

Change-focused leaders are like airline pilots. They develop a plan that if followed will lead to their destination in the most effective way. Without an operational plan, the probability of reaching the desired destination would be small. The plans must, however, be flexible enough to permit prudent adjustments to increase effectiveness. Airline pilots, for example, may need to make slight deviations from their plan to avoid stormy weather. Future events are not always predictable and errors in judgment will be made, but planning often provides clarity of direction, which is so critical to success.

Seven — Leaders plan to the point of overkill

For every leader I have seen fail due to lack of planning, I know of another one who stumbled because he tried to plan for every little detail. Some leaders continue to analyze a terrific plan until it becomes too late to execute it. In this era of uncertainty, the people with the greatest flexibility built into their plans will be able to exert the greatest amount of control over their world. *Some details just cannot and should not be planned.* Trying to control every variable puts us on the entrance ramp to the freeway of destruction.

The United States Marine Corps uses the one-third/two-third rule. This reserves one third of the planning time for a commander while giving the other two thirds for the subordinates to do their preparation. When coupled with the 80 percent rule, which says that delaying a decision so that it can be made with more than 80 percent of the necessary data is hesitation, a premium is placed upon creating a calculated bias for action. One of America's preeminent thinkers, Harland Cleveland, said, "Information, because it is expandable without any obvious limits, means the facts are never all in — and facts are available in such profusion that uncertainty becomes the most important planning factor. Information rich does not mean affluent; it is quite as likely to mean swamped."[5]

Don't Forget This

It is hard for an organization to develop a reputation for boldness if there is hesitation in making routine decisions.

Part of a good plan in today's world is one that allows for quick adaptability. Corporations are moving away from trying to build up huge balance sheet assets. The conventional wisdom said that to control something, we must own it. Today, leased buildings, furniture, automobiles, and outsourcing non-core activities (to name a few), provide the critical adaptability that allows a business to control its response to the changing environment. Alan Mulally, CEO of Ford, went so far as to sell almost all of the company's assets, including plants, buildings, real estate, patents and trademarks, for $23.4 billion in cash. This put them in a much better position to ride out the calamity of the sudden collapse of auto sales.[6] Adaptable corporations are finding it more economical in the long run to hire people as consultants or on a contract basis, institute telecommuting, or design offices with movable walls. The paradox of the information age is money invested in trying to gain control through ownership reduces control because the option of quick adaptability is forgone. Today flexibility is control.

As Richard L. Evans once put it, "We have to remain flexible in living life. Not flexible as to our purpose, but flexible in our reaction to the environment, to people and places, to changing situations and circumstances." Planning of this sort requires a high tolerance for ambiguity.

Well thought out plans can provide us with the added self-confidence that will give us the ability to overcome our fears of the future. Good planning points out problems that can be avoided before they arise. It also prepares us to handle issues that crop up.

When things go wrong in life, lots of people blame bad luck. Poor planning or lack of a plan are seldom cited as reasons for failure. Yet hard work channeled into the wrong direction is one of the surest routes to disaster. Planning is a key event, which cannot be ignored.

Eight — Leaders let expediency drive their decisions

One of the major reasons leaders fail to plan is it takes time away from activities that may be generating immediate results. Unsuccessful people become addicted to activity as if it was cocaine and they lose themselves. They confuse busyness with achievement. Top performers know that developing the patience to plan will allow them to speed past their competitors in the long run.

One of my manufacturing clients has a strategy of locating its plants in small towns. The plant manager told me *half* of the people working there were unsatisfactory performers. When I asked him why he didn't get rid of them, he said, "Bad breath is better than no breath." He said there was 1 percent unemployment in the area and they were *forced* to take what they could get. Expediency drove the strategy and has set this organization on a path to failure.

Bosses often mock their staff for taking their teams off site to do planning at the beginning of a project. The thought is that if you take two days to plan, you are already two days behind schedule just two days into the project. Oh how wrong they turn out to be. Planning is truly an investment with an uncertain payoff, and it takes great intestinal fortitude to resist the pressure of others to jump in and start doing "real work."

Indispensable Tip !

Your boss may do stupid things, but you have got to prevent your boss from causing you to do stupid things. If you are not willing to challenge the boss when you believe he is wrong, you will probably never achieve greatness.

Nine — Fire Fighting

Another major reason why people fail to plan is they can't seem to find a way to get around current crisis situations, which gobble up their time. In the business world, I have seen hundreds of people who handle the same problem week after week that could be solved for good, if only they took the time to develop a long-term solution. I have yet to run into a great performer in any field who did not have to face at some point the decision to keep fighting fires or pay the upfront price to prevent them in the future. Effective leaders decide to pay the price.

> ## Indispensable Tip !
>
> It is hard to have optimal impact when your office is a disaster and you have hundreds of unanswered e-mails sitting in the queue. You have got to get caught up and organized, then stay that way.

Ten — Leaders don't plan for things that can go wrong

It is much easier to be confident when we anticipate and prepare for the inevitable things that are going to go wrong. By developing the necessary tactics to deal with contingencies likely to arise, we build in the ability to sustain our confidence level during rough times. Bill Walsh felt that total knowledge of what could go wrong, and having a plan as to what to do if it did, was essential to success.[7]

With contingency planning, we are buying peace of mind. It is difficult to place a value on the feeling of comfort that comes from knowing *we* are in control of the situation. Having already planned for most of the significant problems allows us to direct our energy into productive avenues instead of into worry or despair.

An old colleague of mine, John Narciso, calls worrying "suffering in advance." When we are insecure or feel there are too many loose ends, we tend to worry. Since anxiety is usually counterproductive during actual performance, we should do our worrying in the contingency planning stage.

During his days as a college professor, Dr. Narciso saw many students agonize over examinations. In a steady stream they would flood his office expressing concerns, such as "I don't do well on tests" or "I really can't afford a 'C' on this course." John's common-sense counsel never varied. He simply said, "It would be a much more productive investment of energy if you would study rather than worry."[8]

Eleven — Leaders allow events to escalate out of control

One story stands out so clearly in my mind because it illustrates the downfall of a successful person and a once proud organization at the same time. I had been doing some work for a large regional bank from mid-1979 to mid-1981. This bank was somewhat unusual at that time in that it earned more income from its currency and securities trading than it did from its lending operations.

The author of this rather aggressive business approach was the bank's chief economist. For a period of seven years prior to 1980, this man had made increasing amounts of money for the bank each year from his trading activities. As a reward for his excellence, huge bonus payouts were awarded. The bank also set aside larger and larger funds, which he could commit on a moment's notice without further approval from the CEO or the board (sounds a lot like the Société Général Bank fiasco created by Rogue trader Jerome Kierval in 2008).

His strategy had been to predict interest rates and either buy or sell bonds based upon his determination of the direction of those rates. In general, when interest rates go down, bonds go up and vice-versa. In the fall of 1980, interest rates were at an all-time high of 17 percent. The chief economist's projections were for rates to drop to more historic levels. Based on his analysis he invested several hundred million dollars in bonds. Rates did indeed begin to drop slightly, but soon began to shoot up in rapid fashion. Within weeks, the rates were at another all-time high of 21.5 percent. The bonds were worth so little money that the bank on paper was technically insolvent. Because selling these securities was out of the question, the bank was forced to incur monthly carrying charges of millions of dollars.

The bank immediately reduced its workforce by 25 percent. Eventually it was taken over by another institution. The chief economist lost his job, prestige and large amounts of his own money. The tragedy is not that he was wrong in his projection of interest rates; rather his real error was in failing to have a contingency plan. Such a plan could have had a trigger point at a level such as 17.5 percent where a bailout would have resulted in a loss less than catastrophic. The signals were all there, but he never once thought his analysis was in error until it was too late. Sounds a lot like the lack of thinking that went into President George W. Bush's excursion into Iraq.

The Story of a Poor Planning Disaster

This points up another paradox. The better we think the original plan is, the more we need to ask ourselves the tough questions and prepare for disaster. Without building in this review upfront, we are more likely to experience the "Titanic effect." The greater the magnitude of the potential disaster, the greater will be the tendency to ignore it.[9] It is almost impossible to believe, but apparently George W. Bush did not even consult Colin Powell, perhaps the most important person in the world to have consulted, before deciding to go to war against Iraq.

Bad situations, which have not been anticipated, tend to escalate into full-scale disasters. In reacting to the crisis we are tempted to "throw good money after bad" trying to salvage the situation. Why is this so? Barry Staw has done extensive research into this question and has developed the following possible explanations.[10]

1. We are motivated to try and recoup past losses. Some leaders in effect, "double down."

2. We seek to protect our self-image by attempting to justify the original rationality of our decisions. It is also a way of putting off the negative consequences that may come if we admit that we made a mistake.

3. We have been taught that consistency is one of the hallmarks of leaders and successful people. Plus we may have actually weathered past storms through intense focus and feel if we buckle down and try hard enough, we can do it again.

None of these reasons are all that irrational.

Worst Case Scenario

Worst-case scenario planning is a delicate balancing act. Human nature as described by Staw will serve to keep us committed to our goals and plans. This is a basic requirement for peak performance. Commitment to a losing course of action however, is stupidity. The only way I know of to obtain the benefits that accrue from perseverance without risking the liability of an "escalation situation" is to prepare ahead of time for a worst-case scenario.

There are two mistakes that are almost always fatal. They are to run out of time or money. When we run out of either (and we usually lose both at once), the game is over.

In preparing for the worst, the difficult questions must be asked. It is easy to get caught up in the hype of our own plans. It is human nature to underestimate the competition. You see it constantly in sports. Playing *devil's advocate* with yourself or, better yet, getting someone else to play that role is often critical to a leaders success.

Most people fail to get the insight of others. Norman Vincent Peale summed it up when he said, "We would rather be ruined by praise than saved by criticism."

The key is balance. Criticism can be paralyzing and totally unwarranted. People on the leading edge usually know more than the people doing the critique. As Einstein once said, "Great spirits have always encountered violent opposition from mediocre minds." However, another perspective may be quite helpful despite that fact. There must obviously be care taken in the selection of a critic. One who has our best interest at heart is essential.

A worst-case scenario plan is not meant to protect us like armor. While armor protects us, it also limits our mobility. Disaster planning is meant to provide protection more in the vein of an early warning system. The emphasis is on avoiding disaster rather than surviving it.

Once a worst-case scenario has been developed we must ask ourselves if we are prepared to accept the consequences should they occur. If we can play out a strategy knowing we won't be devastated beyond repair if the worst occurs, we will be able to devote unwavering energy into achieving success.

Effective contingency planning forces us to think through our priorities, goals and timeframes. It allows us to organize our attack. Potential obstacles to success are pointed out. Critical knowledge, skills and abilities required to translate goals into reality are identified. Planning for problems opens our minds to selecting resources to help us overcome the problems. Well thought out plans force us to take notice of the moves of other people critical to our success, including possible competitors, financial backers, employees, and prospects.

Experience is a demanding teacher; the lesson comes after the exam.

Learning from self-experience is learning the hard way. Failing to learn from our experience is even harder. Wisdom can come from many sources and so it is helpful to learn from the mistakes of others. After Vietnam, the Powell Doctrine was formulated as a template for deciding when and how to go to war. It worked brilliantly in Desert Storm. Then it seems it got tossed in the trashcan, leading to the current tragedy in Iraq.

Among the mistakes most often made is failing to ensure that we recognize and deal with disasters that can be foreseen. When told by President Bush of his intention to invade Iraq, Colin Powell reportedly said, "Mr. President, you will end up owning the place." He certainly saw disaster on the horizon. You do not have to "fly by the seat of your pants." Learn the lesson the easy way — plan for things to go wrong!

Dupont is the best I have ever seen at planning for disasters. They have seventeen teams representing all critical organizational areas with contingency plans in hand ready to deploy on a moment's notice should a crisis develop.

Leading for change means living life on the edge. This makes for greater risk. If this risk is not balanced by contingency planning, critical errors may eventually catch up with us. Like Russian roulette, the possibility for disaster increases with each move. As someone once told me, "Fortune knocks but once — misfortune has more patience."

Winston Churchill said, "The price of greatness is responsibility."[11] This comes from sweating the details — taking a look at the potential pitfalls and insuring against them. Like Lloyds of London, we must make it our business to insure against the catastrophic. I know many individuals who owe their ultimate success to the fact they had a disaster plan.

Traditional *western* culture is ready-fire-aim. I don't advocate that the pendulum swing all the way from an *action bias* to a *planning bias*. But, the goal should be one of being cognizant of and attempting to avoid these eleven most common failures in planning.

CHAPTER 14

GENERATE THE POWER OF THE PYRAMID

The primary job in leading for change is to influence the organization's associates to alter the way things are done in an effort to further the aims of the enterprise. Creating an effective power base to make this happen is essential. All leaders have numerous potential means of influence at their disposal. Understanding the advantages and disadvantages of these various bases of power and picking the right one(s) to use in any given situation is an extremely important consideration.

Building the Power for Change

Visualize a pyramid that is wide at the base and gets progressively smaller at the top as shown in diagram A. It has been my experience that leaders too often start out attempting to use the stages of influence from the top down, which is precisely the *wrong* way to go about it.

Avoiding Coercion

The top four sections of the pyramid can be thought of as "push" forms of influence. People feel pushed into doing what the leader wants done. At the very top is *coercion*. This refers to the negative consequences such as expulsion, isolation, public humiliation, withholding resources, or anything that a person might feel threatened by. There are many problems inherent in the use of this type of power. First, it is very fragile. The organization gives a leader the ability to coerce people but can instantly take it away. Second, it mostly works when the leader is physically present. We all remember the iron-fisted teacher who, when out of the room or when a "substitute" was teaching, saw all discipline go out the window. Third, coercion causes people to do the bare minimum necessary to stop the pain and typically not one thing more. Lastly, people who feel coerced tend to spend a lot of energy trying to figure out how to avoid the pressure or worse, coerce back.

DIAGRAM A

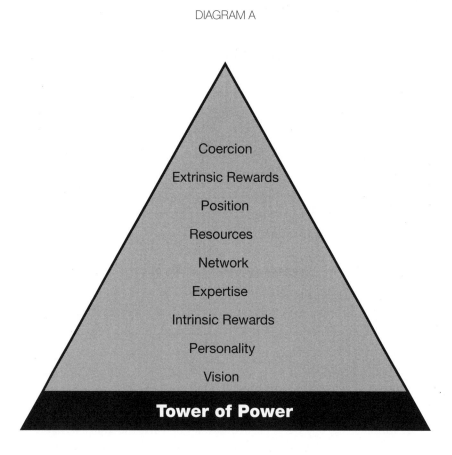

Indispensable Tip !

Coercion should *never* be used as the first option. It should *always* be held in reserve until other possibilities are explored.

In today's world our associates often have more coercive power over us than we would like to admit. They could for instance, hire a contingency fee attorney with no money out-of-pocket to threaten us with litigation, knowing that many organizations will settle out of court. If it goes to trial, we end up spending countless hours in depositions, fulfilling document requests, lining up witnesses and the like. Or they could go to the local news media and allege anything. The story will make page one of the business section and create a public relations nightmare. If we spend the time to investigate the claims and prepare a response, it will be buried in the back section.

Coerced associates could choose to sabotage key organization systems. In the IT world, one string of code tapped in by a disgruntled employee could crash the whole kit-and-caboodle.

If our enterprise is a government contractor or of sufficient size, an associate could file a complaint with a whole host of agencies such as the EEOC, OFCCP, IRS, or comptroller. If you want a real paper chase, just try proving to a watchdog agency that you *didn't* do something.

Finally, deranged associates who feel coerced could always bring in a weapon and open fire. On June 25, 2008, a 25-year-old employee of Atlantis Plastics in Henderson, Kentucky, killed his supervisor and four other employees before turning the gun on himself. A few hours earlier he had felt coerced by his supervisor over not wearing safety goggles and the use of his cell phone on the assembly line. He reportedly called his girlfriend and said he was so riled up he wanted to kill his boss[1].

I'm not saying coercive power is not good to have or that a leader should never use it. Rather, it should be a last resort and not a leader's first option. Yet sadly, even in 2009, far too many people in positions of authority use fear and intimidation tactics all too frequently. The goal of influence in the workplace is to ensure you have not jeopardized your ability to influence these same people again in the future. With coercion, you can expect just the opposite.

Limiting External Rewards

One level down on the pyramid is *external rewards,* or, in a sense, bribery. In the use of this type of influence, a leader engages in a sort of quid pro quo with associates. Essentially the idea is to hold out "carrots" such as pay raises, promotions, desirable task force assignments, favorable geographic locations, or other "perks" in exchange for moving in a desired direction.

This base of influence is also very fragile in that the organization can easily take these things away. At some point a leader literally runs out of things that can be given to associates. And as several military officers have told me over the years, "The thing which causes a soldier to jump on a hand grenade to save a buddy is not combat pay or the thought of a medal awarded posthumously."

Don't Forget This

External rewards tend to motivate for a very short period of time and form a higher floor of expectations for the future.

Once again, it is nice to have these types of things as bargaining chips, but it should be further down the list.

Don't Rely On Your Position

The next stage of the pyramid is *position power.* This refers to the legitimacy of being called CEO, president, senior executive vice president and the like. It also is tied to one's authority to back, approve or support the proposals of associates.

Frankly, after the scandals of inflated body counts in Vietnam, phantom weapons of mass destruction in Iraq, the resignation of Detroit Mayor Kwame Kilpatrick in disgrace, the defrocking of religious leaders Jim Bakker and Jimmy Swaggart, and the Enron, Worldcom, Adelphia, and Tyco fiascos, formal position power doesn't come close to having the impact it once had. Just try telling your teenage son or daughter, "Do it because I'm your father and I'm telling you to do it." This never worked well with my son, and I trust it won't work well with yours either. Public opinion polls in recent years consistently show that the majority of employees do not trust the public pronouncements of their senior-most executives.

> ### 💡 Don't Forget This 💡
> Trying to appeal to Generation X and Millennial associates with formal authority is pointless.

This base of power is also very fragile in that the organization gives you the legitimacy of authority and can instantly take it away. Consider what happens to U.S. presidents and their staffs on Inauguration Day. At the beginning of the day the outgoing president is the most powerful person in the world and hours later is just an ordinary citizen. In his book *Crisis,* Hamilton Jordan, President Carter's chief of staff, reveals that in the hours leading up to the swearing in of President Reagan, he and his staff were making the final arrangements for the release of the American hostages from Iran. There was considerable uncertainty as to the timing of the expected release. Moments after President Reagan was sworn in Jordan tried to call his assistant to check on the status of the hostages. After a brief pause she came back on the line and said simply, "Mr. Jordan, you are no longer cleared for that information." It was at that moment Jordan realized how much of his power had been tied to his position and how quickly it was taken away.[2]

Like the other bases for power outlined so far, having formal authority is great and often helpful, but it should not be relied upon too heavily.

Don't Waste Resources

The last of the "push" forms of influence is *resource power.* This is a less personal form of bribery and includes providing budget, materials, space, time, staff support, data, and the like. Individuals who can provide the most critical and difficult to obtain resources come to have significant power. Think of supply sergeants in the Army or budget directors in government. However, this form of influence has exactly the same limitations as the other form of external rewards outlined earlier.

In an ideal change scenario, a leader might be able to throw massive amounts of money, people, or other resources at the challenge. A New York Yankees approach if you will. But under the more severe resource constraints most organizations are faced with, this option is a non-starter. Most change-focused leaders are forced to seek solutions where they optimize the resources they can amass around some strategic theme. This requires hard choices to be made.

The Push and Pull of Networking

In the middle of the pyramid is *Network.* This form of influence can be used to "push" or "pull." Basically, networking refers to using your relations with influential people to either threaten or help others.

In the threatening use of a network I liken it to "murder for hire." In my consulting practice I never have any formal position inside of the organizations I work with. I couldn't *personally fire,* demote or cause anyone inside the organization to be isolated. But if I could convince people that I have a better relationship with an internal power broker that could do those things, then I have de facto ability to coerce from a distance.

Tales from the Workplace

Let me provide an example of the "pull" use of a network. I was conducting a strategic planning session with one of my clients a few years ago. A competitor had just come out with an innovation that made one of my client's products obsolete overnight. This item represented roughly 30 percent of the organization's revenue. They felt there was no way to respond since it was December and the industry trade shows where all of the buying decisions took place were scheduled to be held less than a month away. Historically in this company it took nine months to create a prototype,

---

get samples made, and produce initial shipment quantities, since all their engineering and manufacturing were done in-house. Thus they were all set to abdicate 30 percent of their revenue base to their competitor.

In pushing the team further it became apparent that all they really needed were prototypes and spec sheets to take to the shows. The product didn't even need to work just yet; it merely had to look like the finished product would look. Fortunately they had already engaged a patent attorney to provide counsel on the specifications and appearance the product would have to not violate their competitor's patent.

I was able to introduce them to two people in my network who were able to do 48-hour turnaround on computer aided design prototypes and two others who could produce in China the initial several thousand units needed within 90 days to stock their dealers' shelves. In the end, they were able to keep their market share and prevent the competitor from making further inroads. While I *personally* had no idea how to make quick prototypes or any experience with manufacturing in China, people in my network did. How much influence do you think that buys me with this client in the future?

The best networker I've heard of is Atoosa Rubenstein, former editor in chief of *Seventeen Magazine*. She counts more than 43,000 friends on My Space. Her goal is to tap into that network to create a web-based business.[3]

Mark Burnett, the father of reality TV, is not afraid to tap into his vast network when searching for ideas or solving problems. He says, "The bottom line is that only results count. How you arrive at them does not."[4]

Pull Forms of Influence

Expertise

The first of the "pull" forms of influence is *expertise.* This is a leader's credentials, degrees, certifications, technical prowess and track record of success. A nice thing about this base of power is that it is not fragile. Once a leader possesses these things, no one can take them away. Most people are much more likely to follow someone who has some kind of proof that they should know what they are talking about[5.]

When Shaquille O'Neal joined the Los Angeles Lakers, coach Phil Jackson gave him a stack of books to read, few of which had anything to do with basketball. Shortly thereafter Shaq was interviewed on ESPN and asked if he planned on reading any of those books.

Shaq said, "Sure." When asked why, he said, "I don't know what these books have to do with basketball. What I do know is that my coach has six championship rings and I don't have any. If he thinks my studying these books will get me a ring, I am all for reading them."

Because of Phil Jackson's past record of success, he was able to influence one of his stars to do something most of the rest of us would be unable to get Shaq to do. Your reputation is your personal "brand." Guard it jealously, and always be on the lookout for ways to enhance it.

The thing experts have to guard against is over-complicating their communication with non-experts. Research indicates that once we learn something it is difficult for us to imagine not knowing it. Thus, experts either omit key contextual data or talk as if everyone understands at the same level they do.

Intrinsic Rewards

The next "pull" form of influence is *intrinsic rewards.* Ask a thousand people — and I have — the question, "Think of a time when you couldn't wait to get to work. A time when you woke up at 1 a.m. tossing and turning with ideas in your head. You took out a pad of paper, jotted down notes and tried to go back to sleep. You continued to toss and turn and seemed filled with adrenaline. Finally, at 4:30 a.m., you gave up on getting sleep, got dressed and drove to work in the dark. You skipped lunch and dinner, and looked at the clock amazed that it was 6:30 p.m. What was going on that caused you to be so excited?"

By the way, if you have never had such an experience it is very sad, because you probably have never truly been "in the zone." Natural narcotics called endorphins and ocitocins are released in the brain during such peak events. They can be just as addictive as real narcotics. Once you have experienced them, it is hard to live any other way.

The answers that kept coming up time and again were *challenge, achievement, recognition, freedom, and growth.* These are as close to universal motivators as you will find. We all differ on the level of challenge, the type of recognition and the kind of growth that will be motivating, but these are the things that cause great effort to be expended in pursuit of a goal.

Tales From the Workplace

To demonstrate the power of becoming a leader that can tap into and fulfill people's intrinsic needs, consider this. One of my clients, an aerospace company, hired the first outsider to run a major division of the organization. He had left as president of a smaller company in Southern California and asked three of his key lieutenants to join him in the new venture. Essentially he offered them the same title, similar pay, same type of industry, and they had to uproot their families and move to the Rocky Mountains. All agreed to do so. When I asked why, each said that they had never worked for a better boss. When I probed further as to what made him so great, each of the three said something to the effect of, "He puts me in ever-challenging situations, gives me a reasonable resource allocation to allow me a fighting chance of success, rewards me when I do well, coaches me when I struggle, allows me the autonomy to do things in the manner I think is best, and keeps me on the steep part of the learning curve so I never get bored." Now that's a boss to emulate!

Well it turns out that this fellow was a "turnaround" manager who normally likes to keep moving around. Sure enough, three years later he left the company to take a job as a division president in the Pacific Northwest. The same three people once again quit their jobs and uprooted their families a second time for the same reason. Within three years, the leader quit yet again to take the presidency of an organization back in Southern California. And you guessed it, the same three people followed him back to the place it all started, this time unable to even afford the quality of house they sold six years earlier because of the rapid appreciation of Southern California real estate. He had become a truly addictive boss by never losing sight of the universal motivators.

Personality Power

Nearing the bottom of the pyramid is *personality power.* Included in this base of influence would be things like approachability, likeability, genuine flattery, authenticity, constructive criticism, personal warmth, and having the other person's best interests in mind.

Think about it: what wouldn't you do for your best friend? Yet unless you work for your best friend, can that person give you a raise? Promote you? Assign you a bigger or better office? Let you run a prestigious task force? Give you more time on tasks or a higher budget allocation? Generally not.

But, I would be willing to bet, if your best friend called you at 2 a.m. from the jailhouse asking you to bail him out, you would immediately spring into action, no questions asked. Why? Because that person fills a need all people feel — to be tightly connected with someone else. Generally our best friends treat us with respect. They praise us when we need a "pick-me-up." When they criticize us, we know deep down that they are truly trying to help us. Personality power is also about humility or lack of ego.

Human nature being what it is, we tend to be far more influenced by people we like than those we don't. When we mirror the behavior, speech or appearance of another person, we are creating rapport. People who are like one another tend to like one another. And people who do things which allow others to feel good about themselves tend to be seen as magnetically attractive.

Skateboard entrepreneur Tony Hawk has a surprising lack of ego for a superstar. People who know him well say they have never seen someone so successful be so humble. Nucor CEO Dan Dimicco flies commercial, does not have his own parking space and makes the coffee in the office if he takes the last cup.[6] The "commoner's touch" gives him extraordinary influence with people. Ford CEO Alan Mulally put his ego aside and had the courage to say that he is largely accelerating a plan for turning around the company created by someone else, acknowledging what he doesn't know about the car business and empowering those on his staff who do.[7]

In my opinion quite a bit of the appeal of Ronald Reagan and Arnold Schwarzenegger can be traced to their personalities. Both made frequent use of self-deprecating humor, smiled often, tried to talk about areas of mutual interest when in conversation with others, and endeavored to end interactions with sincere compliments.

Charm is seductive and everyone is prone to seduction. The importance of personality as a powerful base of influence should not be underestimated.

Vision

Forming the base of the pyramid is *vision,* or essentially "winning hearts and minds." James MacGregor Burns in his seminal work, Leadership, referred to this as "transformational Leadership." [8]

Sometimes a person will be expressive and able to light up a stage like Barack Obama, but this part of vision is the least important. Think about the consumer advocate Ralph Nader, billionaire Warren Buffett or Senator John McCain. For nearly five decades, millions of people have been drawn to the consumer movement Nader started, millions more hang on the every word of Buffett and John McCain became the 2008 nominee of the Republican Party for president of the United States. Yet they are three of the least dynamic people you will ever come across.

So, why do people follow visionary leaders, even those who are not personally electrifying? Generally these leaders tap into some of our most basic needs, including the desire for *direction* and the need to find *meaning*.

Transformational leaders have a clear orienting vision. Passion for the cause. A moral conviction that their cause is just. They hold themselves to very high expectations and serve as role models themselves that others seek to emulate.

Cult leaders, though in the darkest of ways, are the epitome of visionary leaders. The ability of Jim Jones and the People's Temple, David Koresh and the Branch Davidians and Marshall Applewaite and Heaven's Gate to get dozens of people to kill themselves "en masse" shows the incredible power of direction and meaning, even if it is in pursuit of insanity.

One of the movies that I have my coaching clients watch is *The Last Castle*.[9] This story depicts a highly decorated Marine Corps general officer played by Robert Redford, who is imprisoned as a result of an error in judgment, attempting to overthrow the brutal prison warden played by James Gandolfini. The warden has all the "push" forms of power on his side and doesn't hesitate to use them. But the Redford character knows that the true battle will be won by capturing the hearts and minds of not only the other inmates but also the prison guards. Even though it is just a movie, the techniques the general uses-including an orienting vision, passion, strong moral conviction, building the confidence of the prisoners, holding everyone to the highest expectations, and serving as a role model-are each adroitly used to achieve the goal. And, like all other "pull" forms of power, no one can take away a leader's vision.

Essential Knowledge

The total number of power bases a leader can bring to bear in any given situation determines the rate of speed at which a leader can bring about lasting change. Effective change-focused leaders are constantly looking to build up their various power bases and choose the most appropriate ones for the situation at hand.

In attempting to lead others it is best to start at the bottom and work up the pyramid. If sufficient skill is developed in the use of the "pull" forms of influence, a leader may never have to use the push forms. As a Southern gentleman who attended one of my seminars some years ago said, "You don't need to kick down the door if you know how to pick the lock." But as Al Capone reportedly once said, "You can get much further in this life with a smile and a gun than you can with a smile alone." It helps to have the ultimate ability to coerce others as a last resort.

CHAPTER 15

AVOID "ONE SIZE FITS ALL" PERFORMANCE MANAGEMENT:

Performance Driven Leadership

In challenging economic times associates get laid off, contingent work agreements with outside contractors are allowed to lapse, and open requisitions are frozen. The direct consequence is that those who remain are forced to take on additional work.

Of course the intelligent thing to do would be to review all tasks and eliminate the lowest value activities so that workloads can be sized to fit the new under-resourced workforce. This is something that should occur regularly even in flush times. The reality is that executives don't like getting rid of *any* projects, even bad ones, because it entails trampling someone's legacy, walking away from sunk costs, threatening associate comfort zones or potentially causing turf wars.

Usually, supervisory spans of control get larger as frontline leaders are the first herd to be trimmed. Thus supervisory time and attention, which is at a premium even in good times, must be deployed in a manner that will result in the greatest payback for the time invested.

 Don't Forget This

One of the biggest impediments to leader's success is that many spend far too much time doing work themselves and too little time managing the performance of others.

An organization's performance management system refers to the interaction of five elements; target setting, delegation, empowerment, performance appraisal, and compensation. It is the key system that impacts the institution's ability to execute. In many organizations this system could use a complete overhaul.

One key element of a performance management system is to help organizations attract, retain and motivate associates. Yet, during my 32-year career one constant complaint has been that most employees see the system their institution uses as unattractive, de-motivating and causes the better performers to consider leaving on a regular basis. And why not? These systems have changed relatively little since the 1950s and still most often revolve around some version of a bell curve distribution.

Performance Management Systems In Action

I have yet to see an employee opinion survey that did not list as one of its top five complaints the ineffectiveness of the enterprise's performance management system. Consider this common counterproductive scenario. A person (Mike) is told on the first workday of the year what is expected in terms of performance (if Mike is fortunate enough to work for a competent boss). Mike works hard throughout the year to try and accomplish his goals. He is also the consummate team player, regularly assisting his colleagues Mary, Sue, and Betty, and doing things in the best interests of the enterprise as a whole.

Mike may even get feedback along the way telling him that his performance is on track and his team play is appreciated. Then comes the annual performance appraisal and, wham, the hammer drops. Mike is told that indeed he did all that was expected of him. But Mary did more than him. Sue did more than Mary, and Betty produced more than Mary and Sue combined. The result: Mike gets a below-average performance rating.

Mike of course labored all year under the assumption that he was being judged against his goals, something he considered to be reasonably under his own control. He had no idea that in reality, he was *competing* against his teammates. Mike being a smart guy realizes that he got screwed being a team player. He now sees clearly that his goal was not to meet a *standard* of performance, it was really to out-do his co-workers.

Mike can choose to work harder next year, which is of course what the organization hopes he will do. However, Mike could also decide to take the "Tonya Harding approach." He might conclude that it is easier to hinder or eliminate his "competition" by, in this case, hoarding, sandbagging, withholding information, failing to offer assistance, or plain sabotaging their efforts. These are not exactly the types of behaviors managers say they want their employees to practice.

Such a reaction represents the unintended consequences of the traditional performance management system practiced in most large institutions. Given this, why don't they try something different? Basically it comes down to inertia, fear or ignorance of a better way.

One Size Doesn't Fit All

As to inertia, most managers use a "one size fits all" approach to managing people. They argue that management's job is to be consistent, which they wrongly interpret as treating everyone the same. Rarely do they put forth the effort to determine which elements of their people's jobs are the most critical. Nor do they usually create clear standards of acceptable performance for each key accountability. And perhaps, worst of all, they fail to differentiate the amounts of merit increases they give to their people.

One size fits all leadership, compensation, or development is insanity of the highest order. It is especially critical in a resource scarce environment that top performers receive outsize attention. Smart companies have long treated their best customers differently from their marginal ones. The time has come to do this with associates.

Indispensable Tip !

Fear comes in two varieties regarding performance management. One is the fear of doing something different from the norm of other large organizations. The other is the fear that some other approach will blow their compensation budget out of whack. Both of these fears can be allayed.

The Bell-Shaped De-motivation System

The law of large numbers tells us that employee performance will naturally cluster along a bell-shaped continuum. A few will be terrific performers, a few will be substandard, and the many will be in the middle. No argument there.

However, a problem arises because for all practical purposes, managers are "forced" to rate their people along those lines so that the whole enterprise ends up with a "normal" distribution. This is the part that punishes good managers, rewards poor managers and upsets most associates.

Poor managers who run a unit made up of mostly substandard performers are allowed to call some of them adequate and a few exceptional, even though none may really be that good. Great managers who have assembled a unit of superstars are forced to call a few substandard and many adequate, even though none may really be that bad. This creates two disincentives.

First, there would seem to be little reason to try to assemble a team of "A" players, since only a few will be able to be appropriately paid and those under-compensated would probably leave. Second, there is little incentive for a poor performing unit to get better as everyone is already rewarded beyond what their real contribution would say they should be paid.

So the net result of using this system is that the size of the compensation pie stays fixed and the fighting erupts as to how to divide the slices. Most organizations then compound the problem by seldom withholding a slice of any size from anyone and don't really give a much bigger piece to the top performers than they do to the adequate performers. Thus all but a few people at the bottom are unhappy.

> **Indispensable Tip !**
> If you have a targeted merit increase of 3 percent, give your stars 6 percent and give absolutely nothing to your duds.

Also, there is a psychological problem with this approach. Extensive research indicates that nearly 80 percent of people rate *their* own performance as being superior to that of their peers. Thus, calling people average serves to upset them since in their own minds, their performance is above average. And, since people are compared against each other instead of against a standard, there is no *objective* way to tell them that they are wrong. Also, when associates are judged against others, the outcome becomes subjective, thus seeming to them to be outside their ability to control. Frankly, I think anyone using a system like this would be better off just giving everyone an equal cost-of-living adjustment each year and calling it a day.

If done correctly, the following approach outlined here will actually increase the amount of money paid out to associates *but* it will come out of a *substantially* larger amount of top line revenue. Income will increase due to higher productivity, better morale, increased retention of top performers, and the enhanced ability to shed the poorest performers. It is surprisingly simple, though it does require some time and intelligent thought up front. Best of all, the associates are the ones in control over whether they are seen as performing at a superior, adequate or substandard level.

A Tailored Approach To Supervision

Research going as far back as the famous 1959 Leadership Studies at Ohio State University indicates that there is no one style which is "best." To the contrary, "effective" leadership behavior is that which appropriately meets the needs and demands of a specific situation.

A starting point for effective performance management is that the leader must jointly define with the associate the five to ten most critical activities that the associate is going to be asked to perform. The key is to make sure the critical objectives represent a balance between personal goal attainment, team play, leading and developing others, and innovation.

Once these key accountabilities have been defined, there must be agreement on appropriate "measures" for each of the key items. For instance, we could measure quality, quantity, budget/resources consumed, schedule, innovativeness and customer satisfaction, for each accountability chosen. There should be three delineations of possible performance: unacceptable, acceptable and superior. As an example, let's say we chose scores on a customer satisfaction survey as the key metric for one of the associate's critical tasks. If the survey was scored on a five-point-scale, we could define superior as 4.0-5.0. Acceptable could be 3.8-4.0, and anything less than 3.8 would be unacceptable.

So let's recap. To this point we have jointly defined the most critical activities each associate is being asked to perform. We collaborated upon choosing a metric for each activity and agreed what performance level it would take to earn a superior, acceptable or unacceptable rating against each standard. Now we are in a position to determine the associate's current performance against each standard. This will aid us in deciding how we should best interact with them to help them succeed.

Perhaps dozens of factors conspire to determine an associate's level of performance in any given key area. However the most critical are the associate's: 1) level of skill, 2) level of commitment, and 3) personal responsibility level. Setting luck and systemic variables aside, the more skill, commitment and maturity an associate demonstrates, the higher the performance level.

Skill is knowledge that can be put to work by a person to deliver a result. And of course, skill varies depending upon what you are asking a person to do. A highly skilled carpenter may be a terrible public speaker.

Commitment is a multiplier of two things — a person's need to achieve times the person's level of self-confidence. Need to achieve and self-confidence have both stable and situational components. A person could have a generally high need to achieve, but a low need to excel in any given situation. For instance, the person may have a high need to win at poker, golf, business, or a debate, but might not care much about winning in tennis.

The same holds true with self-confidence. A person could generally have a very high level of assurance, but could be lacking in self-confidence when it comes to sexual prowess, formal education, height, or weight.

Situational confidence is affected by one's previous performance in a similar situation, expertise, history of receiving positive or negative feedback, or their internal assessment of how they might stack up against others.

So, taken together, a person may have a high need to achieve in a situation but low self-confidence. Or they could be highly confident but have no real need to achieve in a particular situation. In such cases, their commitment level as a whole would be low. Or, if a person has a high level of self-confidence and a tremendous need to achieve in the situation, then the commitment level will be very high.

Responsibility basically refers to whether or not you can count on the person to show up on time on a regular basis, and *consistently* deliver adequate performance or above. I have talked at length with several general managers of professional baseball clubs and have asked each what the main difference is between a major league player and one in AAA ball. They each said the same thing: The AAA player can do everything a major leaguer can do, they just can't do it as consistently. Also, we know some people may party too much, get sick often, or simply have a lot of "off" days. These types of people cannot be trusted.

There are three distinctively different styles of interaction that can be used with an associate depending upon that associate's level of performance and responsibility. Not only may you be interacting with each associate differently from one another, *you may even interact with any given associate differently* depending upon their level of performance for each critical area of accountability. See diagram one for an overview of the model.

DIAGRAM 1

Performance Driven Leadership™

MANAGE	COACH	SERVE
Give Limited Authority Establish Tight Parameters Provide Lots of Direction Monitor Consistently	Clarify the Vision Explain Guiding Principles Expand Participation Begin to Loosen Parameters Provide the Rationale Behind Your Decisions	Shared Accountability High Autonomy Negotiable Parameters Prevent Major Errors
SUPPORT	Build Associates Confidence Share Your Style/Philosophy Develop Associates Skills Give Frequent Feedback	Remove Barriers Provide Resources Buffer Political Interference Provide Visibility Create New Challenges Invest in Development As Requested Match Praise/Contact to Assoc. Need
EMPOWERMENT		
Praise Associates Progress		

SUPPORT AND EMPOWERMENT

	PERFORMANCE		
0%	P1 UNACCEPTABLE	99%	P2 ACCEPTABLE 100%	110%	P3 SUPERIOR 111%	INFINITY

P1 UNACCEPTABLE	P2 ACCEPTABLE	P3 SUPERIOR
Poor Skill and/or Limited Knowledge and/or Low Need To Achieve and/or Poor Self Confidence and/or Irresponsible	Adequate Skill And/or Knowledge Moderate Need To Achieve Moderate Self Confidence Generally Responsible	High Skill/knowledge Strong Commitment Highly Responsible

H

H

L

Let's list the three styles of interaction and where each style is most effectively used. The approaches are called managing, coaching and serving.

Manage

Managing is used in situations where an associate's current performance is in the unacceptable range. This would be performance from zero to 99 percent of standard. This person is failing to meet expectations in this area of accountability.

One or more of the following factors usually causes substandard performance: limited knowledge, poor skill in applying the knowledge, low need to achieve, poor self-confidence, or a generally irresponsible person.

The style of interaction called managing is essentially designed to make sure the associate does not fail in the short term. Under this style of supervision, the associate will have very limited authority to act outside of some very tight parameters. Some person, machine, or procedure will provide them with lots of direction and they will be monitored almost constantly.

Indispensable Tip !

Even though a leader's overall philosophy should be one of empowering people, some associates for some tasks should have very limited latitude.

If you have ever had to deal with bank teller trainees, you have probably noticed the computer system gives them almost no authority to make large transactions without the approval of a customer service manager. While this is maddening to us as consumers because the limits are set too low, it is an example of how such an approach to limit empowerment can work in practice.

From a support standpoint, a leader's main responsibility is to look for things that the associate is doing well so that she can praise their progress. At this stage of employee development, praise can be a powerful motivator to keep associates trying harder as they come to feel they are making progress.

In today's world the *managing* style will not be used very often. It will be used for developmental "projects." These are people who are thought to have potential to be a good performer at the task in the future despite their currently low-level of performance today. Think about Michael Jordan when he quit basketball mid-career to try his hand at baseball. He had world-class hand-eye coordination, tremendous quickness and a strong work ethic. But he couldn't hit a minor league fastball, let alone a major league curveball.

The other time you will use this style is when the associate is either temporarily or permanently a poor fit with the position. Years ago administrative assistants were asked to junk their IBM Selectric typewriters in favor of the then state-of-the-art technology called word processors. Overnight they went from supremely competent to sub-standard. The same thing happened to machinists who went from manual machines to numerically controlled. In the beginning they needed lots of structure and direction. Or perhaps a former star performer is having problems at home or with substance abuse. Performance may have temporarily slid into the unacceptable range.

A more permanent misfit for the task might be someone who is simply a bad hire and for legal or practical reasons you just can't move them out of the spot to a job that would be a better match for their skills and desires. Someone or something must protect you, them, and the organization from doing the wrong thing. The *management* approach is the best at doing this. Keep in mind that *management* does not mean you have to treat the associate in an abrasive, blunt, critical, or demeaning manner. What you are attempting to do is to provide almost total direction to minimize the chances of errors occurring.

Coach

When an employee is performing at an acceptable level, which means at 100-110 percent of standard, then the *coaching* style of interaction would make the most sense. With this approach you are making a heavy investment in the associate in the hope that ultimately he or she will be able to self-supervise in this activity.

From an empowerment standpoint, coaching means that while you as a manager still have all of the responsibility, you begin to loosen the parameters within which the associate is allowed to perform. You want to take great pains to clarify the vision, explain the guiding principles, and most importantly provide the rationale behind *your* decisions.

Psychologist Jonathan Friedman demonstrated another benefit of explaining the "why" of things. He did an experiment where he individually instructed a group of boys NOT to play with a certain robot toy out of a selection of many toys available under the threat of punishment. When he was present, they did not play with the toy. But six weeks later, in the same room with Friedman absent, most of the boys played with the robot.

In another group, he also warned them *why* it was wrong to play with the robot (because it was someone else's). Six weeks later with him absent, all the boys still obeyed the rule. They didn't want to play with the robot because they understood why it was wrong to do so.[5]

The kind and amount of support you provide changes dramatically as well. The biggest thing you personally can do is to provide a lot of feedback. I see failure to give frequent feedback to associates as one of the most underused developmental tools we have in our arsenal. In professional sports we see coaches giving feedback *every minute* of every practice. Yet in the corporate, government, and non-profit worlds, people are lucky if they get meaningful feedback *once a year*. This does not have to take a lot of time. It can be thirty seconds after a meeting in which the associate did something well or poorly. It can be fifteen seconds in the hallway when you see something good or bad.

Other types of support in the *coaching* style would be taking the time to share our personal philosophy, building confidence, and preparing a skill/knowledge development plan for the associate. It might mean sending them to training. It could be having them "shadow" a great performer for a couple of days. Or, it could mean self-paced instruction over the Internet followed by fifteen minutes a day for two weeks with you.

Serve

The third style of supervision is called *serving*. This is used with superior performers who are at the 111-plus range of performance to standard.

From an empowerment standpoint we can safely *share* accountability with the associate. The employee can be given a lot of autonomy and should be allowed to negotiate performance parameters. Basically the leader's job is to ensure that *major* errors do not occur.

A major error is a breach of safety, an illegal or unethical act, or a difficult to recover from loss. We have a fiduciary responsibility to not let errors of this type occur, no matter how much we have told the associate he or she was empowered.

Your job as a leader is to support superior performers in any way you can. You might even say that the leader *works for* the associate in a high performing scenario. The leader's job is to remove barriers that get in the high-performing associate's way. This might be a policy, procedure, or defective piece of equipment, among other things. Also, you want to put most of the resources in these people's hands since they have obviously demonstrated that good things happen when they are properly resourced.

Another goal of the leader of high performers is to *buffer* political interference. You may never fully eliminate it but you can perhaps minimize its disruptive effects. You may choose to provide technology or an assistant to help them with paperwork or choose to handle a request from above on their behalf. You want your stars to spend as much effort applying their core competency as possible while you minimize all the peripheral stuff that often gets in their way.

Also, you want to give *them* the visibility, not hog it yourself. Instead of you making the presentation to the CEO or board of directors, your associate gets to make the pitch. Rather than you visiting the customer, they get to make the trip.

A lot of leaders are afraid that if they used the *serving* style their organizations would consider them to be expendable and choose to lay them off. In my experience, this fear is unfounded. As the CEO of a Fortune Top 10 company liked to say, "If you ever see a turtle sitting on top of a fencepost, you know that turtle had some help from someone in getting there." Turtles can't climb fence posts on their own. CEOs and board members know that it takes a special kind of leader to effectively attract, develop, unlock, and retain superstars. I expect that virtually every coach who has won a Super Bowl, Stanley Cup, NBA title, or World Series could easily land another job if he wanted one.

Essential Knowledge

A summary of effective performance management:

1. The associate and manager jointly agree on the five to ten most critical elements of the job against which the associate will be measured.

2. The associate and manager jointly decide the key metrics for each critical job element.

3. Unacceptable, acceptable and superior levels of performance for each metric are agreed upon.

4. The boss interacts with the associate in the appropriate manner (manage, coach, serve) for each key area with the goal of helping the associate to ultimately reach the superior level ("A" player status) for each activity.

The associate is compensated by a merit increase at a level established *in advance* depending upon whether their overall performance comes out unacceptable (generally *no* increase), acceptable (generally the organization's targeted average increase) or superior (generally quite a bit more than the average increase) *regardless* of what anyone else in the organization does.

If we do a good job defining the key elements, set the appropriate standards, and delegate properly, the organization will be so successful that finding the money to pay everyone at the superior level in the extremely unlikely event that would ever happen would be no problem. In fact, a firm could easily budget in advance for most associates to receive the maximum merit increase. If they were to attain the level of performance necessary to get that increase, great. If not, the money saved could be diverted into other worthwhile endeavors.

But that really should be the goal of every manager — to have all of their people performing at a superior level for all of their key accountabilities. This approach puts the burden on the leader to do the upfront work correctly and leaves the associate in control of his or her own destiny. There should be *absolutely no surprise* at the end of the year how the associate will be appraised or compensated.

Special Performance Management Considerations in Uncertain Times

Keep Associates Spirits Up

It is easy to get caught up in all the negativity that tough or uncertain times seem to generate. Leaders need to find ways to show all associates that the glass is half-full, not half-empty. Those who prevail through difficulty develop mental toughness. While they may not always know how they will succeed, they believe that through a combination of relying on fundamentals, coupled with out-of-the-box thinking, they will emerge relatively unscathed.

Keep A Closer Eye On Metrics

During times of uncertainty performance against key metrics needs to be analyzed more frequently. Potential problems and opportunities need to be identified so that critical decisions can be made more quickly.

Consider Automation

Too many executives cut the IT budget during downtimes. One way associates actually can be more productive in doing more for the business is if they are armed with the latest technology.

CHAPTER 16

AVOID "ONE SIZE FITS ALL" PERFORMANCE MANAGEMENT:
Turn A One Man Band Into A Symphony Through Delegation

Effective Delegation

A one-man band can create some interesting music, but even the most talented cannot come close to matching the awesome sound of a symphony orchestra. To get truly symphonic performance, the leader of a one-man band needs to go beyond his individual talent and become a conductor of other talented players. In the business world this requires delegation.

Legendary CEO of The Limited, Leslie Wexler, finally bumped up against the wall of what he could single-handedly do to goose organizational performance. He concluded that before he could change his business model that he needed to alter his own style. He said, "I needed to change from sole inventor to the leader, the teacher, the coach."[1]

Just about every manager I have ever met has a horror story surrounding a delegated task gone awry. And as the old adage "once burned, twice shy" goes, their response is usually an over-reaction in the form of "next time I'll just do it myself." Through this fear of failure of others they begin to sow the seeds of their own ultimate destruction. Leaders who don't learn to delegate become overloaded, exhausted, and fail to tap into the unique abilities of the members of the team.

At its most fundamental level, any leader's job is to get the things an organization needs to have done performed *through* the efforts of *other* people. Delegation is the method by which managers attempt to make this a reality. No matter what level of management one holds, it is impossible to be successful in the long run without effectively offloading many key tasks to others.

Despite most managers' instinctive knowledge that delegation is a critical skill, very few seem to possess the ability naturally and, inexplicably, many organizations don't emphasize it as an early developmental priority. In fact, the very reason most supervisors were promoted in the first place is often due to their being the best individual contributor in the unit. This cements in their own minds that they can do everything better than the others, otherwise someone else would have been selected to lead the group.

While it is often true that the manager can immediately do most tasks better than the people on their team, if they don't learn to effectively offload work, that situation will never change. The result will be that the manager fails over time simply due to the physical limitations of the 168 hours we each have in a week.

The whole idea of delegating key tasks to others flies in the face of successful people's desire to control their own destiny. The thinking goes, "If I am going to fail, at least I want to know it is because of something I did, not due to the incompetence of someone else." The great irony is that in the desire to retain control of everything, managers who are unable to effectively delegate are setting themselves up to lose the very control they seek.

In *The Education of an Accidental CEO*, David Novak, CEO of Yum Brands, tells of a conversation he had with basketball Hall of Famer Earvin "Magic" Johnson. Like many star athletes, Magic was a child prodigy. In junior leagues his team would win by 50 points and Earvin would score 80 percent of the points. At the end of the games, not only were Magic's opponents mad, but also his own teammates and their parents were upset that he was such a ball hog. No one else was having any fun. After awhile, Magic became alienated from everyone.

One day Magic realized he was going to have to get more people involved or no one would ever like him. That was when he decided to become a great passer. He found that the team still won by 50 points, but that he would only score about 25 percent of them and his teammates would score the rest. Everyone was happy working together and Magic learned to go from "me to we." Later, while in the NBA, he told Byron Scott that he would help him make the All Star team and told Kareem Abdul-Jabbar that he would help him score more points than anyone in NBA history.[2] Becoming an effective delegator it seems is a lot like developing into a great passer: achieving success yourself by helping others become more successful.

The formula for effective delegation is relatively straightforward. There are two phases to the process. Most managers get tripped up in the first phase and a sizeable number of others in the second phase. The first stage is all about providing associates with the appropriate visibility regarding the task and related parameters. The second involves a milestone feedback loop.

I cannot begin to tell you how often I am approached by people who were delegated a task, worked on it diligently for countless hours and, in the end, missed their bosses' intended mark by a mile. When this happens, the bosses' typical reaction is to throw a fit and complain to themselves about the incompetence of their people.

In my experience the failure of associates to satisfactorily complete delegated tasks is seldom due to the lack of capability or desire on the part of the associate who was assigned the task. It is usually a failure on the part of the manager to describe or articulate *specifically what* they want, *when* they want it, why it needs to be done and the type of *authority* their people have in the assignment.

Perhaps managers skip these steps because they are busy. Or maybe because the task is so straightforward in their mind they simply assume it is clear to the associate. Often it is because the manager may not even be sure what he really wants. In any event, it must be crystal clear in the associate's mind *what specifically you want, by when, why, and the level of authority they have in carrying out the task.*

The best way to ensure that you have properly communicated the "what, when, and why" of a delegated task is to have associates recite back their understanding of all these things. Or they can follow-up with an e-mail clarifying the approach they intend to take.

I know, I know, this seems like overkill, but believe me, you will be shocked how often what they say back to you does not bear the slightest resemblance to what you are asking them to do. What a huge time-saver this will be in the end when you make the effort up front to ensure they are on the proper path. And as a caution, define the outcomes you want and not the steps they should take to get there, unless there is a good reason for an exact set of steps to be followed. Providing *too specific* direction kills their enthusiasm and stifles their creativity.

The second stage of effective delegation is to schedule periodic meetings or request ongoing progress reports at key milestones along the way.

This should occur more frequently during the early phases of the project to make sure things are on track from the get-go. It should also take place more often with associates who are being "managed" for that particular task. The big failure here is that many executives seem to forget they are still on the hook for the results once a task gets removed from their personal "to do" list. By failing to check progress you are, in effect, abdicating instead of delegating.

Mistakes Caused by Delegation

The boss needs to step up and take the hit for a mistake made by her staff on a delegated task. This will almost always cause the person who made the error to try even harder the next time so as to not embarrass the boss.

In her bestselling book *Basic Black*, Cathie Black, CEO of Hearst Magazines, tells the story of how by effectively handling a faux pas by one of her staffers she actually ended up enhancing her reputation as a leader.

A story that ran in one of the Hearst magazines made reference to "The chairman of Estée Lauder, Ronald Lauder and his wife Evelyn." Unfortunately Ronald was not the chairman of the company and Evelyn was not his wife. The correct reference should have been to Ronald's brother, Leonard, who is married to Evelyn. Black said, "It was an innocent mistake, but an incredibly stupid one and once I was told about it, I knew I needed to fess up immediately. The Lauder Company spends millions of dollars on advertising and is a major advertiser in our magazines. I couldn't take the chance that our blunder would leave a bad taste in their chairman's mouth. And since I'd known Leonard Lauder for years, I wanted to apologize to him personally."

It turns out Black had to go to great lengths to even find Leonard, who was somewhere in Europe at the time. Not only did he graciously accept her mea culpa, he was later quoted as saying his regard for Cathie "had shot up into the stratosphere."[3]

Now not all mistakes you own up to will turn out this well. But it is certainly the right way to go about the business of correcting an error made by a staffer to whom you delegated a task.

💡 Don't Forget This 💡

By learning to accept the occasional mistakes of your people, they will be willing to step out and take more chances.

The man who was held responsible for one of the biggest marketing blunders of all time, the introduction of New Coke, resigned in disgrace as part of the fallout of that failed strategy. Nearly seven years later, the Coca Cola Company gave him another chance, saying, "We've become uncompetitive by not being tolerant of mistakes."[4] Today he continues to make positive contributions to Coca Cola's marketing efforts. As future Hall of Fame football coach Mike Holmgren says, "Success in life is going from failure to failure without failing. When a team gets badly beaten it doesn't forfeit the remaining games on its schedule. The coaches and players learn from their mistakes."[5] The key is to have a feedback loop to the associate about what went wrong, why, and how to take a different approach in the future. This of course takes time but, once again, it is time well spent in the long run.

A Three Pronged Approach to Mistakes

1. When you or one of your people make a mistake, see it, own it, admit it, learn from it and forget it. Don't admit your culpability in bits and pieces. Be conservative and announce worst-case scenarios. Any further

news after that will be perceived as good news.

2. Never try to cover up a mistake. We seem to be reminded every week that the cover up is almost always as bad or worse than the crime. Once we have fully accepted responsibility, we no longer have the anxiety associated with trying to hide something. And, if the leader demonstrates humility in the process, he has in effect already torn himself down. There is nothing left for people to do except ease up, empathize, and help the leader rebuild.

3. Tell your associates to quit looking in the rearview mirror. They should not keep beating themselves up about the mistake after the learning from it. To do otherwise risks your people falling into the fear of failure trap, which prevents them from performing in top form. Research indicates the more human the response, the quicker people are to forgive.

To end this discussion of performance management where we began, it is the key system that impacts the organization's ability to execute. Through diligent attention to target setting, delegation, empowerment, performance appraisal, and compensation in the manner just described, you can't help but see an immediate and positive impact on the performance of the institution.

CHAPTER 17

TURNAROUND SITUATIONS: Calling the Bomb Squad

Taking over a failing unit or organization is not for the faint of heart. Similar to what it takes to succeed as a member of a bomb squad, fortune favors those with ice in their veins. Despite the intense and mounting pressure, the leader needs to keep his wits about him. The situation needs to be analyzed before action is taken, but the timer is ticking loudly and one mistake can be catastrophic.

When the bomb squad arrives on the scene they never know exactly what they will face. Bombs consist of varying explosive compounds, have different triggering mechanisms, and the squad has more or less urgency depending upon how the timer was set. Likewise, every turnaround situation is also different. The trigger might be lack of cash, the explosive compound might be the product, service or strategy, and the timer may be set with precious little time left. In all cases it also involves bad people.

The David Schlotterbeck Turnaround Story

Few leaders have done turnarounds more successfully than Dave Schlotterbeck, CEO of CareFusion and a crack turnaround artist.[1] CareFusion is the sixth largest and organically the fastest growing medical technology company in the world, with 13,000 employees and $5 billion in revenue. Dave has successfully turned around seven different organizations in his career. His most famous turnaround was of Alaris Medical Systems. At the time he took over, the stock was trading at 31 cents per share and it was the most debt ridden medical technology company in the world, with 50 percent more debt than revenue. A few years later the company sold for $22 a share, giving people who invested when he took over a 7,000 percent return. Just prior to the sale, the stock was the best performing stock on all three U.S. exchanges for the prior twelve months. Here is the sequence he follows:

1. Recon The Situation

Quickly get a lay of the land. Dave suggests giving yourself two weeks at the very most. He usually targets four days. These will be sixteen-hour days. Talk to your major customers, direct staff, and a cross section of associates at all levels and if you are the new CEO, the board of directors and relevant analysts. Dave's favorite tactic is to talk with thirty people inside all parts of the organization. He asks them how the company got into the problem and what they think needs to happen. He says that inevitably a pattern emerges in the responses almost instantly. In his experience, most associates know the underlying problem. The goal is to gain perspective of the breadth and depth of the key issues.

2. Stop The Bleeding

In a turnaround Dave advises that the leader should unilaterally craft a short-term plan. The goal is to buy time to develop and execute the longer-term plan. Present this to your direct staff, invite their comments, and immediately incorporate any changes they propose that make sense. Then, have the plan typed up, and have everyone sign it. These are the "must dos."

The short-term plan may involve renegotiating credit, attempting to get creditors to settle existing debt at a discount, imposing a hiring and wage freeze, cutting discretionary spending, flushing out inventory, speeding up collections of accounts receivable, delaying accounts payable, laying off non-critical staff, letting go of problem customers, renegotiating union contracts, outsourcing service functions, eliminating marginal products or services, enlisting vendors to give emergency price reductions, selling off equipment or property, and leasing out unused space. Announce the short-term plan at a series of "all hands" meetings.

3. White Hats and Bad Actors

Often, poor performing people in key positions seem to be at the root of the problem. You need to quickly size up your team and separate your keepers from those who may need to be replaced. This should be done in a variety of ways, including one-on-one interviews, daily observation, asking a board member or outside consultant to conduct focus groups, and polling customers or vendors. One huge advantage in turnarounds is that the leader is usually given a level of trust immediately, since people realize a bomb is about to go off and that you aren't the one who planted it.

4. Clear the Area of Your Bad Actors All At Once, But Humanely

This will accomplish three things:

A. You will send a clear signal that there is a new sheriff in town and that incompetence, poor team play, politicking, or other dysfunctional behaviors will no longer be tolerated at any level. Give decent but not "over the top" severance packages. Employees at all levels will be watching how people are treated on their way out. Meet personally with each person who is terminated and explain why he or she is being let go. You don't want people bad mouthing the organization, as it will make it more difficult to recruit their replacements.

B. You will demonstrate that you are capable of bold, decisive action and that there is a firm hand on the tiller.

C. You will be in a position to honestly communicate to your remaining staff that you don't anticipate any more personnel changes at their level. Reassure them that they are the team who will fix things going forward. This will be a huge anxiety reducer and the beginning of getting your staff to pull in the same direction. Dave said the hardest part of turnarounds is in the execution, not in the diagnosis. The diciest part of the execution is changing the culture and getting the senior team aligned.

5. With Your Team, Craft the Medium Range Plan

Take your team off site for several days. The object will be to build the staff into an executive *team* and craft a plan for the next twelve months that the entire senior team can get behind.

Give everyone ten questions to answer. Then ask each member to craft a twenty-minute presentation revolving around their answers to the questions.

- What are our current weaknesses as a business? What can we do to overcome these?

- What are our customers' most frequent complaints about us?

- How can we get additional revenue from existing customers or products?

- What are your suggestions for improving our sales and marketing efforts?

- Where should our new product development efforts be targeted?

- What internal processes most need improvement?

- What are the top three things we as a senior leadership team should do over the next year to make our business more successful?

- What are the top three things the leader (you) should do over the next year to make our business more successful?

- What positions do we need to add to or eliminate from our team? Do we need to structure the organization differently? If so, how?

- What are the most important financial objectives we should focus on over the next year?

Each senior staff member makes his presentation to the others. Then, everyone agrees upon the medium range plan.

6. Meet With Affected Parties and Explain The Plan

It is crucial that key constituents such as all associates, large creditors, important suppliers, the board of directors, and investors know in the appropriate level of detail what the plan is going forward. This may keep people on the fence from jumping ship and begin to create some positive buzz.

7. Make Needed Lower Level Employee Cutbacks ASAP

The lower levels need to know that those who remain are also on the team going forward. It is important that people not be waiting for the other shoe to drop. You want them to be looking ahead to better times.

8. Select New Executive Team Members

Attracting "A" players to fill critical slots vacated by the bad actors who were let go will create confidence in the organization that the plans can be executed and that the company is still a desirable place to work.

9. Create Positive Energy

A. Boost sales commissions.

B. Pay spot bonuses for creative work.

C. Celebrate individual and team successes, no matter how small.

D. Communicate through multiple vehicles more frequently than you would in more "normal" times. Dave suggests being realistic with people. Usually the prior management has not shared the "brutal facts." People want hope, but they also want to know the exact condition of the business.

E. Publicize the most promising new product development effort that you are funding.

F. Have breakfast, lunches, and barbecues with associates and customers.

G. Create upbeat contests of all kinds with many winners.

H. Keep your eyes open for indicators, positive events, even if its small, that tell you things are beginning to change. Take the time to point these out to others who may not have noticed. People need to know that energy they are putting out is producing results. This momentum is crucial to build into the larger successes down the road.

Tough decisions on all aspects of the business need to be made quickly in a turnaround situation. Key people need to be retained. Poor performers need to be let go. Bleeding needs to stop and intermediate goals and plans created and executed. Positive energy needs to be restored. Leading such an effort is one of the most difficult of all leadership challenges. But the results are evident quickly, usually within six months, and the payoff is potentially great.

CHAPTER 18

TAKING OVER A NEW ORGANIZATION:
There's A New Sheriff In Town

There are always three main objectives in any transition. First is to avoid alienating your most valuable associates. Second is to gain insight into the situation you are stepping into. Third is to build your credibility inside and outside the organization.

Avoiding Alienation

One of the biggest mistakes leaders often make when they take over a new assignment is to be too critical of past leaders, decisions, policies, strategies, or performance of the organization. This immediately causes people to hunker down and get defensive. It also begins to set up a "new" vs. "old" schism in the organization.

When a new leader arrives on the scene, there is almost always a lot of angst among the people. At minimum everyone knows they will have to prove themselves to a new boss. Beyond that people worry about their job security or how much they will be expected to change. Since it is human nature to crave stability, both of these thoughts are anxiety producing. Some tension is good and will help you get things moving, but too much can cripple a team. Communicate in both large and more intimate settings, set a positive tone, and listen intently to the concerns of the organization's key associates.

Gain Insight

A common pitfall of executives parachuting into new situations is to spring into unfocused activity before they know the lay of the land. How can someone new to the organization possibly know the solutions until he knows the problems? It is very important to learn the history of how the organization got to where it is today.

Tales From The Workplace

One of my clients had grown from nothing to a nearly $800-million company due largely to the efforts of four people. One of the four gave up the CEO slot and settled into the chairman of the board role. The other three continued to run the company as if it were the "mom and pop" operation they grew up in. It quickly became apparent that the size of the business had eclipsed their talents. So they began the process of adding five outsiders to the executive team over a period of two years.

As each of the newcomers came into the organization they immediately began to make significant changes. Many of their ideas were spot on as to what was needed to turn this enterprise into a more professionally managed operation. However, many other ideas could not possibly have worked in this setting due to several unique factors, not the least of which is that the firm has only a handful of customers. The old guard rejected the new arrivals out of hand, pooh-poohing any suggestions as coming from a position of complete naiveté. The newcomers saw the old-timers as a bunch of bumbling buffoons that time had passed by. Both sides developed animosity and became further entrenched in the "rightness" of their views.

Stepping into a new assignment, you need to know how and why past decisions were made that led to the current situation. You need data on who has what types of talents and who seems to be incapable of handling their roles. It is important to determine who can be trusted and which people in the organization have the most influence.

It should become apparent the appropriateness of accepted norms of behavior and what key systems, policies, procedures, and processes are working and which are broken. Less apparent will be sacred cows that cannot be messed with or potential skeletons in the closet that cannot be disturbed. At some point it should become clear whether the culture is functional or toxic.

In listening mode, it is vital to get a wide variety of inputs from various perspectives. Where appropriate, you might consider talking to current or former customers, suppliers and consultants or outside analysts in addition to people in all parts of the organization.

Facing Five Scenarios

Generally there are five different scenarios a leader might be walking into: startup, turnaround, dark clouds on the horizon, breakthrough, or maintaining excellence.

Startup

This is the one scenario where making immediate decisions will likely have more positive than negative effects. The most important thing is to surround yourself with a talented team as quickly as possible.

In a startup situation a clear and focused strategy is essential so people don't spend a lot of effort spinning their wheels on things that will later have to be undone.

Turnaround

In this scenario it is undeniable that something is broken and major changes need to be made. Despite the pressure for quick action, it is still vitally important to gain insight through the process described earlier. Usually turnaround situations require that you need to remove poor performers. Do this as soon as you can identify who they are. This is where multiple inputs are absolutely critical but in the end you have to use your own judgment. I cannot tell you how many times a client has led me to believe that certain managers were ineffective and others were stars. But after I dug into the situation, I came to find just the opposite.

Spend some money on an outsider to conduct in-depth interviews of your key players, supplemented with 360-degree evaluations and conversations with appropriate stakeholders such as customers or board members. This will shorten your learning curve dramatically as well as give you confidence in your personnel decisions.

Don't forget to let your real stars know that there is a place for them on your team. Never assume they know you consider them to be valuable. In a turnaround, *everyone* gets a little nervous and you may inadvertently lose your "keepers" simply due to the fact that they were never reassured of your high opinion of them.

Dark Clouds on the Horizon

In this scenario the problems are not immediate or critical, but there is surely a storm brewing. Perhaps there are new competitors entering the market or a technological shift in the industry could mean trouble if the organization fails to respond. The challenge here is to get everyone to understand the implications of the new realities.

Whenever possible it is a good idea to get people to see for themselves the need for change. Town Hall meetings across the organization are an excellent vehicle to generate a sense of urgency.

Usually missions will have to be rethought and resources will need to be redeployed to reflect the new priorities. Perhaps the culture will need to change to promote the behaviors necessary to stop the slide.

Breakthrough

In a breakthrough scenario the organization just can't seem to get over the hump to become an undisputed champion. The San Diego Chargers fired Coach Marty Schottenheimer after a 14-2 season because he couldn't win a playoff game. The Dallas Mavericks dumped Avery Johnson even though he was named Coach of the Year in a previous season. The Detroit Pistons sacked Flip Saunders despite his having the highest winning percentage of any coach in history with his length of tenure. None of these men could get their teams over that last hurdle to win a championship.

The idea in a breakthrough scenario is for the leader to make adjustments that will propel the organization to the next level. Usually massive changes would be a mistake. A little tinkering on the edges here and there, plus a revitalization of the environment is typically what is called for. You certainly don't want to disturb the core that has led to success.

Maintaining Excellence

Taking over a winner is not always the dream job it may appear to be on the surface. It is tough to maintain excellence in sports or in business. People and organizations tend to get complacent when things are going well. This is a scenario where inducing some anxiety into the system is actually a necessary tactic to use.

A leader's first order of business in this instance is to fully understand why the organization has been successful. When Coach Mike Tomlin inherited a Pittsburgh Steelers team from Bill Cowher one year removed from winning the Super Bowl, he realized a lot of it was due to Defensive Coordinator Dick LeBeau and his 3-4 defense. Even though Tomlin is a proponent of the 4-3 defense, he realized he did not have the personnel to execute it right away. So he let LeBeau, perhaps the greatest defensive mind the game has ever known, continue to run the 3-4 while he set about opening up the offense. The result was that he was able to take the Steelers back to the playoffs in his first season and won the Super Bowl in his second season, becoming the youngest coach ever to do so.

When Jeff Immelt took over one of America's most successful corporations at General Electric from the legendary Jack Welch, he kept the culture intact, but set about reconfiguring GE's portfolio of companies to focus more on "green" businesses, nanotechnology, and other emerging fields. While the stock price is artificially low due to the overall poor performance of the market, GE continues its tradition of building for the long haul under Immelt's stewardship.

Essential Knowledge

In a nutshell, the leader's job when taking over a successful organization is to preserve the fabric of the enterprise while inventing challenges and making changes that enable the organization to stay at the top of its game.

Building Credibility

There are two parts to gaining credibility. One is to let people get to know you, your style, and your principles. The other is to adopt a few practices that people have been trying to implement but have so far been stymied by the system. Another suggestion would be to get rid of some things that have served to frustrate people.

Some years ago the San Diego Police Department's morale was low. When new Chief Jerry Sanders (currently the mayor of San Diego and a change-focused leader) took over, he did two simple things to bolster morale. First he ordered that the ugly lime green police cruisers be painted black and white to project a more professional image, and second he adopted a proposal that had languished for some time to update the officers uniforms to more of an elite SWAT-type look. These changes cost very little money but had a positive impact on morale and showed that Chief Sanders was interested in and capable of making their work lives better.

Things like painting the facility, providing updated tools, equipment or furniture, or throwing an "all hands" barbecue would be things worth considering. Also perhaps eliminating, shortening, or improving meetings or cutting the number and size of reports in half are ideas that would effectively send a strong signal that you are a different kind of leader.

Drawing a Line In the Sand

From day one a leader can and should clarify his expectations regarding behavior. On President Barak Obama's first day in office, he signed an executive order freezing the salaries of anyone on the White House staff whose salary was $100,000 or more. While this was largely symbolic, it sent a very clear signal of change. Too often, leaders forget the importance of symbolism in the change process. Perhaps it is setting some ground rules for interaction, emphasizing the importance of being on time for meetings, returning all e-mails within 24 hours or tolerating no spelling errors in documents. The idea is to send an unmistakable signal that some things are going to be different immediately.

Prior to Lou Gerstner taking charge at IBM, the company was famous for its Blue Suit, White Shirt look. The company also had become an "Also Ran." On his first day on the job, Gerstner wore a blue shirt. Now, he claims it was just a coincidence. But if you believe that I've got some swampland in Florida I'd like to sell you. Such a small act sent a powerful message that it was time to re-evaluate everything regarding how the organization was doing business.

Any leader will ultimately fail without a good team. Make sure you keep the stars you inherit and don't dally in getting rid of the bad apples. Don't make too many unilateral moves right away — get buy-in. Be careful of trying to do too much — focus. Use your staff and key lieutenants to carry out tasks with people with whom they have already established a good relationship.

Remember that your peers are also a key constituent group. Don't get so caught up managing upward and downward that you fail to develop allies. Don't squander your first 100 days.

CHAPTER 19

AVOIDING BURNOUT: Through The Circle of Life

In turbulent times many leaders tend to pour all their energy into their work. To some extent, spending more time focused on the job is both a situationally driven necessity as well as being a smart political move. After all, if a leader seems both highly committed and indispensable it is less likely the ax will fall in his direction. But to some extent this strategy is also "fools gold."

An imbalanced allocation of resources may well lead to peak performance or happiness for a short time. However, because life gets less fulfilling and complete when there is too much of an imbalance, long-term performance and enjoyment of life suffer.

Don't Forget This
People who invest all their energy into work
that is unenjoyable eventually burn out.

We all know people who became successful in a line of work they

FIGURE A

Circle of Life

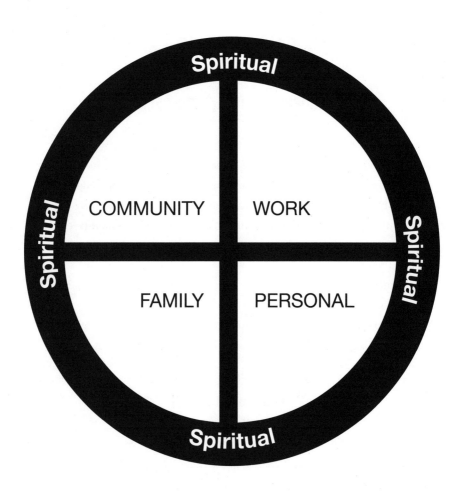

never really liked. Later, they always seem to regret not having done something they really *wanted* to do.

Then there are other folks who over invest in work that they do enjoy, but they make the mistake of sacrificing their health, family, or community in the process. One such person who learned a valuable lesson is Jerry Colangelo, the successful owner of the Phoenix Suns basketball team and the former World Champion Arizona Diamondbacks baseball club. After nearly working himself to death earlier in his career, Jerry said he "resolved to never again get so caught up in my business, no matter how exciting or important, that I allowed it to steal too much time from my family."[1]

The opposite side of the coin is former America's Cup sailing winner Dennis Connor. He claims you can't have a balanced life and still be successful. To become a dominant sailor he settled for being, by his own admission, a mediocre father. He said, "I'm not proud to say it, but my family hasn't been number one. You have to draw up your priorities. My wife knew the situation before we married. We postponed our wedding three times because I had to go sailing."[2] I don't recall of hearing people on their deathbed say they wish they paid less attention to their health or family. Perhaps Dennis Connor might, but he would be an unusual exception.

Likewise, there are many people who invest heavily in themselves and family, but fail to make the sacrifices that could have enabled them to be financially successful in their work. They never seem to have enough money for travel, hobbies, or early retirement.

High performance and personal fulfillment over the long haul requires fusing ability and enjoyment while creating balance in the five core areas of our lives. Figure A depicts the circle of life. The rim is our values or spirituality. In essence it is the glue that holds our work, personal, family, and community lives together. These five areas are interdependent and in conflict for most people. Each segment demands our commitment, time, energy and attention. Since these resources are finite, we are forced to make choices about how they are allocated.

It is difficult to maintain balance because of the "seesaw effect." Once the seesaw begins to tilt, it continues to move in the same direction due to the weight of shifting momentum. It is no different in life. Once additional resources are invested in one area or another, the relative chances for success or happiness in that part of life increase. This further adds to the imbalance. The higher our performance or satisfaction, the easier it becomes psychologically to justify an even larger commitment of resources into that area.

Why not go for success in all areas?

Spiritual Goals

America's most influential spiritual leader, Rick Warren, pastor of one of the largest and best known churches in the world, Saddleback Church in Orange County, Calif., believes it all starts with a spiritual center. In the best-selling non-fiction book, *The Purpose Driven Life*, Rick states, "The purpose of your life is far greater than your own personal fulfillment, your peace of mind or even your happiness. It's far greater than your family, your career or even your wildest dreams and ambitions."

If you don't have a solid spiritual grounding, success in the other areas of your life will be fleeting and will fail to alleviate that feeling of emptiness that the spiritually bankrupt often report experiencing.[3]

Work/Career Goals

People who can find a way to make money doing things they truly love create a virtuous cycle. Because of the passion they put into the job they tend to excel at it. Since they are performing well, they are increasingly likely to love the work even more. If there aren't many other things they would rather be doing, the job really doesn't feel like work. But how do *you* go about finding out what *you* love and what *you* excel at?

When we began life, we were each given a key ring with several keys on it. Few people are talented in just one thing. These keys are our natural gifts. Throughout our lives each time we master a new skill or learn something significant, we gain a new key for our key ring.

Determining our distinctive competence involves taking stock of our natural gifts, learned abilities, and personal desires. Once we have done this, our goal will be to restructure our lives in such a way as to take advantage of these things. When beginning the search for distinctive competencies, the task may seem overwhelming, like trying to take a drink from a fire hose. Things get sorted out quickly however as the process unfolds.

In the late 1980s Rickey Bolden was enjoying a successful and highly lucrative career as a professional football player for the Cleveland Browns. On a steamy August day in the middle of his seventh training camp he suddenly stopped, removed his pads, and walked off the field never to return. He claims he received a personal vision that he should start a ministry.

As a football star, Rickey was indeed talented. But as an evangelist he has blossomed into one of the most compelling speakers I have ever had the privilege of hearing. His leadership has changed more lives than he could ever have touched in his prior occupation. He works with the *broke, busted, and disgusted* to help them ride out the storms of their lives and discover their true calling.

Personal Goals

Robert Louis Stevenson once said, "To know what you prefer and follow your preferences, instead of blindly following someone else's prescription of how you should lead your life, is to have kept your soul alive." We seem to be too obsessed with acquiring things we don't need, with cash we don't have, to please people we don't even care about. Stop acquiring — start enjoying.

As far as making sure your interests are not crowded out by everything else in life, I offer you the following exercise. I do it religiously January 1st and July 4th, and it is the most important thing I do all year.

Step 1: Take out a sheet of paper and write down twenty things you love to do. That is the only criterion. It does not matter if you have done them recently or are even any good at doing them. Just list twenty things you love. If you have trouble coming up with twenty, it might be an indication that your life has gotten out of balance. Force yourself to list as many as you can.

Step 2: Read over the list and circle any of those things you would like to make a commitment to do more of in the coming six months than you have in the previous six months.

Step 3: Take out your yearly planner and schedule time for those things *first*. Otherwise you will wake up at the end of the year and realize you actually did very few of them. This is how you make sure you are living life on your terms instead of someone else's. And, don't feel the least bit guilty about it. This segment of your life is all about being a little selfish as long as it is in balance with the other areas of your life. The people most afraid to die are the ones that know they never really lived.

In my own life I realized that in addition to work, family, community, and spirituality, that I am the type of person who likes to do a little of a lot of different things. So for me, I try to schedule time to attend NFL games, especially the Super Bowl, see at least a few basketball, baseball, and hockey games, water and snow ski, go whitewater rafting, play tennis, run, work out, see many movies, attend a few concerts or plays, travel to remote islands, sightsee, go to museums, host a few parties, and attend a few charity events.

Family Goals

Of course family includes blood relatives. But it can and should include so much more than this. It might include fraternity brothers or sorority sisters. Possibly high school or college buddies. Perhaps current or former neighbors, or co-workers. In short, people who bring or have brought the greatest richness to your life.

My brother-in-law George Bauman died a year ago. His funeral was one of the most impressive I have ever attended. He dedicated his life to serving others. Among many other things George was a former fire chief of the local volunteer fire department. In his Army days, he was a medic. He literally founded the emergency medical services unit in his city. He spent his career as a high school guidance counselor. All vocations that benefited others.

Throughout the viewing and funeral, hundreds of police, fire fighters and EMS first responders paraded past the casket in full dress uniforms, giving one final salute to their departed comrade. Hundreds more of George's neighbors, former students and friends also showed up to pay their last respects.

The funeral procession was led by dozens of police cruisers, fire trucks, and ambulances with lights flashing. Cars stretched for blocks. And, when the hearse passed the fire station on the way to the church, the fire whistle blew one last time as a color guard stood at attention saluting a 50-foot-flag draped atop the extended ladder of a fire truck. At the church, there was a gun salute and military flag ceremony with the folded flag presented to my sister. This was a man with many friends.

Ask yourself, *"What will my funeral be like?"* More importantly, after the ceremony is over and a couple months pass, who would *really* miss you? That list will undoubtedly be a lot shorter. But, *those* are the people I am talking about when I refer to family.

We all get busy and lose sight of the people who really enriched our lives — I am no exception. More than a decade ago I realized that among the happiest days of my life were my college years with my fraternity brothers. I was president of Theta Chi Fraternity and roughly 120 guys were around sometime during those four years. Yet a decade ago I was in regular contact with only three.

So I took it upon myself to encourage the other three to work with me to reconnect with the guys of our youth via a first-ever reunion. We got the names and contact information from the university and national headquarters of the fraternity. We divided up the list and were able to get forty to attend the reunion. In addition to that, since I travel so much I sought to invite others to dinner when I am in their city. That has allowed me to reconnect with twenty more over the years. These days several of us have an annual reunion at my home in Lake Arrowhead.

Most important of all, I realized twenty years ago that my son Chad was the center of my universe. It took me the first year of his life to truly learn this however. Chad was born a few weeks prematurely. I had blocked out two weeks of no out-of-town travel on both sides of his due date thinking this would provide a comfortable cushion. I was conducting one of my seminars in Seattle when the call came from my wife in San Diego that she had just gone into labor. I still had half my program to conduct and most of the class had flown in from out of town to attend, so I couldn't just leave. I was lucky enough to find someone to cover for me the final day. I raced to the airport only to find the flight was delayed an hour. Once reaching San Diego I broke all known speed records getting the twenty-five miles from the airport to the hospital. But when I arrived I was twenty minutes too late. His mother couldn't stand the pain any longer and had the physician induce labor.

Being premature it was not certain if my son would be healthy or even survive the night. They kept him for a few days in the hospital until he was through the worst of it. That first night home he was jaundiced and barely bigger than my hand. I was so afraid he would die that I laid him on my chest all night and prayed for him to grow strong.

After all that you would think Chad would have remained the most important person in my life. But alas, work called and before you knew it a year or so had passed and he didn't command a lot of time on my schedule. Then I had my own near death experience.

A late spring tornado over Lake Michigan sent the airplane I was aboard into a tailspin. A series of *barrel rolls* caused the plane to plunge nearly 13,000 feet. By some miracle the pilot was able to steady the aircraft less than 1,000 feet from crashing into the lake, saving us all from certain death. Suffice it to say, that is when I learned the importance of doing the Three Step exercise previously described, making sure my family would not be crowded out by pressures of daily life.

I realized that life without my son at the center of it would be a shallow life indeed. At that moment I made sure my schedule reflected his importance to me. I began to take him with me on business trips. I carved out time for him on the weekends. I made sometimes heroic efforts to attend his games or musical and theater performances. I once flew from San Diego to Charlotte, North Carolina, to see him and his drum corps perform for 10 minutes just because I had made him a promise to do so. Over the years he became my best friend.

Community Goals

We are all part of something much larger than ourselves. All volunteer organizations seem to have an even greater shortage of leadership than the world in general. And, if you have diligently read this book, you realize how few effective leaders there are in even the best organizations.

Start small; pick something you are passionate about. Perhaps it is the PTA. Maybe the Make-A-Wish Foundation or Habitat for Humanity are more your cup of tea. Volunteer to lead something. It is through the spirit of giving back that we all fulfill those best qualities of our own spirit.

Feeding Off Interdependence

In actuality the five areas of our lives are not walled off from one another. Each is inextricably intertwined with the other. Sir Richard Branson said, "I don't think of work as work and play as play. It's all living. It is like two people sleeping on a waterbed. When one moves, the other always feels the effects."

When I first looked at my time and effort allocation twenty years ago, it was about 70 percent work, 15 percent self, 15 percent family, less than 1 percent community, and 0 percent spiritual. Not surprisingly, my personal life and family life were not that great and community was something of an afterthought. Shockingly though, my work was good, but not at all "A" player level, despite my huge allocation of time and energy. I felt the beginning stages of burnout at the tender age of 35 and was often terribly unhappy.

Today my allocation is about 30 percent work, 20 percent self, 30 percent family, 10 percent community and 10 percent spiritual. With this relative balance I have never felt more effective, especially in business, despite putting in half the time and effort that I used to put in.

For me it all began with an investment in community. Twenty years ago I started giving several weeks a year to charitable and community causes. I was asked to serve on the executive cabinet of the United Way. That modest step has since mushroomed into such wide-ranging causes as Project Rainbow, Make A Wish Foundation, the Union of Pan Asian Communities, San Diego Hall of Champions Sports Museum, and the Boy Scouts.

One instance stands out that changed my perspective. I had just finished an exhausting year on the executive cabinet of the San Diego United Way Campaign. I was so relieved it was over so that I could get on with my regular life. United Way always ends the campaign year with a huge banquet honoring the volunteers.

At the conclusion of the evening, members of the campaign cabinet were each presented with a small gift box. In mine was a handmade wind chime; attached to it was a note that read, "Dear Dr. Hanes, thank you so much for your help in raising money for the United Way Campaign. I am an 18-year-old paraplegic. It took me several weeks to make this gift for you. I wanted to give you this as a reminder of what your hard work was about. Through your efforts the program which has allowed me to develop these skills will be funded for another year." Talk about a lump in the throat misty-eyed moment.

The cabinet members were asked to adjourn immediately to another smaller room for some concluding thank yous. As I entered the room with tears still welling in my eyes from reading the note, next year's campaign chair was at the door shaking my hand with an invitation to join him on next year's cabinet. Three hours before this moment I was exhausted and thankful it was all over. Then in a matter of seconds I couldn't possibly have said "no." I was hooked, and this time for life.

Every minute I spend in the community makes me feel better about myself. And when I feel good about myself, people tell me that my work gets better. They say I seem more passionate about teaching. Then, when my work is going well, people close to me say, "Wow, you seem so energized and alive. You are so much easier and more fun to be around." And when people close to me praise me like that, I can't help but feel better about myself.

When I began to reach out to my extended "family" I got an unexpected bonus. One of my long lost fraternity brothers had by this time become a vice president of a major organization. After reconnecting I was offered a chance to do some work for his company. This provided me with some additional funds that I could devote to the community. This of course started that whole process of feeling better about myself, and so on.

Next, I started investing more into myself. I began to eat healthier, exercise more regularly, and ultimately dropped some excess weight. This gave me more energy and my work got better. With work going well my family became more supportive and this allowed me the chance to do some things that had been pushed into the background, like river rafting.

Finally, my wife Mariann reintroduced me to the spiritual aspect of life that I had long since abandoned. Sexually molested as a child in a Catholic grade school, I had pretty much turned my back on organized religion. With her guiding the way, she has awakened me to the wondrous life that God has in store for me. With newfound inner peace my work got better, which allowed me more time in the community, which made me feel better about myself — you get the idea.

So you see, effort to create balance in my most deficient area led to that virtuous cycle of positive reinforcing actions in the other four areas. Today I have never been happier or more effective in all areas of my life. I know that your choosing to live a more balanced life will do the same for you.

Balanced Life Self-Assessment

1. Do you *really* enjoy your work? If not, what are you going to do to change the situation?

2. Are you paying the proper attention to your health and family? If not, what are you going to do about it?

3. Are you as financially successful as you would like to be? If not, what is your plan to make yourself financially independent?

4. Have you found your spiritual foundation? If not, what will it take for you to do this?

5. Do you set aside enough time for the things *you* really *love* to do? If not, when are you going to do this?

6. What friends would you like to reconnect with? When are you going to make the effort?

7. How can you help the community at large?

CHAPTER 20

CONCLUSION: This Too Shall Pass

Imagine a 1,000-pound marshmallow. It would probably be as big as a tractor-trailer. Now visualize trying to push this huge thing up a hill. The harder you push, the further into the marshmallow you go until you find yourself completely absorbed by it. This is what trying to change an organization is often like. *It* doesn't move. You get overwhelmed by it.

By following the advice put forth in this book, a leader can shrink the size of the marshmallow to a point where it can easily be pushed in any direction he desires.

Basically there are only three reasons to push for change. To resolve an issue, head off an impending problem, or capitalize on an opportunity. Make sure people fully understand the reason you are asking them to change.

Only embark on change if it is vital the change be implemented and you are willing to "buck up" and provide an appropriate resource level so people have a fighting chance of success.

Always remember that people will tolerate massive amounts of pain if they believe they have some choice in the matter, but will resist even minor changes if they feel disenfranchised. This is why it is usually better to institute some changes like a dress code from the bottom up, rather than top down. Co-opt associates into the change process by getting them to make frequent suggestions as to how things should proceed.

At times during the change process people might get discouraged. Leaders may need to "manufacture" a win or focus on a few small wins to reenergize the group. Never be reluctant to take a time out to re-group or to celebrate a success.

People will work harder at change and be able to do it more quickly if they trust the change agent, are clear on what they need to do differently, have the ability to do what you are asking them to do, and see a benefit they value for complying with your wishes. People are also more willing to change if they believe others have to make similar changes.

Remember, a paper towel can only absorb so much water before it becomes saturated. People are the same way. Watch your associates' absorption levels. If they have already gone through a lot of change at work it may be difficult to get them to absorb more. Also, if they have had a lot of change in their home life they may be able to tolerate less at work at the moment than you would ordinarily think.

We Americans are a resilient bunch. In my lifetime alone, our Eastern and Southern coastal areas have survived dozens of devastating hurricanes with names like Andrew, Hugo and Katrina. Citizens in our heartland have had to pick up the pieces after tornados ravaged towns from Alma, Kansas to Xenia, Ohio. In Arizona, California, Colorado and New Mexico, massive wildfires destroyed thousands of homes and displaced millions of people. On the West Coast, earthquakes from Alaska to Southern California collapsed hundreds of bridges and pancaked miles of double-decker highways. Hundred-year floods caused swollen rivers to swallow up homes from Minnesota to Louisiana. Yet each time, those directly affected somehow managed to summon the strength to rebuild, often improving what was there before in the process.

Growing up in Pittsburgh, Pennsylvania, I saw its coalmines abandoned and most of its vaunted steel and aluminum factories shuttered. Yet the city has been reborn, having transformed itself into a high-tech, medical, and biotech hub. The city of Cleveland, Ohio went bankrupt, lost its

NFL team when it chose not to replace its decrepit stadium and had a major river so polluted that it actually caught fire near "the flats." Amazingly, Cleveland's downtown now boasts a thriving theater district, "the flats" is a mecca for nightlife, and its football franchise now plays in a gleaming state-of-the-art stadium. San Diego saw the exodus of much of its aerospace industry, but today is one of our nation's most desirable places to work. In each instance it took perseverance and change-focused leadership to solve these problems and positively alter the course of history. And so it will be with the challenges we are faced with today.

Leading for change usually begins with only you in a rowboat launching off in a new direction. A few people may choose to join you in the boat and help you row. But there will be some people standing on the shore throwing rocks at your boat trying to sink it. The bulk of the people will not be in the boat or on shore. They will be in the water hanging onto the boat trying to decide whether to climb aboard and start rowing, or swim to shore and join the rock throwers. Your job as a leader is to convince them to quickly get into the boat and help you row. Following the strategies for business success in uncertain times will greatly accelerate your ability to do just that!

End Notes

Chapter 1

1 Eileen C. Shapiro, *How Corporate Truths Become Competitive Traps* (New York: John Wiley & Sons, 1991), 121.
2 Interview with Marcie Edwards, June 17, 2008.
3 Interview with Brian Burke, June 26, 2008.
4 USA Today, *Hard Decisions Don't Deter FCC Chief Martin*, (Leslie Cauley, January 14, 2009), 3B.
5 Interview with Christine Fox, July 18, 2008.

Chapter 2

1 Donald J. Trump with Meredith McIver, *Trump: How to Get Rich* (New York: Ramdom House, 2004), 15-16

Chapter 3

1 Business Week, January 19,2009, 42.
2 Michael Jordan, Mark Vencil, Steve Ross. *For the Love of The Game: My Story* (New York, Random House, 1999).

Chapter 4

1 Bradford D. Smart, *Top Grading: How leading companies win by hiring, coaching and keeping the best people* (New York, Prentice Hall, 1999), 2.
2 Ibid., 21.
3 Jim Collins. *Good to Great: Why some companies make the leap... and others don't* (New York, Harper Collins, 2001)41-42.
4 Gene Weingaren, *Pearls Before Breakfast*, (Washington Post, April 8, 2007), 10.

Chapter 6

1 Brian Billick and James Patterson, *Competitive Leadership: 12 Principles For Success* (New York: Triumph Books, 2001), 167.
2 Dean Smith and Gerald D. Bell, *The Carolina Way: Leadership Lessons From A Life In Coaching* (New York: Penguin Press, 2004), 29.

3 Ibid., 18.

4 Andrew Seligman. Associated Press, June 10, 2008.

5 Robert I. Sutton, *The No Asshole Rule: Building A Civilized Workplace And Surviving One That Isn't* (New York: Hachette Books, 2007), 67.

6 Pat Summitt with Sally Jenkins, *Raise The Roof: The Inspiring Inside Story Of The Tennessee Lady Vols' Ground Breaking Season In Women's College Basketball* (New York: Broadway Books, 1998), 66.

7 Ibid., 65.

8 Fortune Magazine, *"Casey Feldman Fortune Q & A."* July 21, 2008, P. 54.

9 J. Richard Hackman, *Leading Teams: Setting the Stage for Great Performances* (Boston: Harvard Business School Publishing, 2002), 55.

10 Frank Lafasto and Carl Larson, *When Teams Work Best* (Thousand Oaks, CA: Sage Publications, 2001), 78.

11 Summitt. Pg. 195.

12 Hackman. Pg. 200.

Note

The concept of teams going through predictable stages comes from Tuckman, B.W. Developmental Sequence In Small Groups, Psychological Bulletin, 63 (1965).

Chapter 7

1 Bill George, *Authentic Leadership: Rediscovering the Secrets to Creating Lasting Value* (San Francisco: Jossey Bass, 2003), 2.

2 Meet the Press with Tim Russert, 12-23-01.

3 Robert Townsend. *Further up the organization: How to Stop Management from Stifling People and Strangling Productivity* (New York: Alfred A. Knopf, 1984), 49.

4 Gordon Bethune with Scott Huler. *From Worst To First: Behind The Scenes Of Continental Airlines Remarkable Comeback* (New York: John Wiley & Sons, 1998).

5   Oren Harari. *The Leadership Secrets Of Colin Powell* (New York: McGraw-Hill, 2002), 35.

6   USA Today, July 11, 2008. *Women Break To The Front of Tech*. Jon Swartz. P. 2B.

7   Interview with Mike Burns, November 2008.

8   Carly Fiorina, *Tough Choices: A Memoir* (New York: Penguin Group USA, 2006), 277-292.

9   Patricia Sellers, Lessons From The Fall, Fortune Magazine, Volume 157, No. 12, June 9, 2008, 70-78.

10 Jim Collins, *Good To Great: Why Some Companies Make The Leap And Others Don't* (New York: Harper Collins, 2001), 21.

11 Stephen R. Covey, *Principle Centered Leadership* (New York: Summit Books, 1990), 219.

12 Cari Ressler and Jody Thompson, *Why Work Sucks: And How To Fix That* (New York: Penguin Group, 2008).

13 Quote often attributed to Steven R. Covey.

14 William D. Hitt, *Ethics and Leadership* (Columbus, Ohio, Battelle Press, 1990), 99.

15 The Canyon Press, Connecticut Lawmakers Want Calhoun Reprimanded, 2-26-09.

Chapter 8

1   Terrence E. Deal and Allan A. Kennedy, *Corporate Cultures: The Rites and Rituals of Corporate Life* (New York: Addison Wesley Publishing, 1982), 4.

2   Terrence E. Deal and Allan A. Kennedy, *The New Corporate Cultures: Revitalizing The Workplace After Downsizing, Mergers and Reengineering* (New York: Perseus Books, 1999), 1.

Chapter 9

1   David Novak and John Boswell, *The Education Of An Accidental CEO: Lessons Learned From The Trailer Park to the Corner Office* (New York: Crown Business, 2007), 162.

2   Kevin and Jackie Freiberg, *Guts: Companies That Blow The Doors Off Business As Usual* (New York: Currency Doubleday, 2004), 140.

3   Joseph A. Michelli, *The New Gold Standard: 5 Leadership Principles For Creating A Legendary Customer Experience Courtesy of The Ritz Carton Hotel Company*, 38.

4   USA Today. The Mets Personality Makeover, June 24, 2008, C1-2.

5   Pat Riley, *Showtime: Inside The Lakers Breakthrough Season* (New York: Warner Books, 1988), 31-32.

6   The gist of the Eisner-Iger story came from Business Week, How Bob Iger Unchained Disney (Ronald Grover, February 5, 2007), 74-79.

7   Michael LeBoeuf, *The Greatest Management Principle In The World* (New York: G.P. Putnam and Sons, 1985).

Chapter 10

1   Geoff Colvin, Leader Machines, Fortune Magazine, October 1, 2007, 100.

2   The Karate Kid, 1984, Delphi Films.

3   Ram Charan, Stephan Drotter, James Noel, *The Leadership Pipeline: How To Build The Leadership Powered Company* (San Francisco: Jossey-Bass, 2001), 33-42.

4   Diane Brady and Jena McGregor, What Works In Women's Networks, Business Week, June 18, 1997, 59.

5   Ibid., Pp. 65-74.

Chapter 11

1   J.R. Moehringer, *23 Reasons Why A Profile Of Pete Carroll Does Not Appear In This Article*, LA Magazine, December 2007.

2   Herzberg, F, Mausner, B., and Snyderman, B., B., *The Motivation to Work* (New York: John Wiley and Sons, 1959).

3   The Economist, December 1, 2007, 84.

4   Interview with Patrick Mahoney, January 2009.

5   CBSnews.com. February 28, 2006.

Chapter 12

1 Ken Blanchard, *Leading at a Higher Level* (Upper Saddle River, NJ: Ft. Press, 2007), 252.

2 Russell L. Ackoff. *Ackoff's Fables, Irreverent Reflections on Business and Bureaucracy* (Hoboken, NJ: John Wiley & Sons, 1991), 2.

3 Gordon Binder and Philip Bashe. *Science Lessons: What The Business Of Biotech Taught Me About Management* (Boston: Harvard Business School Publishing, 2008), 198.

4 Marcus Buckingham and Curt Coffman. *First, Break All The Rules – What The World's Greatest Managers Do Differently* (New York: Simon & Shuster, 1999), 112-115.

5 D. Michael Abrashoff. *Its Our Ship: The No Nonsense Guide To Leadership* (New York: Hachette Book Publishing, 2008), 26.

6 William George. *Authentic Leadership, Rediscovering The Secrets To Creating Lasting Value* (San Francisco: Jossey-Bass, 2003), 5.

7 Sayan Chatterjee. *Failsafe Strategies, Profit and Grow From The Risks Others Avoid* (Upper Saddle River, NJ: Wharton School Publishing, 2005), 18.

8 Conversation with Dan Widen, March 1988.

9 Conversation with Jim and Bruce Nordstrom, February 1989.

10 Ed Lawler. *Creating High Performance Organizations: Practices and Results of Employee Involvement and Total Quality Management* (San Francisco, CA: Jossey-Bass, 1995), 69.

11 Binder. P. 200.

12 Cari Ressler & Jody Thompson. *Why Work Sucks: And How To Fix That* (New York: Penguine Group, 2008), viii.

13 Dov Seidman. *How: Why How We Do Anything Means Everything...in Business* (And in Life) (Hoboken, NJ: John Wiley & Sons, 2007), 253.

14 Emily Ross and Angus Holland, Ibid, 44.

15 Jerry Colangelo with Len Sherman, *How You Play The Game: Lessons for Life from the Billion Dollar Business of Sports* (New York: Amaco, 1989), 172.

Chapter 13

1 Harold Geneen, Managing (New York: Doubleday & Co., 1984).

2 Kevin L. Freiberg and Jacquelyn A. Freiberg, *Nuts! Southwest Airlines' Crazy Recipe For Business and Personal Success* (Austin, TX: Bard Press, 1996), 4.

3 Business Week, March 8, 2002, 6.

4 Ray Didinger. *Game Plans for Success* (New York: Little Brown and Co., 1995), 181.

5 Harland Cleveland. *The Knowledge Executive: Leadership In An Information Society* (New York: Truman Talley Books, 1985), 30.

6 USA Today, Ford Benefits From CEO's Turn To Road Less Traveled, Sharon Silke Carty, December 10, 2008.

7 Didinger, 182.

8 John Narciso and David Burkett. *Declare Yourself* (Englewood Cliffs, NJ: Prentice Hall, 1995), 29-30.

9 Arnold Brown and Edith Weiner, *Super Managing* (New York: McGraw Hill, 1984), 8.

10 Barry M. Staw. *Counter Forces To Change.* In Paul S. Goodman, *Change In Organizations* (San Francisco: Jossey-Bass, 1982), 87-101.

11 Laurence J. Peter. *Peter's Book of Quotations* (New York: William Morrow, 1997).

Chapter 14

1 Associated Press, June 25, 2008.

2 Hamilton Jordan, *Crisis* (New York: Putnam, 1982).

3 Business Week Magazine, Feb. 5, 2007, Say Hello To Alpha Kitty, Jon Fire, P. 24.

4 Mark Burnett, *Jump In* (New York: Random House, 2005), 98.

5 Jeffrey Pfeffer, *Power In Organizations* (Marshfield, MA: Pitman Publishing, 1981), 101.

6 Business Week Magazine, May 1, 2006, The Art of Motivation, Nanette Byrnes. P. 57.

7 USA Today, Ford Benefits From CEO's Turn To Road Less Traveled, Sharon Silke Carty, December 10, 2008. P. 2

8   James MacGregor Burns, *Leadership* (New York: Harper and Row, 1978).

9   Dreamworks Home Entertainment, The Last Castle, 2001.

Chapter 15

This chapter draws heavily the first four referenced works:

1   Rensis Likert, *New Patterns of Management* (New York: McGraw Hill 1961).

2   Robert R. Blake and Jane S. Mouton, *The Managerial Grid* (Houston: Gulf Publishing, 1964).

3   Edward C. Schein, *Management By Results* (Englewood Cliffs, NJ: Prentice Hall, 1961).

4   Paul Hersey and Ken Blanchard, *Management of Organizational Behavior: Utilizing Human Resources*, (Englewood Cliffs, NJ: Prentice Hall, 1977).

5   Robert A. Cialdini, *Influence: The Psychology of Persuasion* (New York: Quill William Morrow, 1993), 91-92.

Chapter 16

1   Emily Ross and Angus Holland *100 Great Businesses and the Minds Behind Them* (Naperville, IL: Sourcebooks, 2004), 255.

2   David Novak with John Boswell, *The Education Of An Accidental CEO: Lessons From The Trailer Park To The Corner Office* (New York: Crown Business, 2007), 75-76.

3   Cathleen P. Black, *Basic Black: The Essential Guide For Getting Ahead At Work (And In Life)* (New York: Random House, 2007), 23-27.

4   Mick Ukleja and Robert Lorber, *Who Are You and What Do You Want: A Journey For The Best Of Your Life* (Des Moines, IA: Meredith Books, 2008), 100.

5   Bob LaMonte with Robert L. Shook, *Winning The NFL Way: Leadership Lessons from Football's Top Head Coaches* (New York: Harper Collins, 2004). 173.

End Notes

Chapter 17

1 Interview with Dave Schlotterbeck, December 19, 2008

Chapter 19

1 Jerry Colangelo with Len Sherman. *How You Play The Game: Lessons For Life From The Billion-Dollar Business Of Sports* (New York: Amacom, 1999), 27.

2 Mark H. McCormack, *The 110% Solution: Using Good Old American Know How To Manage Your Time, Talent And Ideas* (New York: Villard Books, 1990), 56-57.

3 Rick Warren. *The Purpose Driven Life: What on Earth Am I Here For?* (Grand Rapids, MI: Zondervan, 2002), 17.

Organization Environment Index™

Organization Environment. In typical groupings of people at work, there is a set of behavioral norms or expectations. In most cases the behavior of the managers in these groups creates the environment within which everyone must work. Some behaviors create a positive work environment while others make it more difficult for people to perform effectively.

This instrument lists 80 statements which describe some of the behaviors which ultimately determine an organizations environment.

Please read each statement and assign the number which best describes your assessment of how <u>most managers in your organization actually behave.</u>

Be sure and indicate which group of managers you are assessing by checking the appropriate box below. <u>Your assessment will be kept confidential and the data summarized with that of others even if you choose to put your name on this instrument.</u>

Your Name (optional)   Organization Assessed   Date

This assessment reflects my view on (check one of the following)

The Entire
Organization ☐

My Department
(i.e. comp. & benefits) ☐

My Function
(i.e. HR) ☐

My Project
(i.e. wage survey team) ☐

ORGANIZATION ENVIRONMENT INDEX™
INSTRUCTIONS

1. Think about how managers in your organization in general (perhaps not your direct boss, but most others) behave. Use the 5 response options to indicate the frequency that most managers in your organization behave in the stated manner.

2. Respond to each item.

3. Total your scores in each group.

4. Transfer your scores to the graph.

Assign a value of "8"
if most managers behave like this **almost all the time.**
Assign a value of "6"
if most managers behave like this **very frequently.**
Assign a value of "4"
if most managers behave like this **frequently.**
Assign a value of "2"
if most managers behave like this **occasionally.**
Assign a value of "0"
if most managers **almost never** behave like this.

---

1. Show desire to be accountable. _____
2. Accept criticism well. _____
3. Non-defensive. _____
4. Appear realistic & optimistic. _____
5. Are not arrogant / self centered. _____

Total Group A

ORGANIZATION ENVIRONMENT INDEX™

6. Demonstrate concern for people development. ——
7. Are patient with associates who are struggling. ——
8. Listen to associates. ——
9. Provide support & encouragement. ——
10. Give constructive feedback readily. ——

Total Group B

11. Support the Team Upwards. ——
12. Effectively mediate conflicts. ——
13. Share the credit. ——
14. Facilitate information exchange. ——
15. Appropriately include others in decisions. ——

Total Group C

16. Exhibit well developed interpersonal skills. ——
17. Treat people as equally important as results. ——
18. Are approachable. ——
19. Show tact and consideration. ——
20. Are friendly and often stop to chat. ——

Total Group D

21. Do not stand up for their people. ——
22. Exhibit difficulty making decisions. ——
23. Reactive vs. Proactive ——
24. Seem passive, preferring to wait for instructions. ——
25. Avoid risk. ——

Total Group E

26. Switch priorities to please their bosses. ____
27. Too wishy washy or compliant. ____
28. More concerned with "politics" than results. ____
29. Have difficulty dealing with conflict. ____
30. Appear overly concerned with being well liked. ____

Total Group F [ ]

31. Rigidly follow rules/bureaucracy. ____
32. Allow rules to overide common sense. ____
33. Discourage new ideas. ____
34. Fail to question those in authority even when it appears they are wrong. ____
35. Act only "by the book." ____

Total Group G [ ]

36. Seem overwhelmed by their responsibilities. ____
37. Appear evasive and indecisive. ____
38. Blame shift. ____
39. Ignore problems. ____
40. Seldom communicate. ____

Total Group H [ ]

41. Are overly critical of mistakes. ____
42. Overanalyze or procrastinate. ____
43. Micromanage. ____
44. Seem overly concerned with avoiding mistakes. ____
45. Nitpick. ____

Total Group I [ ]

ORGANIZATION ENVIRONMENT INDEX™

46. Set unrealistically high goals for people. _____
47. Take credit for what others do. _____
48. Promote unhealthy competition. _____
49. Seem to create barriers to cooperation. _____
50. Are condescending to lower level associates. _____

Total Group J ☐

51. Relentlessly question and shoot down ideas. _____
52. Possess a negative cynical attitude. _____
53. Use sarcastic humor. _____
54. Appear to look for flaws in everything. _____
55. Seem suspicious and distrusting. _____

Total Group K ☐

56. Tend to dictate rather than guide. _____
57. Show limited confidence in others. _____
58. Rigid or inflexible. _____
59. Use force and intimidation. _____
60. Seem threatened when others are empowered. _____

Total Group L ☐

61. Respect others for candor and conviction. _____
62. Exercise sound judgment. _____
63. Behave ethically. _____
64. Value associates who self supervise or independently problem solve. _____
65. Think "outside the box." _____

Total Group M ☐

66. Fix things so mistakes are not repeated. _____
67. Not deterred by roadblocks. _____
68. Confront poor performance. _____
69. Focus competition against standards of excellence instead of against other people. _____
70. Make sure projects / ideas get implemented. _____

Total Group N ☐

71. Seem comfortable making tough choices. _____
72. At ease with ambiguity. _____
73. Have a bias for action. _____
74. More likely to seek forgiveness than permission. _____
75. Readily assert opinions. _____

Total Group O ☐

76. Seem methodical and systematic _____
77. Create effective work processes. _____
78. Value planning. _____
79. Appropriately analyze alternatives before deciding. _____
80. Think several moves in advance. _____

Total Group P ☐

Total your scores in each group. Transfer your scores to the graph on the next page.

Appendix A

ORGANIZATION ENVIRONMENT INDEX™

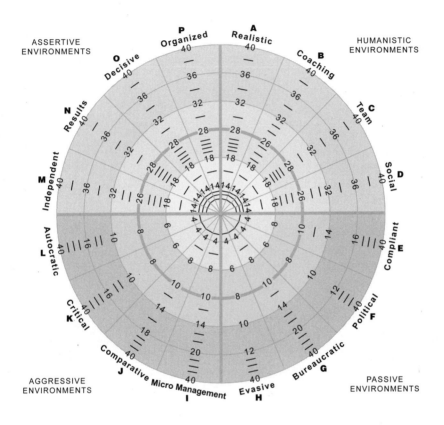

ASSERTIVE ENVIRONMENTS

HUMANISTIC ENVIRONMENTS

AGGRESSIVE ENVIRONMENTS

PASSIVE ENVIRONMENTS

Low Scores = At or Below 25th percentile
Moderate Scores = Between the 25th and 75th percentiles
High Scores = At or Above the 75th percentile

91 - 100
76 - 90
51 - 75
26 - 50
11 - 25
1 - 10

Percentiles

Leadership Team Dysfunction Index™

Effectiveness Dimensions

International, LLC.

Purpose

To give a leadership team insight into productive and dysfunctional activities and behaviors which are occurring within the team as seen by the members of that team.

Directions

The index contains 60 statements. You are to determine the extent of your agreement with each statement as it applies to the team you are assessing. Please assess each of the 60 statements. Please take your time and give your answers some thought. It is important to be honest in your assessment. Feedback will be in the form of a composite of the responses of the team. Your name will not be revealed in the summary report.

Your Name	Organization	Date
_____	_____	_____

Developed by Dr. John W. Hanes
Copyright ©2004 Effectiveness Dimensions International, LLC.
To order online: www.effectivenessdimensions.com

Appendix B

LEADERSHIP TEAM DYSFUNTION INDEX™
INSTRUCTIONS

1. Respond to each item in numerical order.
2. Answer each item as to how effective you honestly see this team.
3. Total your scores for the 5 items in each category.
4. Transfer your scores to the graph.

Assign a value of "6"
if you think this statement **describes this team most of the time.**
Assign a value of "4"
if you think this statement **frequently** describes this team.
Assign a value of "2"
if you think this statement **sometimes** describes this team
Assign a value of "0"
if you think this statement **almost never** describes this team.

---

1. We live up to our commitments. _____
2. We confront team members who do not follow through. _____
3. We hold ourselves to high standards in our work. _____
4. We place great emphasis on not letting down our peers. _____
5. We constructively challenge our peers when appropriate. _____

Total Group A [　　]

6. We solicit and objectively evaluate feedback/criticism from our team members. _____
7. We quickly own up to any deserved blame. _____
8. We place more effort in learning from our mistakes than assessing blame. _____
9. We seem undeterred by setbacks. _____
10. We look for the positives in our teammates and give them the benefit of the doubt. _____

Total Group B [　　]

LEADERSHIP TEAM DYSFUNTION INDEX™

11. We willingly sacrifice budget/headcount
    when it will benefit the team. ____

12. We subordinate departmental priorities
    to enhance overall performance. ____

13. We regularly acknowledge the unselfish
    actions of our teammates. ____

14. We regularly celebrate the overall teams successes. ____

15. We go out of our way to give credit
    to team members who provide help. ____

Total Group C ☐

16. We conceal our weaknesses from one another. ____
17. We look for excuses to avoid spending time together. ____
18. We tend to hold grudges. ____
19. We try and hide our mistakes. ____
20. We often leap to inaccurate conclusions
    about our teammates intentions. ____

Total Group D ☐

21. We talk behind the backs of other team members. ____
22. We say what others want to hear vs. what we really believe. ____
23. We tend to avoid controversial topics in our meetings. ____
24. We personally attack other team members in our meetings. ____
25. We seem to waste a lot of time with "posturing." ____

Total Group E ☐

26. We are not clear on our objectives. ____
27. We have limited understanding of other team members priorities. ____
28. We revisit the same discussions over and over. ____
29. We seem to lack confidence in our decisions. ____
30. We second guess ourselves a lot. ____

Total Group F ☐

Appendix B

ORGANIZATION ENVIRONMENT INDEX™

31. We miss key milestones and deadlines. ____

32. We tolerate sloppy analysis and poor work. ____

33. We improperly allow our teammates to be late for
    or skip important meetings. ____

34. We seem to tolerate lots of excuses. ____

35. We ignore the lack of follow through of other team members. ____

Total Group G _____

36. We blame shift, finger point, sulk or become defensive. ____

37. We tolerate sarcasm, cynicism and negativity. ____

38. We allow some team members to ignore team norms. ____

39. We put up with arrogance and self centered actions. ____

40. We see a lot of jockeying for who gets credit. ____

Total Group H _____

41. We improperly defend our own departments. ____

42. We hoard resources from our peers. ____

43. We fail to share relevant information with our teammates. ____

44. We tend to blow off the suggestions of our peers. ____

45. We see our own departmental teams as more
    important than our leadership team. ____

Total Group I _____

46. We openly admit our own shortcomings. ____

47. We quickly own up to our own mistakes. ____

48. We know about our teammates lives outside of work. ____

49. We know in depth about our teammates backgrounds. ____

50. We sincerely apologize when we are wrong or insensitive. ____

Total Group J _____

ORGANIZATION ENVIRONMENT INDEX™

51. We are unguarded in our discussion of issues. _____
52. We tackle difficult issues in our meetings. _____
53. We engage in constructive conflict within the team. _____
54. We seek out everyone's ideas and opinions. _____
55. We have relatively exciting team meetings. _____

Total Group K

56. We know what our peers are working on. _____
57. We end meetings completely committed to decisions. _____
58. We have clear direction and priorities. _____
59. We move forward without fear of failure. _____
60. We are committed to a common purpose. _____

Total Group L

Additional Comments:

LEADERSHIP TEAM DYSFUNCTION INDEX

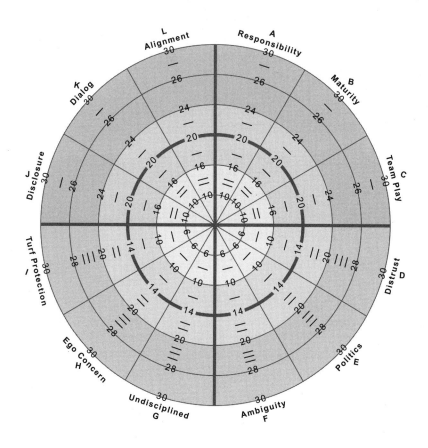

Very Low Scores = At or Below the 25th percentile
Low Scores = Between the 25th and 50th percentiles
Moderate Scores = Between the 50th and 75th percentiles
High Scores = At or Above the 75th percentile

91 - 100
76 - 90
51 - 75
26 - 50
11 - 25
1 - 10

©2004 Effectiveness Dimensions International, LLC. To order
online: www.effectivenessdimensions.com
Developed by Dr. John W. Hanes

ACKNOWLEDGEMENTS

This book is a collaborative effort and is the result of the contributions of many great people:

My Family: Mariann, Chad, Ryan and Dwight, whom I love deeply. They bring constant joy and help me keep the other elements of life in proper perspective.

My Parents: Jack and Betty grounded me with solid values and sacrificed mightily so that I might get a college education.

My Mentors and Teachers: Jim Wright, John Kindler, Tom Downham, Jerry Edge and John Hanson, who showed me the ropes of the business world. Joe Rost, Don Penner and Bill Hitt, who were the greatest of teachers.

My Editors: Alan Rinzler, who prodded me to re-conceptualize the book, and Paul Zieke whose trained eye helped me do justice to the English language that I so often find a way of butchering.

My Agent and Consultant, Andrea Hurst, who led me through the maze of the publication process. Without her expertise and professionalism, this book would not have seen the light of day.

My Assistant: Marlene Pegler, who diligently typed revision after revision and provided encouragement and invaluable insights along the way.

My Professional Partners who agreed to be interviewed for the book: Dave Schlotterbeck, CEO of CareFusion. Brian Burke, president and general manager of the Toronto Maple Leafs, Christine Fox, president of the Center for Naval Analyses, Dr. Michael Burns, CEO of Ferndale Laboratories, Marcie Edwards, general manager of Anaheim Public Utilities, and Pat Mahoney, president of West Coast Arborists. Each of you brought the concepts in the book to life and added valuable perspective.

My Clients: Over the past 23 years they have taught me far more than I have ever taught them.

My friend and investor, Launie Fleming. Without your belief in this project it would not have made it to market.

My Project Manager, Stephanie Chandler at Authority Publishing. You are a wizard. Your attention to detail and coordination skills throughout the publication process is truly amazing.

Despite all this help I am sure I failed to cite someone or some work that along the way contributed to my development as an educator. For these I ask your forgiveness and accept full responsibility.

ABOUT EFFECTIVENESS DIMENSIONS

For nearly 24 years, Effectiveness Dimensions International has been in the business of helping leaders and organizations increase their effectiveness by leading for change. Nearly 24,000 managers have attended our award winning three-day seminar Team Top Gun from more than 800 organizations.

Some examples of our services include:
- Executive coaching
- Organization culture analysis
- Team leadership effectiveness weekend
- High potential programs
- Meeting facilitation
- Leadership effectiveness weekend
- Team Top Gun alumni program
- Psychometric assessment instruments
- Executive candidate assessment
- Team development
- Keynote speaking engagements

To order additional copies of Change Focused Leadership go to: www.changefocusedleadership.com

Headquarters
Effectiveness Dimensions International, LLC
P.O. Box 839
Lake Arrowhead, CA 92352
www.TeamTopGun.com
+1 909.336.3675